THE LIBRARY OF
SOUTHERN CIVILIZATION

THE LIBRARY OF
SOUTHERN CIVILIZATION
Lewis P. Simpson, Editor

SOCIAL RELATIONS
IN OUR SOUTHERN STATES

Daniel R. Hundley
Courtesy Mrs. J. Dexter Nilsson

—❧❦—

SOCIAL
RELATIONS
IN OUR
SOUTHERN
STATES

—❧❦—

DANIEL R. HUNDLEY

Edited, with an Introduction, by
William J. Cooper, Jr.

LOUISIANA STATE UNIVERSITY PRESS

Baton Rouge and London

LIBRARY OF CONGRESS CATALOGING IN PUBLICATION DATA

Hundley, Daniel Robinson, 1832–1899.
  Social relations in our Southern States.

  (Library of Southern civilization)
  Reprint of the 1860 ed. published by H. B. Price,
New York.
  1. Southern States—Social life and customs—1775
–1865. I. Title.
[F213.H93 1979]   309.1'75'03   78–23811
ISBN 0–8071–0554–6
ISBN 0–8071–0559–7 pbk.

For Dr. and Mrs. Michael Holmes

CONTENTS

ILLUSTRATIONS

ACKNOWLEDGMENTS

I HAVE thoroughly enjoyed working on *Social Relations in Our Southern States*. Especially gratifying has been my contact with descendants of Daniel R. Hundley, who shared my enthusiasm and made significant contributions to my work. I owe a special debt to Professor J. Mills Thornton III, who pointed me toward the Hundley family. Signal assistance came from Mr. Daniel H. Hundley of University City, Missouri, from Mr. Thomas McCrary of New Market, Alabama, and from Mrs. J. Dexter Nilsson of Rockville, Maryland. At the Louisiana State University Press, Leslie Phillabaum, Beverly Jarrett, and Martha Hall have once again been magnificent. Lewis P. Simpson, editor of the Library of Southern Civilization, has given his complete support to this project. For incisive critical readings of my Introduction I am grateful to Anne C. Loveland and Karl A. Roider.

INTRODUCTION

DANIEL R. HUNDLEY
Interpreter of the Antebellum South

DANIEL R. HUNDLEY set a special mission for his *Social Relations in Our Southern States*. He wanted it to provide an accurate picture of the South that would dispel erroneous notions derived from "intemperate newspapers and exaggerated romances of the Uncle Tom school." According to Hundley, objectivity was sadly lacking in accounts of the South because they had been written "in praise or blame—generally the latter—of Southern peculiarities." As a result most Americans "remain to this day in profound ignorance of the Summer land." Instead of following this pattern of egregious partisanship Hundley asserted that he would "endeavor to portray, truthfully at least, what has been presented to my own mind, from my present standpoint." Acutely aware of his assault on partisanship, Hundley announced that he had no intention of whitewashing southern faults. On the contrary, he was determined to "state the plain, unvarnished truth" even though "it may occasionally scratch."[1]

Hundley declared that he possessed a unique per-

1 Hundley, *Social Relations in Our Southern States* (New York: Henry B. Price, 1860), vi, 8, 20 (cited hereinafter as *SR*).

spective for accomplishing his self-appointed task. He claimed for himself a notable objectivity—an objectivity based on his travels in nearly every state, his residence and education in both South and North, and his financial interests in the two sections. He told his readers that his special background would enable him to overcome the simplistic and polarized attitudes that had dominated previous descriptions of the South and southern society.[2]

II

Daniel Robinson Hundley is an elusive figure. The *Dictionary of American Biography* does not include him; nor does any other major biographical directory of nineteenth-century men such as *Appleton's Cyclopedia of American Biography*, *Lamb's Biographical Dictionary*, or the *National Cyclopedia of American Biography*. Only in two old publications dealing specifically with Alabama do biographical sketches of Daniel Hundley appear, sketches most notable for their brevity.[3] No Daniel R. Hundley papers exist in any manuscript depository, though his descendants possess a diary.[4] Hundley and his writing

2 *Ibid.*, 19–20.

3 W. Brewer, *Alabama: Her History, Resources, War Record, and Public Men From 1540 to 1872* (Montgomery: Barrett & Brown, 1872), 313; Thomas McAdory Owen, *History of Alabama and Dictionary of Alabama Biography* (4 vols.; Chicago: S. J. Clarke, 1921), III, 869.

4 The diary, which used to be on deposit in the Southern Historical Collection, University of North Carolina, was removed in 1952 by the depositor. I am extremely grateful to Mrs. J. Dexter Nilsson, a great-granddaughter of Daniel R. Hundley, for giving me access to a portion of it. Mrs. Nilsson has also placed a copy of that portion in the Department of Archives, Louisiana State University Library.

have been the subject of three published articles, but only one has more than rudimentary biographical information.[5] His own publications provide the chief source of biographical material with supplementary data available from several different sources.

The youngest of six children, Daniel R. Hundley was born on December 11, 1832, into a landholding and slaveholding family of north Alabama. His father John H. Hundley, a Virginian, migrated to the Huntsville area in 1818, then in 1824 went back to his native state to marry Malinda Robinson. Returning to Alabama with his new bride, John Hundley continud his farming activities. Later he turned away from active farming to the ministry and the practice of medicine, though he retained his land.[6]

We have no information on Daniel Hundley's youth before he left home for college. His father's religious convictions probably played a substantial part in the choice of Bacon College in Harrodsburg, Kentucky, where Hundley received an A.B. degree in 1850. Named for Sir Francis Bacon and chartered in 1837, Bacon College grew out of the religious dissension that wracked Baptist-dominated Georgetown College. Plagued by

5 Tommy W. Rogers, "Daniel R. Hundley's Contribution to Folklore," *Alabama Historical Quarterly*, XXX (Fall and Winter, 1968), 203–218 and "D. R. Hundley: A Multi-Class Thesis of Social Stratification in the Antebellum South," *Mississippi Quarterly*, XXIII (Spring, 1970), 135–54; Blanche Henry Clark Weaver, "D. R. Hundley: Subjective Sociologist," *Georgia Review*, X (Summer, 1958), 222–34, which has helpful biographical information.

6 Mrs. J. Dexter Nilsson to William J. Cooper, Jr. (hereinafter cited as WJC) November 4, 1976; *Alabama Records, Madison County*, XXV, 95 and CLXI, 35, in Alabama Department of Archives and History; Weaver, "Hundley," 223.

money problems, Bacon had been its healthiest before Hundley arrived, but it survived precariously until 1855 when it "no longer showed life." Although the name was lost forever, the college was resurrected in the late 1850s as Kentucky University. After the Civil War it became one of the building blocks that went into the construction of the University of Kentucky. All of his life Hundley retained a definite loyalty to his alma mater, where he delivered the alumni address at the 1860 commencement.[7]

From Bacon, Hundley moved on to the study of law at better-known educational institutions. First he studied at the University of Virginia for a year; then in 1852 he registered at Harvard University. At Harvard he completed the law requirements in one year. The law faculty recommended the LL.B. degree after only one year for Hundley and four other students because the five had attended another law school for at least six months. Accordingly, on July 20, 1853, Hundley was awarded his law degree.[8]

Upon graduation from Harvard, Hundley did not return to the land or to the law of his native Alabama. In November, 1853, he married his first cousin, Mary Ann Hundley of Virginia, whose father Elisha E. Hundley

7 James F. Hopkins, *The University of Kentucky: Origins and Early Years* (Lexington: University of Kentucky Press, 1951), 43–50, 73; Daniel R. Hundley, *Prison Echoes of the Great Rebellion* (New York: S. W. Green, 1874), 59; Daniel R. Hundley to James A. Noyes, nd [1897], in Daniel R. Hundley Biographical Folder, Harvard University Archives, Nathan M. Pusey Library, Harvard University.

8 *SR*, 19; Weaver, "Hundley," 223; *Harvard College Papers*, Second Series, XX (1853–54), 99, 109, in Pusey Library.

had considerable wealth and wide financial interests, including real estate in the Chicago area. To that city the young law graduate moved in order to manage his father-in-law's holdings. Details of Daniel Hundley's business activities are unknown, but family tradition gives him poor marks for business acumen. As for Hundley, he liked his northern home. "I had many warm friends in Chicago," he remembered, "and I preferred living there to living in Alabama." Even so, he kept in close touch with his first home. The Hundley clan still had property in Alabama, and his own family wintered there every year.[9]

No evidence suggests that Hundley took an active role in politics prior to the crisis of 1860–1861. Claiming to "subscribe to no party creed or shibboleth," he condemned "party shackles" while professing loyalty only to "the constitution and laws of my country." There is no reason to doubt his assertion that his first political post came during the presidential contest of 1860 when he was an election judge in Chicago.[10] Although Hundley was not active in the political wars before 1860, that inactivity did not mean that he had no interest in public affairs.

Not only did he have a keen interest; his interest had an outlet. In the late 1850s he contributed two articles

9 Mrs. J. Dexter Nilsson to WJC, November 4, 12, 1976; "Hundley Manuscript Diary," May 13, 1861; *SR*, 19–20; Hundley, *Prison Echoes*, 6.

10 Daniel R. Hundley, *Work and Bread; or the Coming Winter & the Poor* (Chicago: James Barnet, 1858), 18; Hundley to Wm. B. Figueres, December 1, 1860, printed in Huntsville *Southern Advocate*, December 12, 1860.

to *Hunt's Merchants' Magazine*.[11] In one of them he extolled the "national freedom" and the "commercial prosperity" enjoyed by the United States, both North and South. This happy state of affairs he attributed to "the *virtue* and *manhood* of our fathers." Hundley believed that losing the priceless legacy of character would endanger American political and economic health, notwithstanding the country's material advantages. To prove his contention that moral corruption would engulf the unwary he pointed to the fall of previous commercial empires from ancient Phoenicia to the Hanseatic League. He thought his argument unanswerable. Hundley's second article berated "the pharisaical spirit" that permitted "philanthropists" in England and the North to denounce southern slavery while remaining silent about a much greater evil. In Hundley's view the transportation of nonwhites to labor in the British West Indies wrecked many more lives and was far crueler than slavery in the South. He urged the enemies of evil to train their weapons upon their own devils rather than spend all their time assaulting the South.

Following the Panic of 1857, Hundley wrote a thoughtful pamphlet on the danger posed by unemployment and the urban poor.[12] The deprivation visited by the panic upon sincere, hard-working men moved and frightened him. To alleviate the plight of the unemployed and the hungry he called for a tax to create "a charity

11 "The Evils of Commercial Supremacy," *Hunt's Merchants' Magazine*, XXXVI (March, 1857), 316–17, and "The Traffic in Coolies," *ibid.* (May, 1857), 570–73.

12 Hundley, *Work and Bread* (quotations on pp. 14 and 22).

fund," which could provide essential financial support during emergencies. Hundley contended that failure to act would mean permanent pauperism in American cities. If such a condition ever came to pass, Hundley maintained that social upheaval would threaten the country. He was not censuring urban America; he praised American society for being "as near perfection now in our own social organization as we need ever expect to be." But he insisted that Americans had to preserve the virtue of all citizens, a virtue that underlay social contentment. Otherwise a desperation born of a terrible fear could vitiate the virtue America spawned and Hundley cherished.

These pieces served as a preface to *Social Relations in Our Southern States* which Hundley published early in 1860. In *Social Relations*, he touched upon some of the themes discussed in his previous writing. More important, in his first book he strived to cool the rapidly warming sectional passions by merging his self-proclaimed special objectivity with an appeal to the moderation and good sense of all Americans.[13]

This attitude presaged Hundley's stance during the secession crisis. Identifying himself as one who "has loved this Union," he took a public stand against what he defined as extremism. With that epithet he branded both southern secessionists and northern antislavery zealots, among whom he included the Republican party. Not surprisingly, Hundley vigorously advocated the presidential candidacy of Stephen A. Douglas, "who used

13 For a full discussion of *SR* see below pp. xxviii–xlv.

the most superhuman exertions to enlist conservative men of all classes in his support." His dedication to Douglas' cause brought about his first political post, service as an election judge in Chicago "to prevent the Republicans from committing frauds upon the ballot-box."[14]

After Abraham Lincoln's election Hundley gave up on the Union. Returning to Alabama, he cried that the Republican victory had destroyed "the *fact*" of the Union. He called for "a united South" and "a defiant South" to "secure her rights *out of the Union* now" or forever lose them. When a business trip to Chicago in April, 1861, turned into a nightmare, including a narrow escape from antirebel vigilantes, Hundley became an evangel of secession.[15]

He directed his special efforts toward Kentucky, then holding to an uneasy neutrality. In a public letter addressed to the "Citizens of Kentucky," Hundley admitted that he was not a native son, but insisted that he shared much with Kentuckians—his college days, his political conservatism, and his devotion to "one of the loveliest regions of the country." His message offered Kentucky a clear choice: either align with her sister states of the South or be ground down by the despotic North. He preached a gospel both urgent and militant: "Do not deceive yourselves with the delusive hope that

14 Hundley To Wm. B. Figueres, December 1, 1860, printed in Huntsville *Southern Advocate*, December 12, 1860.

15 *Ibid*; "Hundley Manuscript Diary," April 21–24, 1861. En route back to Alabama, Hundley feared that his property in Chicago would be confiscated; but on May 9 he received word that it had been sold, though at a substantial loss. *Ibid.*, May 1, 4, 9, 1861.

we can ever have peace until it is won by the sword. You must strike now and strike as freemen only strike, whose liberties are endangered. Strike, then, and God defend the Right!"[16]

Hundley was obviously prepared to fight, and fight he did. He raised a company in his north Alabama neighborhood, was elected its captain by acclamation, and took it off to Memphis to join the Confederate army. The new soldier cut a dashing figure; he was tall, six feet two inches, with dark eyes and complexion. This martial effort led to temporary marital distress, because Mary Ann Hundley wanted the new captain at home, not on the battlefront. To his diary he confessed, "I feel that duty calls, honor calls, my country calls and I must obey."[17]

Thus Daniel Hundley went to war, and by all accounts served honorably. In April of 1862 he became colonel of the 31st Alabama Infantry. With his regiment he fought in east Tennessee, in the Vicksburg campaign where he was wounded, and in the battles to defend Atlanta. In the great effort against William T. Sherman's southward plunge into Georgia, the 31st Alabama belonged to Edmund W. Pettus' brigade of John B. Hood's corps in Joseph E. Johnston's Army of Tennessee. Engaged constantly during the Confederate retreat from Dalton toward Atlanta, Hundley fought for

16 Hundley to Citizens of Kentucky, April 27, 1861, printed in Talladega (Ala.) *Democratic Watchtower*, May 15, 1861 (originally published in Louisville *Daily Courier*, April 29, 1861).

17 "Hundley Manuscript Diary," May 14–15, July 8–13, 15, 17–18, 20, 22–23, 25, August 4, 8–9, 1861; the description is from Hundley's Service File, Military Service Records, National Archives.

the last time on July 15, 1864, when he was captured in open battle near Big Shanty. Colonel Hundley was transported to Johnson's Island in Lake Erie where he remained a prisoner for the duration of the war.[18]

For his time as a prisoner Hundley left a full record— a detailed diary—which he published in 1874. In the aftermath of a daring and exciting, albeit unsuccessful, escape attempt in January, 1865, his diary was confiscated. He did not see it again until early 1874 when it was returned to him under mysterious circumstances. Having taken the oath of allegiance just prior to his release from Johnson's Island, Hundley proclaimed himself resigned to Confederate defeat.[19] Even though he had accepted the defeat, he believed the diary should appear unaltered.

The diary is certainly a war document. In it he condemned his captors as well as the treatment he received. Phrases such as "coldblooded despot and human butcher," "the vulgar dictator at Washington" (both referring to Lincoln), and "the bloody monster" (referring to a Union general) abound. "I have learned pretty thoroughly by this time," Hundley railed in October, 1864, "how to conjugate the verb *to hunger* in all its moods and tenses. I am hungry all the time." But through all the hardships Hundley affirmed that he and his compatriots retained an almost unbelievable optimism about Confederate fortunes. Not until the end was at hand did he

18 Hundley's Service File; Hundley, *Prison Echoes*, 17–22; Mrs. J. Dexter Nilsson to WJC, November 4, 1976.

19 Hundley, *Prison Echoes*, 4–6, 14; a copy of the oath dated July 11, 1865 is in Hundley's Service File.

acknowledge the ultimate failure of his cause. The prison diary is a monument to man's struggle to overcome adversity.[20]

Upon his release from Johnson's Island on July 25, 1865, Hundley journeyed to the ancestral acres in Alabama where he spent his remaining years. He seems not to have taken a very active part in the drama of Reconstruction. His models were the great Confederate general and the great Union president. In 1874 he wrote: "Since the end of the war, taking for my example the noble and spotless Robert E. Lee, I have endeavored faithfully to perform the humble duties of my private station with 'malice toward none and charity for all.'" Those tasks included practicing law, serving once as county solicitor, and briefly editing the Huntsville *North Alabama Reporter*. According to family tradition, however, his income in the postwar years came neither from legal practice nor newspaper work but from the family farming operations managed by his brother. Hundley did announce a "work on the results of the Rebellion," but it never appeared.[21]

A local editor stated that ill health forced a quiet life on Hundley. Whether that is true or not, Daniel R. Hundley was not a public person and had not been one for many years when he died at home in Mooresville on December 27, 1899. Even in Alabama his death did not make news outside his immediate neighborhood;

20 Hundley, *Prison Echoes*, *passim* (quotations on pp. 53, 101, 164, 173).

21 *Ibid.*, 6, 14; Hundley's Service File; Mrs. J. Dexter Nilsson to WJC, November 4, 12, 1976; Weaver, "Hundley," 233.

newspapers in neither Birmingham nor Montgomery noticed it.[22] And today Daniel Hundley is remembered not for the whole of his life but for a book he wrote at age twenty-eight, *Social Relations in Our Southern States*.

III

Daniel Hundley published *Social Relations in Our Southern States* in 1860. Although no evidence reveals his thoughts about its reception, I do not think they were joyous. He hoped that an analysis of the South by a southerner who admitted "there is much in the Slave States to call forth either unqualified approbation, or equally unqualified denunciation" would spark northerners and Englishmen to view the South rationally and to realize they had nothing to fear from it. He believed that an identical generalization could be made "with equal truth and pointedness" about any other society, "free or slave," as well as the South.[23] But few paid any attention either to his hopes or to his book.

There was practically no reaction—in the South, in the North, or in England. Searching for reviews of *Social Relations*, I went through almost twenty periodicals such as the *Southern Literary Messenger*, *DeBow's Review*, *North American Review*, *Harper's Monthly*, *Atlantic Monthly*, *Hunt's Merchants' Magazine*, *Edinburgh Review*, and *Blackwood's*. All of them noted and reviewed many books, but only *DeBow's Review* printed a review

22 Huntsville *Daily Mercury*, December 28–29, 1899. The only obituary notice I found outside of Hundley's neighborhood was a brief one in *Confederate Veteran*, VIII (February, 1900), 82.

23 *SR*, 13.

of *Social Relations*. That review was generally positive, though it expressed strong reservations about Hundley's treatment of the southern upper classes. Most of the review, however, did not deal with *Social Relations* at all; instead the reviewer, J. T. Wiswall, spent most of his space discussing his own theories of the origin and value of an aristocracy.[24]

One can only speculate about the reasons for the inattention to Hundley's book. Most of the major periodicals in 1860 were basically literary journals; they noticed and reviewed mostly *belles lettres* and history. *Social Relations* fit neatly into neither category. This selectivity could explain its inclusion in *DeBow's Review* but not in the *Southern Literary Messenger*.[25] Yet such selectivity could not account for the exclusion from *Hunt's Merchants' Magazine*, especially since Hundley had been a recent contributor to its pages. Probably more important than the genre of *Social Relations* was the timing of its publication. Appearing at a time of increasing sectional tension and polarization, its call for moderation had little appeal. Hundley's literary fortunes matched the political fortunes of his hero, Stephen A. Douglas. Hundley called for the North to understand a South that deserved both praise and blame. In 1860 these views were not especially popular anywhere in the United States.

Although contemporaries paid little attention to *Social*

24 *DeBow's Review*, XXVIII (May, 1860), 551–66.

25 This might also explain the omission of Hundley from basic works like Jay B. Hubbell, *The South in American Literature, 1607–1900* (Durham: Duke University Press, 1954) and Louis D. Rubin, Jr. (ed.), *A Bibliographical Guide to the Study of Southern Literature* (Baton Rouge: Louisiana State University Press, 1969).

Relations, it has become an invaluable source for students of the antebellum South. Even so, historians did not always recognize its worth. The first serious notice of *Social Relations* came from the first great historian of the antebellum South, Ulrich Phillips. In an essay prepared for *The South in the Building of the Nation*, Phillips described *Social Relations* as "a general treatise upon social types," which "stands alone among the productions of Southern writers." Phillips thought that Hundley made "particularly useful contributions" with discussions of social class among whites and general conditions among slaves.[26]

Phillips' comment did not, however, lead to the immediate widespread use of *Social Relations*. Phillips himself employed it little in his major books on slavery and southern society. Among his fellow historians of the South, probably the most important was William E. Dodd, who used *Social Relations* not at all in his two influential general studies, *The Cotton Kingdom* and *Statesmen of the Old South*.[27] This pattern of neglect set by Phillips and Dodd was followed in the 1920s and

26 Phillips, "Economic and Political Essays in the Antebellum South," in Julian A. C. Chandler *et al.* (eds.), *The South in the Building of the Nation* (12 vols.; Richmond: Southern Historical Publication Society, 1909), VII, 188–89.

27 In his *American Negro Slavery* (New York: D. Appleton, 1918), 200, Phillips cited Hundley on the ostracism of the slave trader, but in neither *Life and Labor in the Old South* (Boston: Little, Brown, 1929) nor *The Course of the South to Secession* (New York and London: Appleton-Century, 1939) did he use *Social Relations*. Dodd, *The Cotton Kingdom: A Chronicle of the Old South* (New Haven: Yale University Press, 1920) and *Statesmen of the Old South: Or from Radicalism to Conservative Revolt* (New York: Macmillan, 1911).

1930s by other scholars of the antebellum South, including Jesse T. Carpenter, Francis P. Gaines, and William S. Jenkins.[28]

Since 1940, however, *Social Relations* has been widely used by historians. They have heeded Phillips' early appraisal rather than the example of their predecessors. This turnabout occurred in part because historians began writing a new kind of social and intellectual history that drew upon a wider variety of sources. Certainly the rediscovery of Hundley and *Social Relations* has enriched the study of the antebellum South. Even more impressive than the number of historians utilizing *Social Relations* is the variety of uses to which they have put it. Examples abound. For Clement Eaton, *Social Relations* underscored the importance of the yeomen in antebellum southern society. Carl Degler recently called Hundley "the antebellum South's prime contemporary commentator on social mobility." Although W. J. Cash found *Social Relations* full of enthusiasm for "the Southern gentleman," William R. Taylor discovered that Hundley gave other groups more force than the gentleman. Bertram Wyatt-Brown gave *Social Relations* high marks for its discussion of family pride, but he asserted that Hundley "shamelessly romanticized southern life." In direct contrast to any romantic ideal, Kenneth Stampp drew upon *Social Relations* to help make his case for the

28 Carpenter, *The South as a Conscious Minority, 1789–1861: A Study in Political Thought* (New York: New York University Press, 1930); Gaines, *The Southern Plantation: A Study in the Development and Accuracy of a Tradition* (New York: Columbia University Press, 1924); Jenkins, *Pro-Slavery Thought in the Old South* (Chapel Hill: University of North Carolina Press, 1935).

maltreatment of slaves and the evils of slavetrading.[29]

Obviously Daniel Hundley did not write a simple book setting forth a simple view of the South.

IV

In writing *Social Relations* Hundley strove to keep his pledges; in large part he avoided both emotionalism and simplism. The society he described was far from simple; the South that emerged from the pages of *Social Relations* was complex and complicated. Throughout his discussion of white society Hundley juxtaposed the seemingly opposite themes of unity and diversity. He depicted a society greatly influenced by the power and pretension of social class, but simultaneously he insisted that the watchword of the society was democracy. While he praised the worth inherent in an agricultural society, he eagerly welcomed industry to the South. He called slavery a noble institution but acknowledged that an ugly reality often violated his ideal formulation. A curious mixture of traditional values and contemporane-

29 Eaton, *The Mind of the Old South* (Baton Rouge: Louisiana State University Press, 1964), 115–16 and *The Waning of the Old South Civilization, 1860s–1880s* (Athens: University of Georgia Press, 1968), 4–6; Degler, *Place Over Time: The Continuity of Southern Distinctiveness* (Baton Rouge: Louisiana State University Press, 1977), 56; Cash, *The Mind of the South* (New York: Alfred A. Knopf, 1941), 20; Taylor, *Cavalier and Yankee: The Old South and American National Character* (New York and Evanston: Harper and Row, 1969), 337; Wyatt-Brown, "The Ideal Typology and Ante-Bellum Southern History: A Testing of a New Approach," *Societas*, V (Winter, 1975), 5n., 8; Kenneth Stampp, *The Peculiar Institution: Slavery in the Ante-Bellum South* (New York: Alfred A. Knopf, 1956), 180, 256–57.

ously modern ideas informed his analysis of southern society.

No claim about the South aroused Hundley's ire more than the assertion "that in the South, aside from the negro slaves, there exist but two other classes—Poor Whites and Cavaliers." This gross misrepresentation, which had "misle[d] the mass of Free State citizens," Hundley attributed to "windy Northern demagogues."[30] Hundley's proper denial of that charge and his effort to correct it became the chief organizing principle of his book. His chapter titles point to a dramatically different analysis of the white South. Instead of two different classes he found seven, and he spent 75 percent of his pages describing them.

Hundley divided southern whites on the basis of their moral values, their personal and social mores, and, generally, their *weltanschaung.* In his scheme wealth or economic status occupied a singularly unimportant position.[31] Wealth obviously separated the rich from the poor, but, except in that very broad sense, Hundley had little use for it. Occupation assumed greater importance for him; for example, it was crucial in differentiating the middle classes from the yeomen. The former were engaged in town or urban as well as in agricultural jobs while the latter were solely farmers. Although occupation provided a partial help in describing different classes and groups, it did not explain behavior.

Hundley's discussion of the planter class clearly re-

30 *SR*, 81.
31 For a somewhat different development of this point see Rogers, "D. R. Hundley: A Multi-Class Thesis."

vealed his limited use of occupation as a explanatory
tool. His treatment of the planters emphasized his perception of the mainspring of social organization and behavior. Hundley cataloged the planters into primarily
three groups—the southern gentleman, the cotton snob,
and the southern yankee.[32] All three clearly had the
same occupation, though he found southern yankees in
other areas as well. Although the three groups had more
or less the same economic standing, Hundley argued
that the three were composed of very different people
who had radically different values. Hundley, then, did
not bequeath his interpretation of the planters to their
most influential modern student, Eugene Genovese, who
groups them together and gives them a common world
view.[33]

Of all Hundley's planters, his ideal was the southern
gentleman. And in him Hundley anticipated the ideal of
a later, equally perceptive interpreter of the South, for
Hundley's gentleman shares much with W. J. Cash's
Virginian. Hundley's gentleman was "a man every inch,
bold, self-reliant, conscientious; knowing his own convictions of duty, and daring to heed them." Like the Virginian, the southern gentleman possessed all the characteristics of conventional gentlemen, but in addition
was "peculiarly the outgrowth of the institutions of the
South." With an aristocratic heritage he acted according to his own code and refused ever to become "the

32 He also placed some members of the middle class in the planter
category, but they were not so important as planters as the three primary groups.

33 Eugene D. Genovese, *The Political Economy of Slavery: Studies
in the Economy and Society of the Slave South* (New York: Pantheon
Books, 1965).

SLAVE OF PUBLIC OPINION." Motivated by gentility and warmth of spirit, the southern gentleman never
allowed financial gain or garish display to corrupt his
values. Education for education's sake, a deep respect
for religion and family, abiding concern for slaves—
these qualities underscored his distance from ordinary
men. A man of the outdoors, the southern gentleman
was a magnificent physical specimen. "Good size" and
"graceful carriage" highlighted his "faultless physical
development," which led to "remarkable powers of endurance." Hundley, again like Cash, made no claim that
these gentlemen pervaded the South; on the contrary,
they were "not quite so plentiful as blackberries in
summer-time, or New England robins in spring." [34]

In direct contrast Hundley condemned the southern
yankee and the cotton snob for lacking all ennobling
characteristics. The southern yankee "invariably boasts
but one armorial motto, and that is, *vincit omnia AURUM*."
Besides love of money, cruelty to slaves, meanness of
temperament, and disregard for family marked the southern yankee as a disreputable inhabitant of Hundley's
"Summer land." Unpleasant physical characteristics com-
plemented character faults. With phrases such as "heavy-
jawed" and "beetle-browed," Hundley dramatized the
southern yankee's physical inferiority to the southern
gentleman. The cotton snob stood alongside the southern yankee in Hundley's lineup of social criminals. Ill
bred and the personification of *nouveau riche*, the cotton
snob flaunted his new wealth. Vulgar display, debauchery, disdain for religion and proper education, a total

34 Cash, *Mind of the South*, 3–14; *SR*, 20–76 *passim*, esp. 21, 23,
27–29, 31–34, 63–64.

lack of concern for others, including his own family, denoted a "ridiculous and contemptible" class, which brought reproach and obloquy upon the South.[35]

The origin and history of the values that Hundley used to distinguish his three groups of planters provide the key to Hundley's own values. For Hundley one source chiefly accounted for the radical differences among southern gentlemen, southern yankees, and cotton snobs. Because of their ancestry these three types confronted the world in their own particular ways. Hundley took pains to spell out the genealogy of the planters.

He drew the family trees in some detail. The southern gentleman always derived from "good stock . . . usually of aristocratic parentage," which gave him a "faultless pedigree." In the southeast his European ancestors were English cavaliers and the better class of French Huguenots. Farther to the west "the progenitors of the Southern Gentleman were chiefly Spanish Dons and French Catholics." The less fortunate southern yankees and cotton snobs had to make do with a considerably less impressive family tree. The former "[sprang] from all manner of forefathers, though in most cases from persons of the middle class." The latter carried an even heavier burden, for "in nine cases out of ten he is the son of the Southern Yankee."[36]

Throughout Hundley's analysis of these three types of planters, he made clear that in his mind each was either blessed or cursed from birth. Both the values that Hundley cherished and the characteristics that he ab-

35 *SR*, 130–32, 157, 161–62, 166–67, 170–71, 175–76.
36 *Ibid.*, 27–28, 131, 165.

horred were intimately associated with family and blood. He "contend[ed] there is a great deal in *blood*," and the family was absolutely critical, for it held and passed on traits, both noble and ignoble.[37] It served as the agent of transfer: the dead bequeathed; the living inherited. For Hundley this law was immutable. Change had little place in his scheme—once a gentleman always a gentleman, once a snob always a snob. Although Hundley made no provision for yankees and snobs to move up to gentlemen, and allowed little room for changes in values, his system did not preclude social and economic mobility. He believed that in southern society a man could advance his social position and his financial fortune. But such improvement rarely entailed any fundamental shift in moral values.

The physical and emotional characteristics were static; combined they composed Hundley's iron law of social organization, which included physical description, personality, and values. He extended its sway throughout southern society. Although Hundley's emphasis on ancestry and his insistence on the immutability of inherited values appears terribly antiquated, his outlook fitted perfectly with the work of contemporary European students of society. The European social scientists, ethnologists they called themselves, classified virtues and defects of people and races just like botanists and zoologists defined the particular characteristics of flora and fauna.

Such diverse fuels as physiology and nationalism propelled European ethnology. By the mid-century eth-

37 *Ibid.*, 251 (italics in original).

nologists shared a general belief in the efficacy of explaining personal as well as cultural values by specifying physical and social characteristics, characteristics handed down from generation to generation. Probably the most influential scientific statement advocating this ethnology was Count Arthur de Gobineau's *Essay on the Inequality of Races* published in the mid-1850s. Gobineau concluded that he found "in the physical nature of men themselves the factors of race that explain men's minds and institutions." These attitudes spread far beyond the books and conversations of the ethnologists. Even men of letters became imbued with the theories propounded by Gobineau and his scientific brethren. When Stendahl described Italians as "slender, almost thin, very dark, with blazing eyes and a sallow complexion; he lives on coffee and a very few abstemious meals," he gave expression to the power of the new science. Talk of Celtic, Nordic, and Mediterranean characteristics permeated the continent. For the disciples of ethnology physical characteristics as well as inherited cultural traits explained everything from political success to artistic genius.[38]

Although no direct evidence indicates that Hundley ever read the European ethnologists or even their American followers like Dr. Josiah Nott of Hundley's own Alabama, he had a great deal in common with them. Except for anatomical measurement that fascinated the

38 Jacques Barzun, *Race: A Study in Superstition* (Rev. ed.; New York, Evanston, and London: Harper & Row, 1965), Chaps. 3–5 (quotations on pp. 52 and 84). See also James Cowles Prichard, *Researches into the Physical History of Man*, ed. George W. Stocking, Jr. (Chicago and London: University of Chicago Press, 1973), lxvi, ci, cii.

ethnologists, but held no interest for Hundley, a striking similarity marks Hundley's analysis of personality
and society and the work of the ethnologists. Both shared
a penchant for classification as well as the conviction
that classification permitted the separation of man into
various types. In this separation physical traits identified social groups and provided clues to values.

Of his three groups of planters, Hundley clearly preferred the southern gentleman, but he never allowed
favoritism to blind him. As William R. Taylor has noted,
Hundley recognized that in the South of 1860 his beloved ·
southern gentleman was an endangered species. Both
the southern yankee and the cotton snob had greater
numbers and more force than the idealized gentleman.
To the southern yankee in particular, Hundley awarded
the prize for energy and drive. The yankee had "contributed no little to the present unprecedented prosperity of the Slave States." From clearing new ground for
planting, to promoting the use of fertilizer, to building
railroads, the southern yankee operated at the center of
southern material progress.

The southern yankee had even "stimulated the Southern Gentleman to activity and enterprise." Hundley
granted the southern yankee that role while condemn-
ing the motive: the southern yankee had "only sought
to make money and to advance his private interests." In
contrast, the southern gentleman, reacting to the example of the southern yankee, had been "influenced by
public spirit and patriotic pride." Still, Hundley gave
the devil his due; the southern yankee had "ever been
foremost" in southern economic growth. Admitting the
southern yankee's contribution, Hundley not only re-

vealed his belief in the power of strength and energy, he also identified himself with the social manifestation of Charles Darwin's biology. Yet, perhaps the southern gentleman was not doomed to extinction. Because Hundley believed so strongly in ancestry and family as shapers of values, he could imagine the gentleman becoming more energetic while also retaining his nobler qualities. Possibly, then, Hundley thought the gentleman could survive along with the yankee.[39]

Although the planters occupied the highest level in the southern social system, they did not compose the central class in southern society. Long before Frank L. Owsley, Hundley bestowed that honor upon the yeomen and the middle class. Determined to correct the widespread notion that a social vacuum existed between planters and poor whites, Hundley emphasized the importance of the overlooked middle. The "poor white trash" as Hundley called the lowest order of whites, he relegated to a negligible role in the South. In his scheme the middle classes "constitute[d] the greater proportion of [southern] citizens, and [were] likewise the most useful members of her society," while the yeomen were "most deserving of esteem." For Hundley two separate groups existed in the middle. The middle classes engaged in a variety of occupations including farming and planting, but many of them lived in towns where they followed nonagricultural pursuits. In contrast the yeomen lived on the land where they were the staple of southern agricultural society. Hundley pointed out still

39 Taylor, *Cavalier and Yankee*, 337; *SR*, 156–57.

another difference; the middle classes enjoyed slightly more economic success than the yeomen.[40]

Emphasis on difference does not, however, explain satisfactorily Hundley's treatment of the two groups. As I have previously noted, Hundley never put much stock in either financial status or occupation as molders of character and shapers of values. The sources that generated character and values for Hundley indicate not differences, but marked resemblances between the middle classes and the yeomen. These resemblances are so pronounced that the two groups can be merged into one for discussion. Both groups descended chiefly from the middle ranks of English colonists. Hundley depicted the middle classes as appearing in all shapes and sizes, but he stressed "broad shoulders and angular outline." At the same time he noted that "physical heartiness" set yeomen apart. Describing the social characteristics of the two, Hundley used a common language. Hospitable, civil, God fearing, independent of mind—for possessing these qualities in plenitude Hundley praised the middle rank of southern society.[41]

The importance of the combined middle class stemmed chiefly from its contribution to the South, not merely from its numbers. Hundley's middle classes were certainly not mindless men following wherever the planters led. Quite to the contrary, as men of "the stoutest independence" they acted as equals with the planters in

40 Frank L. Owsley, *Plain Folk of the Old South* (Baton Rouge: Louisiana State University Press, 1949); *SR*, Chaps. 2, 5, 7 *passim* (quotations on pp. 77 and 192).

41 SR, 81–82, 84, 94–95, 193, 198–99, 207, 216–18.

managing southern society. No yeoman, Hundley declared, "had learned to fear mortal man"; nor would he "under any circumstances humiliate himself to curry favor with the rich or those in authority." Politics, a politics dominated by a pervasive interest and a broad suffrage, gave the middle class its influence. Extremely well versed in "the lore of politics," the middle class participated actively in that southern passion. Hundley commented favorably on their significant contribution to the roster of southern political leadership. He also believed that the middle ranks of southern society as well as the upper ranks were much more involved in politics than their northern counterparts. Phrases such as *comprehensive knowledge, clearer perception, better versed*, governed Hundley's account of these men in the middle and politics. From my own work in antebellum southern political history, I am convinced that Hundley knew whereof he spoke.[42]

The numerical majority and the political activity of the middle class insured that without its concurrence the issues of the planters could never dominate southern politics. Hundley recognized that political harmony prevailed because the middle class and the upper class viewed politics through an identical lens. Ties formulated by economic interests, political culture, and race pride merged the two great components of southern white society into one. Thus, unity, not diversity, was the benchmark of the society. The unity drew a firm strength from a political system that allowed the mean-

42 *Ibid.*, 54–55, 82–84, 198–99, 201; William J. Cooper, Jr., *The South and the Politics of Slavery, 1828–1856* (Baton Rouge: Louisiana State University Press, 1978).

ingful participation of all white males. In Hundley's mind this unified white society had one overriding mission—to defend slavery.

The slaves were at the bottom of southern society, but they also formed the foundation for the society. Hundley simply could not envision the South without slavery. And without doubt he bowed before the southern myth; Hundley's slaves were happy, well-fed "simple creatures." In fact much of his long discussion of slavery could fit perfectly into any traditional defense of the peculiar institution. He also castigated the self-righteous opponents of slavery who "damn incontinently" a people and an institution of which they know nothing. Hundley styled them "the latter-day Popes, from whose decree there is no appeal." [43]

While Hundley did follow the conventional road on slavery and abolition, he simultaneously gave his account his own stamp. In the southern slave system he found imperfections and admitted evils. And he dealt with both publicly, a rare phenomenon in the South of 1860. In Hundley's story Simon Legree with his "crime and oppression" could be found in the southern countryside. On the plantations of an evil slaveowner, especially the southern yankee, "the crack of his whip is heard early, and the crack of the same is heard late, and the weary backs of his bondmen and his bondwomen are bowed to the ground with over-tasking and over-toil." Then there was "the most utterly destestable" slavetrader, whom Hundley pilloried with abandon—"a coarse, ill-bred

43 Not only does Hundley make slavery the subject of his longest chapter, he also treats various aspects of it throughout the book (quotations from *SR*, 285 and 357).

person, provincial in speech and manners, with a cross-looking phiz, a whiskey-tinctured nose, cold, hard-looking eyes, a dirty tobacco-stained mouth, and shabby dress." Hundley scorned this villain who "habitually separates parent from child, brother from sister, and husband from wife."[44]

In spite of these horrors Hundley insisted upon the morality and essential humanity of southern slavery. He argued that abuses could not destroy the legitimacy of noble institutions. Holding to his Calvinist heritage, Hundley wrote that abuses would never totally disappear because of the essentially evil nature of man. Refusing to accept the doctrine of perfectibility, he asserted, "There is in every man a private devil of his own, who can turn his bosom into a hell or heaven." Drawing analogies with institutions generally beloved in mid-nineteenth-century America, he asked if Christianity should be abandoned because of the tortures of the Spanish Inquisition, or if marriage should be cast aside because of divorce? Hundley answered his own questions with a resounding negative.[45]

Although Hundley vigorously defended slavery, even with its admitted abuses, he advocated placing the peculiar institution "upon a more humane basis than it rests upon at present." He especially wanted to alter laws "allow[ing] families to be broken up and sold to separate masters." And he was "persuaded that the Southern people, if left to themselves" would accomplish just such reforms. But first "all apprehension of intermeddling from outsiders" would have to disappear. To effect

44 *Ibid.*, 132, 140–41, 320.
45 *Ibid.*, 14, 284–92.

that end Hundley called upon all true friends of the slave to cease their warfare upon the South's peculiar institution. Then, but only then, maintained Hundley, the condition of the slave would improve.

To Hundley the only valid inquiry regarding slavery concerned whether or not the blacks themselves had been improved and uplifted. Arguing in the affirmative, Hundley repeated the traditional southern story. Savage and heathen blacks had been civilized and Christianized; moreover they were engaged in productive labor that benefited the entire world, not only their masters and the South. To prove his contention Hundley contrasted the well-being of the southern slave to industrial laborers and free blacks in the North, but especially to black Africans. He drew a bleak picture of factory workers, the "weak, hollow-eyed women and sickly hued men" who suffered from "lack of nourishment, and proper rest" in their "miserable tenant houses." The northern free blacks Hundley described as weighted down with the yoke of discrimination. "*We heap upon them,*" he cried, "*moral obloquy more atrocious than that which the master heaps upon the slave.*"[46]

Even though Hundley made the usual southern bow to the plight of industrial workers and of northern blacks, he devoted considerably more attention to Africa. He presented a grim catalog of savagery, despotism, and ignorance pervading black Africa. In his own mind his case was irrefutable because his evidence came from "the latest and most reliable travelers," such as Heinrich Barth, David Livingstone, and James Richardson.

46 *Ibid.*, 61, 133, 290, 295–300 (italics in original).

These men were simultaneously exerting a powerful influence on British and European opinion regarding Africa. In view of the barbarism dominating black Africa, Hundley called on all antislavery men in the North and in England to reassess their condemnation of southern slavery.[47]

In his appeal to northerners and Englishmen, Hundley urged the general recognition of race mission. Making a Darwinian case, he asserted that the specific black-white relationship in the South was simply one manifestation of the cultural superiority of the white race. For him, as for many of his contemporary students of society, race equaled culture, and racial superiority meant cultural superiority. Claiming correctly that northerners and Englishmen shared his views on white supremacy, Hundley spelled out the similarities between slavery and other forms of cultural supremacy. For the North, it was the treatment of free blacks. For England, it was the treatment of the natives in India as well as the coolie traffic in which the English transported Indians, Chinese, and Africans to their West Indian islands to serve as peasants. Both the northern and the English practices Hundley chastised as far crueler than southern slavery, though he understood them as examples of racial-cultural superiority.

Notwithstanding his dislike for practices in India and the coolie traffic, Hundley envisioned England as standing on the brink of its great opportunity. He called for England to take over Africa, and he was convinced that

47 *Ibid.*, 302–13; Philip D. Curtin, *The Image of Africa: British Ideas and Action, 1780–1850* (Madison: University of Wisconsin Press, 1964), Chaps. 12, 13, 15 *passim*.

"in time" the English, in conjunction with the French, would do so. To Hundley, such an eventuality was inevitable. It would signal a magnificent chapter in English history and in the destiny of the white race. As Hundley saw it, the English would turn the wilds of Africa into a prosperous garden just as their kinsmen had changed the forests of the South into an agricultural showplace. This great work by England—its sharing in shouldering the white man's burden—did not necessarily mean enslavement of the Africans. On the contrary, Hundley maintained that it might be accomplished "in the name of Freedom, as the English now rule the Indies." Offering that alternative Hundley made his major point. It mattered not whether the inferior race was enslaved; total domination by the stronger was the critical requirement. He willingly accepted different methods of attaining the goal, which he regarded "as certain as fate."[48]

Despite the sincerity of his invitation Hundley never understood that the antislavery forces in England and in the North made their fundamental opposition exactly where he thought he had been so generous. Racial domination most antislavery men readily accepted, even, as Hundley noted, in cruel forms. But slavery they viewed as qualitatively different from any other kind of discrimination or domination. Apostles of free-labor ideology, they demanded the maintenance of the form of voluntary choice, a condition symbolized by a joint contract and the payment of a wage, even if the contract and the wage mocked free choice and resulted in "nearly abso-

48 *SR*, 151–52, 316–20.

/

lute subordination." Such an argument totally perplexed
Hundley, who found it thoroughly artificial. For him it
created a difference where none existed.[49]

With his paean to the white man's burden Hundley
placed the South in the vanguard of the great work
charged to the white race—to uplift the lesser races. He
predicted that effort would increasingly occupy the attention and talents of the white nations, to their everlasting credit. Did this faith in uplift mean that Hundley envisioned a slaveless South at some future point?
The answer is yes, but only at some incalculably distant
time. Although "the negroes in the Southern States
have been improved almost beyond computation," Hundley still found them "totally unprepared for emancipation." Emancipation, then, was so far away that white
southerners did not have even to contemplate the possibility.[50]

Inviting the North and especially England to join the
South in a world dedicated to racial uplift through domination, Hundley hoped to guarantee the safety of the
South. He believed an objective description of his society to be the surest way to persuade reasonable northerners and Englishmen that the South was no more evil
or dangerous than their own societies. Although Hundley
cared passionately for the South, he did not camouflage

49 Eric Foner has a full statement of the content and impact of free
labor ideology in his *Free Soil, Free Labor, Free Men: The Ideology of
the Republican Party before the Civil War* (New York: Oxford University Press, 1970). In *The Problem of Slavery in the Age of Revolution,
1770–1823* (Ithaca and London: Cornell University Press, 1975),
489–501 (quotation on p. 492), David Brion Davis has a suggestive
discussion of its origins.

50 *SR*, 324.

the sores disfiguring it. Although he was convinced that
unity overpowered division in southern society, he did not
deny the existence of division. Thus, in large part Hundley achieved his goal of objectivity. He presented a more
realistic account of the artebellum South than did any of
his contemporaries, or have most subsequent historians.

Daniel R. Hundley
age fifteen

Mary Ann Hundley
wife of Daniel R. Hundley

Daniel R. Hundley
as a Confederate officer

SOCIAL RELATIONS
IN OUR SOUTHERN STATES

SOCIAL RELATIONS

IN

OUR SOUTHERN STATES.

BY

D. R. HUNDLEY, ESQ.

———•●•———

"In forming a judgment, lay your hearts void of foretaken opinions; else, whatsoever is done or said will be measured by a wrong rule, like them who have the jaundice, to whom every thing appeareth yellow." SIR PHILIP SIDNEY.

"FAITHFUL are the wounds of a friend; while the kisses of an enemy are deceitful." KING SOLOMON.

———•●•———

NEW-YORK:

HENRY B. PRICE,

PUBLISHER, 884 BROADWAY.

1860.

JOHN A. GRAY,
PRINTER & STEREOTYPER,
16 and 18 Jacob St.

TABLE OF CONTENTS.

PREFACE.

------◆------

In one of his letters to Fum Hoam, First President of the Ceremonial Academy at Pekin, in China, Lien Chi Altangi, the Discontented Wanderer, gives us an amusing and graphic account of his introduction, by the Man in Black, to a certain bookseller in London. This bookseller was named Fudge, and being asked by the Man in Black whether he had recently published any thing new ?—

"Excuse me, sir," says he, "it is not the season; books have their time as well as cucumbers. I would no more bring out a new book in summer, than I would sell pork in the dog-days. Nothing in my way goes off in summer except very light goods indeed. A review, a magazine, or a sessions' paper, may amuse a summer reader; but all our stock of value we reserve for a spring and winter trade."

"I must confess," says Lien Chi Altangi, "a curiosity to know what you call a valuable stock, which can only bear a winter perusal."

"Sir," replied the bookseller, "it is not my way to cry up my own goods; but, without exaggeration, I will venture to show with any of the trade. My books at least have the pecullar advantage of being always new; and it is my way to clear off my old to the trunk-makers every season. I have ten new title-pages now about me, which only want books to be added to make them the finest things in nature. *Others may pretend to direct the vulgar ; but that is not my way ; I always let the vulgar direct me ; wherever popular clamor arises I always echo the million. For instance, should the people in general say that such a man is a rogue, I instantly give orders to set him down, in print,*

a villain ; thus every man buys the book, not to learn new senti-
ments, but to have the pleasure of seeing his own reflected."

Sagacious Fudge ! Neither is the race yet extinct. I dare
say the Fudge family is as numerous now as it was in the days
of Goldsmith. And we have our popular writers, too—the Fudge
beau ideal of a great genius—who worthily, even when handling
the gravest themes, follow the precedent furnished by the inimitable author of the Infernal Guide. " Ah ! sir, that was a piece
touched off by the hand of a master ; filled with good things
from one end to the other. The author had nothing but the jest
in view ; no dull, moral lurking beneath, nor ill-natured satire to
sour the reader's good humor; he wisely considered that moral
and humor at the same time were quite overdoing the business."

But, my readers, this I would have you to understand at the
very commencement of our acquaintance ; you will assuredly find
the writer of the following pages no Fudge, nor in the least ambitious to touch off such a master-piece of wit as that same In fe-
nal Guide. I have endeavored to speak my sentiments plainly,
to narrate facts impartially, and to treat a grave theme in a manner becoming its gravity and great importance. Read for yourselves, and determine. For, however faulty these papers may be
thought in other respects, I have endeavored to portray, truthfully
at least, what has been presented to my own mind, from my present stand-point. Others, I know, gazing it may be, from a higher point of observation, have professed to see the same objects in
a different light; and they may possibly be right and I wrong;
for, fully conscious of the imperfectness and general obliquity of
all men's vision, I am not so fool-hardy as to swear that the shield
whose legend I read so plainly, bears the same device upon its
other side. At the same time, however, permit me to suggest to
those who may not view the matter in dispute the same as I do,
that a peep at both sides will do no harm ; since otherwise, they
might be induced to wage a Quixotic war in defense of what may
prove (when it is too late, alas !) of no greater merit or importance
than that same senseless cause of quarrel which resulted in the
untimely death of both the foolish one-idead knights of the old
days of chivalry.

Jan. 1*st*, 1860.   THE AUTHOR.

Social Relations

IN

OUR SOUTHERN STATES.

———•••———

CHAPTER I.

THE SOUTHERN GENTLEMAN.

> "He is a noble gentleman; withal
> Happy in's endeavors: the gen'ral voice
> Sounds him for courtesy, behavior, language,
> And every fair demeanor, an example:
> Titles of honor add not to his worth;
> Who is himself an honor to his title."
>
> John Ford.

Perhaps it would be altogether superfluous to remind our readers, that the fashion has been for several years, at least since the unlooked-for success of *Uncle Tom's Cabin*, to write books about the South. Englishmen, Frenchmen, Down-Eastern men, the Bloomer style of men, as well as countless numbers of female scribblers, have not ceased to drum upon the public tympanum (almost to deafness, indeed) in praise or blame—generally the latter—of Southern peculiarities,

social habits, manners, customs, observances, and domestic institutions. And yet we dare to presume, the
untravelled reader who has never crossed the line which
separates the North from the South, possesses but a
very confused, and, in the main, erroneous opinion,
touching the veritable and distinguishing characteristics of his much-abused fellow-citizens of the Slave
States. Indeed, we are morally certain, if he have derived his information from no other sources than intemperate newspapers and exaggerated romances of the
Uncle Tom school, he remains to this day in as profound ignorance of the Summer Land, as was poor
John Brown when he made his foolish raid into Virginia at the head of his three and twenty fanatical followers. In truth, the Quixotic enterprise of these
madmen is mainly due to the persistent misrepresentation of the South by the rancorous journals and unscrupulous demagogues of the Free States. Certainly,
it is no easy matter for an entire stranger, let him be
ever so capable and unbiased, impartially to delineate
the peculiarities of any people whatever. But when a
writer's perception is rendered crooked by reason of
prejudice, while his love of the almighty dollar and
the plaudits of the rabble, urges him to cater to the
tastes of his readers, who clamor unceasingly for senseless detraction and bloody murder—what are we to
think of his productions? Certes, that they are to be
credited by no manner of means; and whoever looks
to such a source for any useful information, might just
as reasonably expect to gather lilies off a bramble-bush,
or to find the age of a maiden aunt in the family register.

And yet, if this can be truly said of all peoples—
that one not to the manor born is incompetent fairly to
discuss their social relations—of the South it can be
said most truly and pertinently. Spreading over a
vast area of country, and boasting but few large cities
or great commercial centres, the different phases presented by Southern society are almost as various as the
extent of her territory is diversified; and while it
must not be denied that she sometimes does shock our
humaner sensibilities with brutal displays of one sort
or another; still these, happily, are the exceptions to
the generally pleasing character of the landscape—the
shadows, if you will, whose very darkness only serves
to render more conspicuous those heights of moral
grandeur, and more gratefully pleasing those broad
savannahs of genial hospitality, which stretch all the
way from Little Delaware to the cactus-clad banks of
the Rio Grande. If the South has her Big Cypress,
Okefenoke, and Dismal Swamps, she can also point to
her noble Blue Ridge, her graceful Cumberland and
other mountain ranges, as well as to many a lovely
river embowered in forests of magnolia, beechwood,
hemlock, the wide-branching cedar, and the stately
pine.

It must not be forgotten, either, who were the early
pioneers in the settlement of the Slave States. New-
England was settled mainly by persons in the humbler
walks of life, and who were essentially possessed of the
same habits of thought and modes of speech; whereas
the early pioneers in the occupancy of the South possessed no such homogeneal characteristics, but differed,
on the contrary, widely in every particular—the two

1*

extremes being, on the one hand, the high-bred English courtier of aristocratic mien and faultless manners, and on the other, the thick-lipped African, fresh from the jungles of Congo and still reeking with the bloody stains of cannibalism; while between these were some half-dozen other classes, possessing different degrees of culture and refinement—all of whom yet have their descendants in the South, changed in many particulars from their original and aboriginal ancestors, but for all that, distinctly the representatives of the several classes whence they derive their origin.

Now, as the reader is aware, this very important fact has been persistently ignored by all those outside enemies of the South who are ever "harping on my daughter," and seeking to engender strife and all uncharitableness between the two sections of our common country. We know a few of the "unco pious" do occasionally condescend in their pulpits, and through the medium of *quasi*-religious newspapers, to refer in well-set phrase to the *Convict Fathers* of the South; but, as a general thing, the honey-tongued libellers of the Southern half of our Confederacy, appear to be totally unconscious that her citizens were ever divided into other than three classes—Cavaliers, Poor Whites, and Slaves. Can it be ignorance which prompts this discreet silence in regard to a solemn truth of history—a fact so essential to a proper understanding of the true relations of society in our Southern States? And yet if it be not ignorance, what are we to conclude? Why, that the accusers of the South fear to face the subject squarely, and hence are constrained to resort (with malice prepense) to base and unmanly subterfuges, in the hope of still longer bamboozling their poor dupes and trusting disciples ; thus proving to the world how exceedingly nice is their sense of honor:

> " Like dastard curres, that having at a bay
> The noble stag embost in wearie chase,
> Dare not adventure on the stubborn prey,
> Ne byte before, but rome from place to place,
> To steal a snatch when turned is his face !"

Now, as we conceive, the only proper method of arriving at any just conception of a nation's merits or demerits, as of an individual's, is, to study closely its antecedents—its past history, in a word. It would not be wise to judge of every individual man by the same standard ; wherein, then, consists the wisdom of judging of communities of individuals after the like fashion ? You say, that Jones is short, and Smith is tall, and Brown is corpulent. Because, sir, (being corpulent yourself, ah ! ha ?) you think a rotund beer-barrel to represent the highest style of man, physically speaking, do you dare to laugh at Jones and Smith—to call the former a duck of a man and the latter a bean-pole ? Consider the misfortune of their birth ; how Jones' father was a dapper little gentleman of four feet six, while Smith's mother stood five feet eleven in her stockings. Consider, also, that while you are so enthusiastic in your admiration of Brown, Jones and Smith, on the other hand, feel for you and that jolly fat dog of a Brown, all the pity and commiseration which a profound sense of your unfortunate corpulency awakens in their friendly bosoms. So, too, when nations fall out and call one another hard names, they are only playing on a larger scale the petty parts of Messrs. Jones, Smith, and Brown. Thus have John Bull and Monsieur Jean Crapeaud lampooned each other for a thousand years; and both these have united in discharging their limping pasquinades at Brother Jonathan, ever since that immortal Fourth of July, on which this last-named individual came of age and cut loose from his mother's apron-strings, to "set up on his own hook." And it is in the same spirit that the Cavaliers of Virginia have never ceased to "poke fun" at the sharp-nosed inhabitants of New-England, while the latter have returned the compliment in kind, with all sorts of brobdignagian stories in regard to the outrages on human rights daily perpetrated in the Southern States. A Yankee who visits the South, rarely troubles himself to consider what sort of society he ought reasonably to expect, in view of the different characteristics and dissimilar natures of her early settlers; but, having free access to the firesides of only one or two classes of her citizens, and ignorantly assuming those to be representations of all the rest, he very naturally blunders, often ludicrously, and always most egregiously, whenever he attempts to delineate the same. He reminds one of the sapient Englishman who went over to Boulogne, in France, tarried one night only, and returning home the next day, reported that all the women in France possessed red heads; and all because his hostess of Boulogne was blessed with such a flaming capillary ornament! In illustration whereof, we may further observe, that all the gentlemen of Mrs. Stowe's novels are represented as being anti-slavery in sentiment, though slaveholders; while every Southerner who entertains an honest conviction that slavery is right, is invariably made to appear as a brute, a bully, a hardened wretch—one who is to be looked upon as any thing else than a gentleman or a Christian. How false in fact such a presentation of the subject is, must be obvious to every unbiased mind; and yet the fair authoress is not to be charged with having intended to convey a false impression No more can the Hon. Miss Murray be accused of a similar intention, while presenting a diverse report in her Letters; for this lady's associations led her to see a very different phase of Southern society from that presented to Mrs. Stowe, whose anti-slavery sentiments were well known, and who, for that reason, would be very apt to affiliate with persons of kindred convictions. Viewing the matter in this light, we are willing to concede, that both these ladies, as well as all other reputable authors who have devoted their attention to the South, are equally honest, so far as intentions go: and this, too, whether they have written in praise or blame of Southern institutions.

Indubitably, there is much in the Slave States to call forth either unqualified approbation, or equally unqualified denunciation; owing entirely to the nature of the individual's sympathies who so applauds or denounces. We will even go a step further, and declare in all good conscience, that there is much in the South to call forth honest praise from honest men, as well as much to grieve the spirit of the most rational and conservative of philanthropists. But we have yet to stumble on that community, free or slave, of which the same remark can not be made with equal truth and pointedness.

All human society, indeed, is faulty, more or less, and ever must remain so; and it is, therefore, a grave error either to praise or to denounce unqualifiedly, any system of human government whatever, however good or bad. Nothing good can ever come of such a policy, dictated, as it of necessity ever must be, by a very circumscribed knowledge of man's imperfect nature, as well as by the most intolerant bigotry or the narrowest prejudice. Thus, in spite of fifty years' unceasing denunciation of her peculiar domestic relations, the South is stronger to-day than at any former period, and fifty-fold more prosperous than when the denunciation first began. This, the reader will probably remark, is hardly to be considered as an unfavorable result, and so it is not; but there is an evil still, which has resulted from the indiscriminate blame of Southern institutions, and that is the indiscriminate praise of the same, indulged in to excess by the too intemperate and hot-headed advocates thereof; until, in consequence of the wild vagaries of the two extremes, so totally erroneous a public sentiment has been created, that few persons, if any, whose opinions have of necessity to be based upon the testimony of others, possess as accurate information as they should touching the true state of society south of Mason's & Dixon's line.

While one portion of the Northern people inclines to believe, that the citizens of our Southern States are so many Chevalier Bayards, *sans peur et sans reproche;* living upon their broad estates in all baronial splendor and hospitality, but being, nevertheless—like the slave-holding Catos and Brutuses of republican Rome, and the equally slaveholding Solons and Leonidases of

democratic Greece—still true to the Constitution, the
Commonwealth, and the Laws; another portion of the
same community (and for the honor of humanity, we
pray Heaven this portion be not so large as we fear)
entertains in regard to the same people opinions not
quite so flattering, to say the least. What evil thing
has not been laid to the charge of the poor Southerners,
indeed, by the very Christian, refined, and amiable
people, of whom this latter portion of the Northern
community is composed, it were difficult for even the
most experienced Tombs lawyer to suggest. Only
think of an ex-minister of the Gospel, who publicly
declares that the hanging of John Brown, horse-thief,
traitor, and murderer, by the Virginia authorities, would
make the gallows as glorious as the cross! Oh! for
shame! shame upon you, Massachusetts, when you can
applaud to the echo such blasphemous utterances!

We hope our readers are not growing impatient, for
we shall endeavor to get rid of this prosing style in a
few more paragraphs; when we shall proceed immediately to the discussion of more entertaining topics. But
we can not resist the temptation to prose just a little
bit longer while we are in the vein.

And what we wish to impress upon the reader's mind,
is this (and we have been drawn to the subject almost
unawares): The greatest villainies that were ever perpetrated, were perpetrated in the name of God and
Justice. The bloody guillotine was erected to further
the ends of justice. The Order of Jesus and the Holy
Inquisition were instituted in behalf of God and justice.
And alas!·even while the Rabbins and Pharisees hanged
the King Immanuel upon the cursed tree, they loudly

professed that they were doing the will of Jehovah! Mark, however, had there been no public sentiment to justify the High Priest and Levites who consented to the death of Christ—a public sentiment which had been created and fostered by the false teachings and rabbinical traditions of the Levites themselves—such monstrous sacrilege never could have been consummated. Just so at the present time; did not a lamentably false public sentiment sustain our modern Levites in their political crusade against men as righteous as themselves, they never would dare to speak as the Phillipses and Beechers have spoken about John Brown, neither would they persuade themselves that to preach "Jesus Christ and him crucified" (which was the sole ambition of the noble Paul) consists in beating their drums ecclesiastic in a rage of fanatical zeal, or in actively consorting at primary political caucuses with every drunken vagabond who has a ballot, and who votes it according to *their consciences.*

Now, as every well-informed person knows, the fact is indisputable, and has often been boasted of by the infidel press, that anti-slavery sentiments were first propagated by the ultra socialists and communists—those miserable *sans culottes*, who, during the memorable French Revolution, raised the cry of *Liberté, Fraternité et Egalité,* and in the madness of their drunken folly enthroned a nude harlot in the Temple of Justice as the goddess Reason, the object of their admiration and worship. At that time England and Massachusetts were virtuously engaged in supplying the slave-marts of the world with cargoes fresh from Guinea and Loango, and our Northern divines had not the least suspicion that the Bible condemned slavery. But, sansculotteism being quelled in France, soon found a foothold in Exeter Hall, and thence spread to the United States. For a long time the clergy resisted the storm of radical ideas, but being only men like the rest of us, and having an eye to benefices, calls, surprise-parties, and the like, as well as "itching ears" to catch the sweet voices of the rabble, they have at last almost surrendered in a body in the Free States, and now seek to lead in the new crusade; yea, some of them have even gone so far as to doff the surplice to assume the uniform of a new master, and are now prominent political leaders: know how to pull the wires and the wool over the eyes of honest citizens, equal to the shrewdest; can turn off a five-dollar whisky-skin as coolly as the bloodiest Blood Tub, and entertain for the frailer-daughters of Eve a benevolent regard which is truly affecting.

In truth, in some sections of New-England, the clergy have made this thing of *free wool* a part of their creeds —the great Open Sesame of their churches; the real party or sectarian shibboleth: the only test of piety, or benevolence, or humanity, or civilization; until, and we declare it with shamefacedness, in the transcendentally mystified atmosphere of that highly enlightened region, the *substance* of things is no longer regarded, only the *name*. Does the reader doubt our assertion? Behold, then, the proof! We quote a brief passage from the writings of one of the most popular of New-England authors:

"Russia has sixty millions of people: who would not gladly swap her out of the world for glorious little Greece back again, and Plato, and Æschylus, and Epa-

minondas, still there?   Who would exchange Concord
or Cambridge in Massachusetts for any hundred thousand square miles of slave-breeding dead-level?"

Now, this is all good enough as high-sounding rhe-
toric, but it is also high-sounding nonsense as well.   Is
the writer ignorant that his " glorious little Greece," the
whole pocketful thereof, was only " slave-breeding dead-
level," in its palmiest days ?   Is he ignorant that " Plato,
and Æschylus, and Epaminondas," and all the rest of
the Grecian worthies, were slaveholders as much as
George Washington, or Henry A. Wise, or Gov. Ham-
mond? with this difference, that these are Christian
slaveholders, while those were profane heathens, ignorantly worshipping gods of wood and stone?   And yet
this amiable orthodox anti-slavery philosopher and dia-
lectician of the "Modern Athens," would rejoice to see
Christian Russia blotted out of existence, merely to
have back again " glorious little Greece," with all her
thirty thousand obscene gods and goddesses, and her
slaveholding populace, whose morals were so bad, that
Thucydides, after having driven in a car drawn by six
nude Cyprians through the public thoroughfares of
Athens, was by popular ballot elected to the highest
office in the gift of his fellow-citizens !   Need we wonder the Old Bay State, while under the control and
guidance of such perspicacious logicians, despite her
acknowledged wealth and refinement, exerts no greater
influence in the land than she does?   Verily, in the
days of Cotton Mather, when her godly sons were sorely
exercised about Quakers, Baptists, witches, hobgoblins,
broomsticks—and the like precious theological matters,
they were not more befogged and befooled, than are

their descendants of to-day on the subject of "slave-breeding dead-level." If, however, they will grant us a patient hearing, we hope to enlighten them somewhat in that regard, at least in so far as our own Slave States are concerned. Russia must take care of herself·

Of course, in order faithfully to perform the delicate task we have voluntarily undertaken, (for it is a delicate matter to presume to discuss the social relations of any community,) even if we were an author of well-established reputation, and long acquaintance with the public, it would behoove us to show some personal fitness for the work; but much more is this the case, when a young and unknown literary aspirant lays claim to a public audience. We trust the reader will pardon a seeming egotism, therefore, when we proceed first to state, that the writer has enjoyed more than ordinary opportunities for observing the different phases of Southern society. Born in the South, his education was chiefly acquired at . Southern institutions of learning, in the States of Alabama, Tennessee, Kentucky, and Virginia. 'Tis true he left the University of Virginia to conclude his professional studies at Harvard University, Massachusetts; but this was because he had a strong desire to come in contact with the Northern people, and Northern prejudices, on their own soil; to correct his own sectional prejudices, should these require correction, as well as to demonstrate to those with whom he might have occasion to associate, that not all slaveholders are such "outside barbarians," as the enemies of the South strive so laboriously to make the Northern public believe. He has, besides, travelled in nearly every State in the Union, and for four years has been a freeholder and house-

keeper in a Free State. Indeed, his pecuniary interests
in the North and South are about equal, so that there
will not be a sufficient preponderance of selfish interests
to bias his judgment one way or the other. We shall
aim all the time at strict impartiality. And although
we do not deny that we entertain very warm sympathies
for all classes of persons in the Slave States—not excepting those who are there held as property and sold
as chattels—we are yet perfectly well aware, that many
of them are in very bad odor with all honorable men,
as they rightly deserve to be. When, therefore, we
come to speak of such, while we shall take care to set
naught down in malice, we shall endeavor nevertheless
to state the plain, unvarnished truth; even if, as the
great English novelist has suggested, it may occasionally scratch.

Having premised the above, more to introduce the
writer to the reader than his subject, we now proceed
to introduce to him the latter. And, *imprimis*, we beg
to make him acquainted with the SOUTHERN GENTLE-
MAN. We know the usual practice with writers is, as
with hod-carriers, to begin at the bottom-round of their
argument and thence ascend to its topmost; but we are
pleased to reverse the usual order, and so beginning at
the topmost, shall endeavor to descend as easily as possible until we reach the " mud-sills," known in the old-
fashioned vernacular of the South as slaves.

In our description of the Southern Gentleman—his
family and friends—his negroes, horses, dogs, and estates—his manners, speech, opinions, excellencies, and
faults—all indeed that appertains to him—we wish the
reader to understand from the beginning, that we in-

tend to confine ourself to such a gentleman as is peculiarly the outgrowth of the institutions of the South. Of course there is at the South a conventional gentleman, as there is at the North, or in England, or on the continent of Europe; but he is no more *the Southern Gentleman*, than was the Count D'Orsay such a gentleman. Although born in the Southern States, and never having been any where else, may be, he is yet simply a gentleman—the universally accredited gentleman of the civilized world. This conventional species of gentleman may be either an honest man or a knave—a *blasé* libertine, a wine-bibber, a coxcomb; or a hero as well, a Christian, and a sage. We know there are those who will cry out against this definition of the world's gentleman; but let them bawl until their lungs are sore, yet they can not thereby change the facts. What was Beau Brummell, but a spendthrift, drunkard, and coxcomb? What was my Lord Chesterfield, but a polished sepulchre, fair outside to look upon, within black and unsightly with every rank corruption? What was King George the Fourth—that most "perfect gentleman in all Europe"—but a base deceiver, a proud and selfish ruler, and a heartless hypocrite? And coming down to these degenerate times, what shall we say of P. Barton Key? And do you presume, honest reader, that "the tower of Siloam," which fell upon him, crushed in his person all the polished, but false, Keys in the land, who are accustomed habitually to unlock the treasure-house of their bosom friend and steal thence his diamond without price? What, too, shall we say of Bulwig, the learned novelist, the titled playwright, and minister of her Christian Majesty—Bulwig, who notoriously beats his wife, and shuts her up in a mad-house without cause? Has not this same Bag-wig, as Yellowplush blunderingly calls him, shot into the very centre and bull's-eye of fashion? Is he not looked upon in all respects as being no less a gentle-man than was our own immortal Washington, or is that purest of our statesmen and chastest of our orators, Ed-ward Everett? Certainly: and all because the learned Baronet has read Chesterfield with profit, and possesses a certain external polish—a certain suavity of manner and speech, soon mastered by such as frequent courts and the palaces of the great—as well as a complete knowledge of all those conventional laws of etiquette, which the artificial nature of our social intercourse has rendered almost indispensably necessary to the comple-tion of a polite education. Neither are such mere or-namental accomplishments to be despised; but whoever would lay too great store by them, let him not forget, that while blossoms and green leaves render the tree beautiful to look upon, still much more greatly to be prized are its black, misshapen roots, which, striking deep down into the earth, hourly extract from the soil those juices which supply both leaf and flower with all their fragrance and beauty.

Now, we are not going to say, that the Southern Gentleman does not frequently possess as much of Chesterfieldian polish as most others, for then we should say that which is not true; but we do say, that a great many persons in the Southern States possess equally as much polish and refinement, who are yet not to be con-·sidered as Southern Gentlemen, *par excellence;* while many of those who are to be so considered are not always what the *beau monde* calls *au fait* in matters of dress and deportment. Many of them are quite old-fashioned, indeed, and would crack in a trice any simpering coxcomb's skull who should dare to whirl their daughters through the indecent mazes of some of those most popular modern waltzes, suitable to Germany and other parts of Europe perhaps, but as yet exotics in these States, and like all exotics so far of but feeble growth—though much affected by the codfish-ocrats of our large cities, as well as by all the ambitious inland villages, which so love to ape the vices of a metropolis, since they can not aspire to its virtues.

And we would also like to impress now at the commencement upon the mind of our reader, that the genuine Southern Gentlemen, like all real gentlemen, are not quite so plentiful as blackberries in summer-time, or New-England robins in spring. To intelligent Northerners, who have travelled much, this information is superfluous, we know; but a great many citizens of the Free States — amiable, educated, and naturally shrewd people—on visiting the South for the first time, manifest great surprise because they meet there, as at home, many ill-bred and vulgar persons; just as they are disappointed, oftentimes, to discover that the Southern landscape is disfigured now and then with a reedy swamp, a long stretch of barren sand-hills, or many continuous miles of monotonous piney woods. They have been so accustomed from infancy to hear and read of Southern hospitality and wealth, as well as of the splendors of natural scenery in all Southern latitudes, they seem to anticipate at every step a princely mansion, and at every turn magnolia groves. Filled with

such ideal conceptions of the Summer Land, it is not at
all strange that such persons can not refrain at times
from expressing their disappointment, when they come
to realize the facts.

We remember travelling once on the Mississippi in
company with an old gentleman from New-York, (it
was in the autumn of '57,)—a respectable member of
the middle classes, intelligent and courteous, though
somewhat of a cockney. He was quite a portly old
gentleman—must have stood at least six feet in his
stockings—with a red face and very white hair ; a bachelor withal, hearty and jovial, and a pretty fair specimen of what one might fitly call an Old Boy. Being
such an Old Boy, he was not above associating with
young gentlemen many years his junior, but seemed on
the contrary to prefer such company to that of the se-
niors; and so we became quite familiar. He was on his
first visit Southward, and it was quite amusing to note
the changes which came over his bachelor visage as we
neared the tropics. He came aboard at Cairo, and besides having had to stay in that dull Illinois town one
whole night, the ticket-agent at Chicago had swindled
him out of a dollar, selling him a through-ticket to
Memphis at a higher rate than the usual railroad and
steamboat fares combined amounted to ; and these two
trials united had left our Old Boy in no very pleasant
humor, although he was a jolly old bachelor. The
steamer happened to be one of the best of the Louisville
and New-Orleans packets—stately in its proportions,
luxuriously furnished, and was besides fairly packed
with first-class passengers. The bustle of landing, etc.
etc., together with the novelty of the whole scene to

our bachelor's eyes, for a while made him forget his
misfortunes, as well as his ill-humor; and the Old Boy
manifested almost as much delight as any Young Boy
would on his first escape from the maternal apron-
strings. Rubbing his hands together with delight, and
thridding his way nervously from deck to deck among
the hundreds of travellers, in the brief space of half an
hour he must have informed near upon twenty differ
ent individuals that he was a New-Yorker, Sir; and
was on his first visit to the South, Sir; and hoped to
spend the winter in the same, Sir! And at least half-
a-dozen times he must have asked, pointing to the colored waiters, "And these are the slaves? eh, Sir, all
slaves?" while at the moment he was evidently inclined
to think very favorably of an institution which had
succeeded in manufacturing into such decent and respectable, not to say important-looking personages, the
raw material originally imported from Africa.

In truth, so long as the bustle and confusion lasted,
our bachelor acquaintance seemed pleased with every
thing about him. So long had he been used to the
continuous hum and noise of a large city—so long had
he been accustomed to being jostled about at every
turn—that to him *unrest* seemed to be the only species
of *rest* of which he knew any thing. This fact became
painfully apparent after his first day's travel on the
Mississippi; we say painfully, for it was (save that it
was ludicrous as well) really painful to witness the misery the old gentleman suffered day by day, as we
steamed further and further down the broad bosom of
the Father of Waters. He was evidently a kind-hearted
man, national and patriotic, and did not wish to say

2

any thing out of the way; but it was still plain as a pikestaff that in his own mind he connected the vast solitude, in the awful stillness whereof he seemed to be dying, with the "curse of slavery." For a long time he endured the horrors of his situation with the patience of a martyr, (and what he must have suffered in mental agony and bodily worriment before he did speak, it is frightful to conjecture;) but at last, after having walked his boots almost off, and after numerous ejaculations, as if to himself, while standing by the taffrail, of "Well! well!" "It's no use!" "Yes! it must be so!" "It must be so!" he came up to us in a pompous manner, and says he, very energetically, giving his inexpressibles a nervous hitch at the same time, and striving hard to *look* unutterable things—says he: "WHERE'S YOUR TOWNS?" The question was so characteristic, and was uttered with such a meaning look and gesture, we could not refrain from turning aside to have a quiet laugh. And yet at least one half of the Northern people, used all their lives to the bustle of cities and towns, and the noisy clatter of mechanical trades, if similarly situated with our earnest New-York acquaintance, would propound just such a question as he did—never once reflecting that cotton, sugar, rice, wheat, corn, tobacco, and all other agricultural products, grow only in the country, and very *quietly* too at that. Hence, even while they are passing a princely plantation—hid from view though it be by the dense forest on the river's bank—whose proprietor could with a single year's crop buy up half-a-dozen New-England villages, they will whisper confidentially in your ear: "Ah! Sir, how unlike our thrifty Down East villages!" Observe, however, we are casting no stones at any body in particular. Nor yet do we complain of any man for doing what it is perfectly natural he should do, until he has learned to do better. It is natural for the city cockney to find the country dull, and to wonder without affectation how people manage to live there; and it is equally natural for the sun-embrowned farmer, after one week's sojourn in the town, to find it excessively boring, and to wonder how any body can make money honestly where they neither sow turnips nor raise garden "sass."

But let us return to our subject.

To begin with his pedigree, then, we may say, the Southern Gentleman comes of a good stock. Indeed, to state the matter fairly, he comes usually of aristocratic parentage; for family pride prevails to a greater extent in the South than in the North. In Virginia, the ancestors of the Southern Gentleman were chiefly English cavaliers, after whom succeeded the French Huguenots and Scotch Jacobites. In Maryland, his ancestors were in the main Irish Catholics—the retainers and associates of Lord Baltimore—who sought in the wilds of the New World religious tolerance and political freedom. In South-Carolina, they were Huguenots—at least the better class of them—those dauntless chevaliers, who, fleeing from the massacre of St. Bartholomew and the bloody persecutions of priests and tyrants, drained France of her most generous blood to found in the Western Hemisphere a race of heroes and patriots. In Florida, Louisiana, Texas, and other portions of the far South, the progenitors of the Southern Gentleman were chiefly Spanish Dons and French Catholics

Thus it will be seen that throughout the entire extent of the South, (for the new Southern States have been settled almost wholly by emigrants from those named above,) wherever you meet with the Southern Gentleman, you find him *hijo dalgo*, as the Spaniards phrase it : however, there are many notable exceptions in every Southern State.   For, owing to the repeal of the Law of Primogeniture, and the gradual decay of some of the old families, as well as the levelling effects of many of Mr. Jefferson's innovations, particularly the subsequent intermarriages between the sons and daughters of the gentry and persons of the middle class, (of whom we shall have something to say in the next chapter,) there are scattered throughout all the Southern States many gentlemen of the genuine Southern character, whose ancestry was only in part of the cavalier stock.   Indeed, Mr. Jefferson himself was a fit representative of these ; for, while his mother was a Randolph, his father was only a worthy descendant of the sturdy yeomanry of England.

Besides being of faultless pedigree, the Southern Gentleman is usually possessed of an equally faultless physical development.   His average height is about six feet, yet he is rarely gawky in his movements, or in the least clumsily put together; and his entire *physique* conveys to the mind an impression of firmness united to flexibility.   If the reader has ever read Lieutenant Strain's account of his perilous Darien Expedition, he will have had presented to him a fit illustration of what the superior physical structure of the Southern Gentleman enables him to undergo, in the remarkable powers of endurance possessed by Capt. Maury.

We mention this subject, because the Northern people entertain in regard to it such very erroneous opinions. They have been told so incessantly of the lazy habits of Southerners, that they honestly believe them to be delicate good-for-nothings, like their own brainless fops and nincompoops—those amazingly good fellahs, who dawdle at watering-places during the summer months, and dance attendance all winter upon some fair Flora McFlimsy, who is in all respects as utterly stupid and worthless as themselves. Only those Northerners who have travelled in the Southern States, or whose associations otherwise have made them familiar with the gentlemen of the South, possess any correct knowledge of the physical perfectness of the latter. This these owe in part, doubtless, to those mailed ancestors who followed Godfrey and bold Cœur de Lion to the rescue of the Holy Sepulchre, or to those knightly sires, may be, who, like Front de Bœuf and most of the other gallant gentlemen of those days, were great with battle-axes, and in every other kind of physical prowess, but who also always signed their names with a *cross*.

Much more reasonably, however, we think we may attribute the good size and graceful carriage of the Southern Gentleman, to his out-of-doors and a-horse-back mode of living. For we might as well here inform our readers, the genuine Southern Gentleman almost invariably lives in the country. But let them not conclude from this circumstance that he is nothing more than the simple-hearted, swearing, hearty, and hospitable old English or Virginia Country Gentleman, of whom we have all heard so repeatedly. The time has been when such a conviction could have been truthfully entertained; but that was long ago. In those good old times the Southern Gentleman had little else to do than fox-hunt, drink, attend the races, fight chicken-cocks, and grievously lament that he was owner of a large horde of savages whom he knew not how to dispose of.

But times change, *et nos mutamur in illis.* The new order of things which succeeded the innovations of Mr. Jefferson made it necessary for the Gentlemen of the South, for all the old families who had before lived upon their hereditary wealth and influence, to struggle to maintain their position, else to be pushed aside by the thrifty middle classes, who thought it no disgrace to work by the side of their slaves, and who were, in consequence, yearly becoming more wealthy and influential. Besides, after the repeal of the Law of Primogeniture, the large landed estates, the former pride and boast of the first families, very soon were divided up into smaller freeholds, and the owners of these, of necessity, were frequently forced to lay aside the old manners and customs, the air and arrogance of the grand seignor, and to content themselves with the plain, unostentatious mode of life which at present characterizes most gentlemen in the South. The result of all which has been, that the Southern Gentleman of to-day is less an idler and dreamer than he was in the old days, is more practical, and, although not so great a lover of the almighty dollar as his Northern kinsman, still is far from being as great a spendthrift as his fathers were before him.

But, notwithstanding the old style of Southern Gentlemen has in a measure passed away, the young South is nurtured in pretty much the same school as formerly—at least so far as physical education is concerned—and participates more or less in all those rollicking out-door sports and amusements still common in England to this day. Scarcely has he gotten fairly rid of his bibs and tuckers, therefore, before we find him mounted a-horseback; and this not a hobby-horse either, (which the poor little wall-flower of cities is so proud to straddle,) but a genuine live pony—sometimes a Canadian, sometimes a Mustang, but always a pony. By the time he is five years of age he rides well; and in a little while thereafter has a fowling-piece put into his hands, and a little black boy of double his age put *en croupe* behind him, (or in case mamma is particularly cautious, his father's faithful serving-man accompanies him, mounted on another horse,) and so accoutred, he sallies forth into the fields and pastures in search of adventures. At first he bangs away at every thing indiscriminately, and the red-headed woodpeckers more often grace his game-bag than quail or snipe; but by degrees he acquires the art and imbibes the spirit of the genuine sportsman, and ever after keeps his father's hospitable board amply supplied with the choicest viands the woods or fields or floods afford. By floods, the reader will please understand rivers, creeks, and ponds; for our young Southerner is as much of a fisherman as a Nimrod. When he tires of his gun, he takes his fishing-rods and other tackle, and goes angling; and when he tires of angling, provided the weather is favorable, he denudes himself and plunges into the water for a

swim, of which he tires not at all.   Indeed, he will remain in the watery element until the sun blisters his
back, and if thus forced to seek *terra firma*, he does it
"upon compulsion," and under protest.   As a general
thing, the blue-noses of Nova Scotia, or the natives of
South-America, are not greater lovers of the healthy
exercise of swimming than the boys of the South, of
all classes.

In his every foray, whether by flood or field, our
young gentleman has for his constant attendant, Cuffee,
junior, who sticks to him like his shadow.   At the
expiration of five years or so of this manner of living,
(provided there is no family tutor, and in that case his
mother has already learned him to read,) the master is
sent to the nearest village, or district, or select school,
returning home every night.   Sometimes this school is
from five to ten miles distant, and so he has to ride
from ten to twenty miles every day, Saturdays and
Sundays alone excepted.   Again Cuffee is sent with
his young master, and morning and evening the two
are to be seen cantering to or from the school-house,
the negro taking charge of their joint lunch for dinner,
(to be eaten during "play-time,") and the master carrying on the pommel of his saddle or his arm the bag
which contains his books and papers, and maybe a
stray apple or peach to exchange with the village
urchins for fishing-rods, or to present to some school-
boy friend, who has a rosy-cheeked little sister, with a
roguish black eye and a silvery laugh.

And although every day in the week, from Monday
to Friday inclusive, is thus occupied, both master and
slave sit up nearly all of Friday night, cleaning guns,

arranging fishing-lines, and discussing enthusiastically the sports to be followed on the morrow. These change very materially, as our young Southerner begins to get higher and higher in his teens. He very soon surfeits of the tame pastime of shooting squirrels and ducks, woodcock and plover, or chasing of hares; when for a short while, say a couple of years, his chief delight is to hunt wild turkeys—a rare sport where turkeys are abundant and when one has a well-trained dog. But even this soon ceases to be attractive, and is succeeded by fox-hunting. Preparatory to entering upon the latter rare old English sport, our young gentleman gets some one of the many dusky uncles on his father's plantation, to procure him a deep intoned horn; which procured, he proceeds immediately to exchange his pony for the fleetest and most active of his father's stud. On a great many Southern plantations there are kept hunting horses, regularly trained for the sport as in England; and it is astonishing in what a little time they become as fond of the same as their riders. Even mules, after having been used a few times, will prick up their heavy ears at the sound of a merry horn, and will follow the hounds with all the eagerness of the best-blooded of their sires.

Having selected his steed, and mounted Cuffee on another, (usually a mule, by the way,) our young fox-hunter gives his horn a merry wind in the "wee sma' hours atween the twal" in the morning, answering to which well-known call, Ringwood, and Jowler, and Don, with all their yelping and barking mates, soon gather together and hasten after their master to the appointed place of rendezvous. Here soon assemble the

2*

sons of the neighboring gentry, or such of them at least as intend to participate in the morning's sport. Masters and negroes, horses and dogs, all sniff keenly the bracing morning air, and, after a brief parley, having settled the preliminaries, away they all hie to some old field filled with broom-sedge, or to some scarcely penetrable copse—these being Reynard's usual habitats; and ere a great while the rattling music of the "pack in full cry" breaks on the stillness of the hour:

> ———" For the fox is found,
> And over the stream, at a mighty bound,
> And over the highlands and over the low,
> O'er furrows, o'er meadows the hunters go :
> Away ! away !   As a hawk flies full at his prey,
> So flieth the hunter, away, away !
> He flies from the burst at the cover, till set of sun,
> When the red fox dies, and the day is done !"

Ah! it is impossible for your pale denizens of the dusty town, whose horizon on every side is bounded by dull brick walls and flaming sign-boards, to appreciate the wild delight of a steeple-chase ride through brake and briars, over gullies and fences, adown green lanes and under the overshadowing boughs of majestic forests, with a whoop and halloo, and hark, tallyho! and all the accompanying bustle and excitement of a regular old-fashioned Virginia fox-hunt!   We say Virginia fox-hunt, not that it is peculiar to the Old Dominion, but because the red fox most abounds in that ancient commonwealth, and this is the fox which gives the longest run and the greatest sport, and to win whose "brush" is the ambition of all aspiring hunters.   Fox-hunting is more or less followed in all the Slave States, both by the sons of the gentry and of the middle-class planters and farmers; and such has been the practice ever since the first settlement of the country. It was originally introduced by the English cavaliers, was a favorite pastime with the Father of his Country, and in those days was adhered to by the lovers of the sport, even until their "frosty pows" admonished them that the greatest of huntsmen, Death, was about to "earth" them in his turn, as they had "earthed" many a noble fox before. At present, however, it is chiefly patronized by boys and young men, and in consequence, occupies much less of public attention than formerly, or than it still does in England. Nor have we ever known an instance in the South of a lady's indulging in the sport, which is a common practice in the old fatherland; and the foxes are so plenty, the copses, woods, and other breeding and hiding-places, being so abundant, instead of having to take the precaution to insure a continuance of the breed, as our English cousins have to do, the Southern farmers complain that the cunning rascals only breed too fast, despite the hunters and their hounds.

We are thus particular to speak of these matters, since they are so imperfectly understood in the Free States, wherein every species of pastime which hinders the making of money is regarded as sinful; and wherein also the usual custom is, to hunt foxes with any kind of dog, while such a thing as a horse, or merry-sounding horn, is never once thought of. We remember being in Concord, Massachusetts, on a certain occasion, indeed, having driven thither from Cambridge in a sleigh, and stopping at a country-looking tavern, the bar-room whereof reminded one of the South-west. This licensed rum-hole was full of rough, unpolished people, dressed like laborers and farmers, and dogs—old dogs and young dogs, puppies, sluts, and snarling curs. After we had sufficiently thawed our frozen fingers to listen to the conversation of the bipeds in the room, (one of whom, in a kind of drunken glee, held an overgrown pup between his knees, and, while the brute made frantic efforts to lick its master's face, descanted in a doting, maudlin way on the *pup's pints*—for one we thought the master could boast of more *pints* than the dog,) we gathered that some of the company present had just returned from a fox-hunt; and learned, to our astonishment, that they actually had taken guns along to shoot poor Reynard, in case their "mongrel curs" should fail to catch him—which indeed happened; while, from the manner in which they recounted over and over again the various incidents of the chase, laughing the while immoderately, they certainly fancied they had had a deal of sport.

Now, the sport of a properly conducted fox-hunt consists in its adventurous character, in the wild excitement and general *abandon* of the long chase, and the eager cries of the hounds—all which are heightened and rendered more delightful by reason of the "merry bold voice of the hunter's horn." Even when one is not a participant in the chase itself, there is an indescribable charm in listening to the various sounds which accompany it. Let any person, no matter how prejudiced he may be against the sport, only be aroused from his slumbers some still frosty morning, when the sky is cloudless and the moon is just beginning to wane in the first blush of the dawn, and all at once have borne to his ears, as in a dream, the distant winding of the hunter's horn, the echoing shouts of a dozen horsemen, the deep and varied cries of fifty hounds in hot pursuit, the whole mellowed by the distance and sweetly confused—at times almost indistinct, as the huntsmen dash madly through some sequestered glen—then again ringing clear and melodious as they brush past the brow of a neighboring hill, only to be lost so soon as they drive helter-skelter down its thither side; and he will prove singularly phlegmatic and lacking in enthusiasm who does not feel, for the moment, that he can heartily and conscientiously approve the sentiment so beautifully and musically uttered by Barry Cornwall :

> "Sound, sound the horn! to the hunter good,
>   What's the gully deep, or the roaring flood?
>   Right over he bounds (as the wild stag bounds,)
>   At the heels of his swift, sure, silent hounds.
>   Oh! what delight can a mortal lack,
>   When he once is firm on his horse's back,
>   With his stirrups short, and his snaffle strong,
>   And the blast of the horn for his morning's song?"

After fox-hunting succeeds deer-hunting, which, in the Southern States, among gentlemen, is usually conducted somewhat after the same fashion as the former, or by what in hunter's parlance is called "driving," although scholars, and men of quiet contemplative natures, frequently prefer to "still-hunt," which is likewise much in favor with all "pot-hunters;" these latter adopting such a mode of killing their venison from necessity, and their inability to afford the horses and dogs necessary to a successful drive, while the former, being usually of a taciturn bent of mind, find opportunities in still-hunting to gratify their penchant for meditation and solitude.   And truly there is a wondrous charm in being all alone in the shadowy woods—shut out as it were from the bright sunlight above, which only trickles down in little golden showers through the thick green leaves over one's head—and where the stillness is so profound, you distinctly hear even the faintest wimbling of the wriggling wood-worm in the very heart of the old log on which you sit down to rest. How pleasant a place, indeed, for one to look after the interests of his *Chateaux en Espagne!*   In reality you sit on a very common sort of rusty old log, and rest your gun idly on your knee, while a red-headed wood-pecker drums in a very prosy monotone on the decayed branch of the old oak over your head, and little gray squirrels skip about around you, stopping now and then merely to taste a savory acorn, or chasing one another from root to root and tree to tree; but oh! what different scenes does the arch magician Fancy spread out before you!   You are in your own enchanted castle, and your trusty vassals are keeping faithful watch in the tower and at the portcullised gate.   You are "monarch of all you survey," and dream your dream of love, or fame, or wealth, with none to molest you or make you afraid.   But when the dream has ended, (as all such dreams will end, alas!) and you awake to find the sun fast sinking in the West, it is not so pleasant to trudge homeward many a weary mile, through marsh and bog and reedy swamp, with the gloomy shades of darkness fast gathering around your head, and the brambles and tangled grass growing every minute more tangled and intricate beneath your feet. Besides, one is sure almost to get wood-ticks and chigas on his person, by reason of his contact with the old log on which he sits down to ruminate; and these pestiferous little varlets render his night-dreams for a long time the very antipodes of the pleasant day-dreams in which he may have indulged, while they managed to fasten on his breeches.

But, even conceding that "still-hunting" has its charms for quiet people of an imaginative turn, despite a few drawbacks of the kind we have adverted to, we still think that most persons would prefer "driving." This is in truth a right royal sport, and engages the attention of the Southern Gentleman in matured life, after he has given up most other field-sports, although it is followed by the younger men and boys also. It is most popular in the far South and South-west, because of the greater abundance of deer in these parts of the country; for in the more northerly Slave States it is rarely indulged in more than once in a twelvemonth, and then parties of gentlemen have to retreat to the mountains in the autumn, and participate in what is called a camp-hunt, which lasts from two to six weeks. Driving, to prove successful, requires a skillful horsemanship, a quick eye and steady aim, thoroughly trained horses and dogs, and a partial familiarity at least with the geography of the hunting-ground, as well as the "range" of the deer thereon. Above all things else, however, the hunter should be endowed with steady nerves; for even the oldest and most experienced hand sometimes trembles and fails to draw the trigger until the right moment has been lost forever; while, if you were to station an ordinary cockney sportsman at a "stand," and some lordly "monarch of the forest" were to come bounding towards him, with tail waving like a banner in the breeze, his kingly head thrown back and the branching antlers thereof tossing a proud defiance to both hounds and huntsmen, ninety-nine times in a hundred he would be suffered to pass by unharmed, receiving only a bewildered stare from his ambushed enemy, who for the moment is totally oblivious that he has a gun in his hands; or even did he recall this circumstance, it would be all the same, since a hundred guns would be of no service whatever to a man already nearly shaken out of his boots by the terrible "buck-ague."

It is mainly owing, as we conceive, to such out-door sports as we have briefly described above, and others like them—which are common in most parts of the South—that the Southern Gentleman possesses that fine physical development which we have already adverted to. Such pastimes, aided materially by plenty of pure country air, do almost if not wholly counteract the pernicious influences of certain dissipations—unfortunately too prevalent in the South—but more particularly the dissipations and close confinement incident to college-life. Herein, indeed, lies the chief reason why the Southern people, though living in a warmer climate, are far less nervous and spasmodic than their fellow-citizens of the Free States. The latter pay so little regard to the proper culture of the physical man—have so persistently banned and anathematized all rollicking

field-sports and healthy out-door amusements, and at
the same time have taken such great pains to stimulate
into undue and excessive activity the mental faculties—
that we are by no means surprised the London *Times*
should conclude that the Americans have physically
deteriorated in the last hundred years. Nor do we
wonder that Spiritualism, and every other blind fanaticism of the hour, should possess the minds of men,
whose bodies are unsound and whose secretions are altogether abnormal. We do not wonder that, from
Maine to Minnesota, there should have been one general bonfire on the success of the Atlantic Cable, while
the English continued to eat their roast-beef as quietly
as usual, and scarcely a bell was rung in a single Slave
State. Comparisons are "odorous," we know, as the
learned Dogberry hath said; but the writer means nothing unkind by these remarks. We entertain for our
Northern fellow-citizens the highest regard, take them
en masse. Among them we have many personal friends
also; but we never allow our friendships to blur our
vision. The fault is not confined to one class alone at
the North, but to all those above the laboring or farming classes. Foreigners, when they visit America, see
it and speak of it. Sir Charles Fox, one of the Commissioners of the Crystal Palace, while in Boston, visited one of the high-schools for girls. On coming away
he remarked to his friend: "You seem to be training
your girls for the lunatic asylum." Such was the impression made upon this practical Englishman by their
wonderful intellectual achievements, in connection with
their pale and sallow faces. And as for the Northern
boys, here is what Mr. Theodore Sedgwick said, in a

recent address before the Alumni of Columbia College, New-York:

" From the time that the boy whose fortune it is to be educated is immured in school, till the period when he is again to be immured in a lawyer's office or counting-room, and from that time again until he enters upon the profession of his life, no systematic attention whatever is paid to the subject of physical education. All the health, all the exercise that he gets, he gets by nature or by chance. No regular opportunity is provided for it—no authoritative encouragement is given to it, no stimulus, no prize; all the ambition, all the zeal, all the ardor of his young, ignorant, and unreflecting nature is concentrated on the vigil and the midnight lamp. Severe labor, long terms, short vacations, crowded rooms, late hours, bad air—what is the result?"

Must we answer for Mr. Sedgwick and our readers? Who are the leaders of the Northern masses at this time? Theodore Parker, Wendell Phillips, Ward Beecher, Dr. Cheever, John Brown, and their "compatriots!"—men whose early excesses of one kind or another have impaired their reason, and who ought, as has been found necessary in the case of Gerrit Smith, to be confined in a *Maison de Santé*.

" To this complexion will it come at last!"

Believe us, our readers, without a sound body a well-balanced mind is not to be thought of. In all seriousness, we think a good digestion has about as much to do with great thoughts and great actions as a good brain. The fable of the freedman Æsop is as true to-day as it was when the old fellow uttered it. If you keep a bow bent too long, in time it will lose its elasticity; and if you tax the mind too greatly, both it and the body must suffer. It is all work and no play, you know, that makes Jack a dull boy.

Now, as has been intimated already, the natural manner of living in the Slave States helps to cover up a multitude of Southern shortcomings—tobacco-chewing, brandy-drinking, and other excesses of a like character —which would otherwise without doubt render the masses of the Southern people as fickle and unstable, as nervous and spasmodic, as the masses of the North. God knows dissipation and debauchery are rife enough in all conscience over the whole land; and our own opinion is, neither the North or the South would be justifiable in casting the first stone at the head of the other. Such irregularities, however, are not so frequently committed by the gentlemen of the South as by a certain class of underbred snobs, whose money enables them for a time to pretend to the character and standing of gentlemen, but whose natural inborn coarseness and vulgarity invariably lead them to disgrace the honorable title they assume to wear. The real gentlemen of the South are restrained by considerations of family pride, and family prestige, if by none more honorable, from participating in those disgraceful practices so well calculated to tarnish the family escutcheon, and to render themselves the unworthy descendants of the compatriots of the Hero of Mt. Vernon. Perhaps in no one place in the South is the truth of the above observation illustrated with greater force and clearness than at the University of Virginia. Here congregate from all portions of the South the flower and bloom of her chivalrous youth, as well as the scum and dregs of her whisky-swilling snobs and bullies. While the writer attended this first of our Universities, there were about five hundred students, either actually or nominally pursuing their studies in its various departments. Of this number, at least one hundred were more or less dissipated; while of these not more than a dozen at the farthest could have been the sons of gentlemen. The rest were either needy adventurers—beggared in purse as in character—living in a kind of shabby-genteel way, and indulging in cards, and wine, and loose women only to that extent which insured their becoming intimate with vulgar greenhorns and new-rich swells, whom they hoped to fleece, and who formed the larger proportion of those given to dissipation; for, besides themselves, and the *chevaliers d' industrie* whom they helped to support, and the single dozen of gentlemen already named, there were but a few others, and these, singularly enough, were State students. What is meant by "State students" may need some explanation. The University of Virginia is a State institution, (as the reader is doubtless aware,) and undertakes to educate free of charge a certain number of Virginia young men every year—boarding and lodging them gratuitously also, unless we misremember; at all events they have lodgings separate and apart from the rest of the students, and dress very poorly, being usually selected from the most destitute families in the State. Under such circumstances it is hard to credit the statement, but it is true, that some of this very class are the most dissolute and worthless of all the young men who attend the University lectures. At first they come clothed in suits of russet, with freckled sun-tanned faces, large red bony hands, loose matted locks of hair, and having in their pockets neither scrip nor purse. But so soon as they begin to associate with the "spreeing fellows," by some sort of talismanic influence they seem to become transformed almost in a day—completely metamorphosed in their whole appearance. 'Tis true for a time they appear somewhat awkward in their flash apparel, and do not get rid very soon of their shuffling country gait; but they attempt, to the best of their ability, to imitate the swaggering strides of their more wealthy associates, and on the whole succeed pretty well, considering their "chances." They remind one, however, in some of their assumed airs, of Dr. Livingstone's friend, Sambanza, a high functionary attached to the court of the royal Shinte, king of the Balondas, in Central Africa. Shinte's chief dress consisted of a series of heavy brass rings, which reached, one above the other, from his ankles to his knees; and owing to their great weight, his sooty Majesty was perforce obliged to walk in a right royal straddling fashion. Sambanza, too poor to wear the same amount of brass on his legs as his royal master, made up the deficiency by another species of brass not wholly unknown in this country; and so out-Shinted Shinte himself in his performance of the fashionable royal straddle, making believe that he bore on his own stout calves all the brass in heathendom!

We shall not deny that one will occasionally meet in the South, as elsewhere, persons of the smallest possible calibre of mind—whose respectable position in society is owing to no merit of their own, but to that of their fathers—who imagine that their social *status* is a license to do wrong with impunity; but our readers need never fear to set down as a *parvenu* that Southerner who is openly and notoriously dissipated in his habits, or loose in his morals. They may sometimes mistake their man, but we apprehend they will do so very rarely. One of the most mortifying trials we ever had to endure was a day's journey by rail through a Northern State in company with one of that class of drunken, snobbish, but ignorant as conceited Southerners, who claim to be Southern gentlemen, but whose claim is about as reasonable as was that of the painted jackdaw to a place in the dove-cot. So long as such worthies can manage to hold their tongues, they succeed in deceiving strangers very well; but, like most other shallow-pated fools, they would burst could they not wag their unruly little members upon all occasions. Our companion, in personal appearance, was presentable enough, but his speech spoiled every thing; and yet claiming to know an intimate friend of ours, we could not well treat him with that contempt which his conduct merited. He was near upon "half-seas over" most of the time, and rendered himself peculiarly obnoxious to every body by insulting the sun-imbrowned but honest yeomanry who occupied the same car as ourselves—sneering at the customs of the country in a tone of supercilious *hauteur* altogether insufferable, and for which he deserved to be ejected from the train. On another occasion, we attended Chapel at Harvard, in company with another Southerner of the same stamp—a purse-proud upstart, as different from the gentlemen of his native State as a boor is from a prince. This fellow's impudence and ill-breeding passed all bounds. Notwithstanding the chaplain was occupied with the morning services, he kept continually staring about the room, occasionally nudging us with his elbow while he indulged in the most disparaging remarks relative to different young gentlemen present, and in a tone sufficiently loud for the subjects of his criticisms to hear plainly every word he spoke. We never felt less devotional or much savager than we did on this occasion. It is a consolation to know that we have seldom met with such glaring instances of ill-breeding—only a few times in the persons of Southerners, and about as many in the persons of fanatical Down-Easters, whom either self-interest or some worse motive had induced to visit the Southern States. We recall at this moment one instance of the latter, which we will put on record as a set-off to what we have said touching the former, and because, also, it may enable some good people to see themselves as others see them.

The instance to which allusion is made attracted our notice while traveling in Virginia, in the depth of winter, on the route from Richmond to Washington by the Orange and Alexandria railroad. The train was crowded with passengers, and had been delayed for some hours by a heavy snow-drift—the thermometer standing meanwhile below zero, while the fires in the stoves seemed to give out not the least bit of warmth. It was truly a most uncomfortable situation, but the Virginians present took the matter pleasantly, chatting and laughing as unconcernedly as if they were in their own parlors. There chanced, however, to be some rude and untutored Yankees aboard, seated in different parts

of the "coach"—as they call a rail-car in the Old Dominion—though, as afterwards appeared, evidently belonging to one and the same party. For some time
these ascetic individuals discreetly kept their own coun-
sel and their tongues between their teeth; but becoming cold and restless, one of them presently popped his
sharp nose out of a window, designing, doubtless, to
take a survey of the adjacent landscape. Through the
driving snow nothing was visible but old field pines,
with here and there a shivering darkey holding a lantern in one hand and a shovel in the other; without
exaggeration, a gloomy picture enough, and was so reported by our observant Yankee, in a loud vulgar tone,
and broad accent, as if addressing himself to the rest
of his party. For immediately, like as when you have
thrust a burning stick into a coil of snakes in winter
time, the whole batch of Down-Easters opened their
"shrivelled jaws" at once, and began right off a most
abusive tirade against the noble old "Mother of States
and Presidents;" taking occasion meanwhile to sneer
at the institutions and people of the South, cheering
each other on to the glorious work, by laughing long
and delightedly at their own coarse and vulgar witi-
cisms. Filled with shame and mortification at such an
unlooked-for display of ill-breeding on the part of their
fellow-travellers, every gentleman present, whether Virginian or Yankee, remained silent until the poor boobies
had sufficiently vented their spleen; and this was the
only notice taken of them; for the moment they again
relapsed into moody silence, the conversation once
more became as lively and general as before the ungra-
cious interruption. Doubtless there were those present

who, in their ignorance of the "land of steady habits," imagined these loutish New-England provincials to be fair specimens of the noble stock of Puritans ; as it is equally probable, that many of the pale students of the Chapel mistook the vulgar fellow from the South for a genuine representative of the chivalry ; and with just about as much truth in the one case as in the other.

But to proceed once more with our subject.

When the Southern Gentleman has fully completed his academic labors—has honorably gone through the University Curriculum—if his means be ample, he seldom studies a profession, but gives his education a finishing polish by making the tour of Europe ; or else marries and settles down to superintend his estates, and devotes his talents to the raising of wheat, tobacco, rice, sugar, or cotton ; or turns his attention to politics, and runs for the State Legislature. Should, however, the patrimonial estate be small, or the heirs numerous, (and the generous clime of the South renders the latter supposition highly probable,) he then devotes himself to some one of the learned professions, or becomes an editor, or enters either the Army or the Navy. But of all things, he is most enamoured of politics and the Army ; and it is owing to this cause, that the South has furnished us with all our great generals, from Washington to Scott, as well as most of our leading statesmen, from Jefferson to Calhoun. In order to attain either eminence or success, men must do whatever they undertake *con amore.* Hence the popular outcry against the undue political influence of the Slave Power, or the Southern Oligarchy, is just as senseless and absurd as if the little retail grocer, who sells brown sugar

3

by the two-penny paper package, should denounce his fellow-citizens because they prefer "loaf" of the best quality, and in order to obtain it patronize his more wealthy neighbor on the opposite side of the street; for the laws of supply and demand govern in both cases— the *best* in the market will always be most eagerly sought after, as well as command the highest prices.

The Northern people have interested themselves chiefly in commerce, manufactures, literature, and the like ; and we behold the result in the ships, the steamers, telegraphs, the thousand practical inventions, the works of art and genius they have already furnished the world. On the other hand, the South has interested herself in agriculture mainly, political economy, and the nurture of an adventurous and military race ; and the fruits of her labors are to be witnessed in her long lists of Presidents, Cabinets, Generals, and Statesmen, as well as in her teeming agricultural resources, which add every year some two hundred millions of dollars' worth of exports to our country's commerce. It is also traceable to this marked difference between the two great sections of our Republic, that, while the North has not extended her limits Northward a single degree since the birth of the Constitution, the South has already seized on Florida, Louisiana, and Texas, and her eagle eye is even now burning with a desire to make a swoop on Cuba, Central America, and Mexico. Understand us, however. We do not claim that the South has any thing to boast over the North, no more than do we believe the latter possesses any superiority over the former. They each have their own separate sphere of action, and both, in their respective spheres, have done nobly and well. They each have their own "manifest destiny" too; but by Union alone can they ever hope to achieve the same—by a union such as existed when the first guns fired off in behalf of Independence reverberated along the bleak hills of Massachusetts—a Union of Hearts and of Hands—a Sacred Union which we trust will never be dissevered.

One chief reason why the North has never yet furnished what might be truly called a great party leader, is the fact that the Northern people are too intent on other pursuits to find time to study, much less to master, the great science of Political Economy. And moreover, owing to the great diversity of interests in the Free States, their public men are not continued long enough in service—an indispensable requisite to the thorough accomplishment of the statesman. If there were in the North some one predominating interest, no matter what, which would command always a popular support, it would not be a great while before a change for the better would be observable in her public men. As matters now stand, however, the wealthy and influential citizens of the Free States are so divided in interests—some being producers, while others are manufacturers; some being for protection, and others opposed thereto—that there seems to be only one subject upon which they can consent to agree; and in that not a single Northern citizen is interested, and all the addresses about which are only so many appeals to the passions of the unthinking rabble, who know not how to understand any more a profound State-paper than a doggerel political hymn sung by political mountebanks to the tune of "Du-dah" or "A Few Days," and who always

elevate to office, by their " sweet voices," the oily demagogue who most flatters and cajoles them.

And so the practical effect of the unstatesmanlike
proceedings consequent upon such a state of affairs has
been to drive away from politics the choicest spirits in
the North, until it is a common observation in the Free
States, that no person who wishes to live "cleanly and
like a gentleman" ever condescends to dabble in politics
at all. Hence many Northerners of wealth and culture
spend most of their time abroad, in idleness and fashionable dissipation, until they gradually lose all respect
for their native land, as well as all love for free institutions, and in the end become nothing better than mere
tuft-hunters and toad-eaters. Instead of leading useful
lives themselves, and rearing up sons and daughters of
whom a free people might be proud, they waste their
own time and talents, and educate their children to be
nothing better than obsequious flunkies to a titled and
debauched aristocracy. This is why the historic names
of New-England are so rapidly passing off the stage of
modern action, the unworthy owners of the same preferring to bask in the questionable smiles of Old World
princes to doing yeoman's service in the country of
their ancestors, (we shall not call it their own country,
for theirs it is no longer.) A son of one of these degenerate sons—a descendant of one of our most illustrious
families, of one of those noble gentlemen who stood
shoulder to shoulder with the ever-loved Washington
during the Revolutionary War—we once chanced to
know. He was at that time a minor, as was the writer;
but at the age of twenty-one he would fall heir to an
annual income of thirty thousand dollars, and in this

respect our fortunes were very dissimilar, alack-a-day! But how do you presume he was preparing himself to use his fortune? A *man* with thirty thousand a year could accomplish much good for himself and his fellow-men; a *fool* with the same income would accomplish his own ruin, and perhaps the ruin of many others more deserving than himself: and, alas! the fool's part was the sole ambition of this unworthy scion of a noble stock. Although bordering on twenty years of age, he reasoned like a little child—amused himself like a boarding-school miss, with gilt-edged story-books and costly bijouteries for presents to his acquaintances, and felt as much pride in never knowing his lessons (that being vulgar in his eyes) as ever his great-grandfather felt while winning those laurels which have rendered the name illustrious. He had spent even then the greater portion of his life in Europe—had already tasted those forbidden pleasures which in Paris are to be had "for the asking"—and he solemnly asseverated that, so soon as he came of age and thereby got rid of the control of his governor, he should return to Europe again, and every year thereafter make it a point of honor to squander his whole income in riotous living, gratifying all the lusts of the flesh, the lusts of the eye, and the pride of life! Now we shall not charge that the sons of all American gentlemen who desert their native shores to play second-fiddle to some Lord Tom-noddy in the Old World, are so utterly brainless as this unfortunate youth; but let them beware, for if they are not, their children will yet come to be such, since it is God's will that every man who is not a natural fool should have something to do, and whoever fails to find that something to keep alive the manhood that is in him, will eventually become both an unnatural as well as a natural fool.

Now, when the facts in regard to politics and parties in the North are duly weighed, we do not see why any intelligent man should express surprise that all our national parties should have originated in the South, or that the leaders of those parties should, generation after generation, prove to be Southern men. Neither is it astonishing that the Northern people, after having denounced every Southern statesman in turn, should in time come to adopt their several opinions. Thus, when Mr. Jefferson overthrew the New-England Federalists, and inaugurated the principles of Democracy, nearly every political pulpit in New-England thundered anathemas against his administration, and both priests and people vilified him without measure. But to-day the worthy old Federalists celebrate with all the honors the tough old Democrat's birth-day, and his chief panegyrist and encomiast is one who, when he was alive, thus damned him in flowing numbers:

> " And thou, the scorn of every patriot name,
> Thy country's ruin and her council's shame!
> Go, scan, Philosophist, thy Sally's charms,
> And sink supinely in her sable arms ;
> But quit to abler hands the helm of State,
> Nor image ruin on thy country's fate."

So too when Jackson "set his face like a flint" against a National Bank, and all other great moneyed monopolies, he was denounced all through the Free States as an illiterate tyrant: but the name of Jackson is now an household word, and his memory is sacredly enshrined in the hearts of his countrymen. And as for the States-Rights doctrines of Mr. Calhoun, they are already beginning to find favor in the North; and by another decade we expect to see the name of Calhoun placed side by side with the names of Jefferson and Jackson; while the coming Southern leader, who shall inaugurate whatever *new* policy the shifting fortunes of our growing Republic must in time demand, will be vilified at first by the Northern people, until they learn to respect the wisdom and foresight of his measures, when they will inevitably applaud the same as heartily as they before condemned, and will embrace his principles with as much alacrity as the people of the South will ever continue to welcome the literary productions of Northern authors and the practical inventions of Northern mechanics, and to applaud the matchless eloquence and profound learning of those Northern statesmen whose constituents have the good sense to keep them in public life long enough to enable them to master the science and philosophy of government.

But to return.

No matter what may be the Southern Gentleman's avocation, his dearest affections usually centre in the country. He longs to live as his fathers lived before him, in both the Old World and the New; and he ever turns with unfeigned delight from the bustle of cities, the hollow ceremonies of courts, the turmoil of politics, the glories and dangers of the battle-field, or the wearisome treadmill of professional routine, to the quiet and peaceful scenes of country life. The glare of gas and the glitter of tinsel, the pride, the pomp, the vanity,

and all the grace and wit of *la bonne compagnie*, he sur-
renders without a sigh of regret, and joyfully retires to
the seclusion of his own fireside, grateful for the auspi-
cious and happy exchange.   The old hall, the familiar
voices of old friends, the trusty and well-remembered
faces of the old domestics—these all are dearer to the
heart of the Southern Gentleman than the short-lived
plaudits of admiring throngs, or the hollow and unsat-
isfactory pleasures of sense.   Indeed, with all classes in
the South the home feeling is much stronger than it is
in the North; for the bane of hotel life and the curse
of boarding-houses have not as yet extended their pernicious influences to our Southern States, or at best in
a very small degree.   Nearly every citizen is a land-
holder, and therefore feels an interest in the perma-
nency of his country's institutions.   This is one reason
why the South has ever been the ready advocate of
war, whenever the rights of the nation have been trampled on, or the national flag insulted.   But if the patriotic feeling is strong in the breast of even the poorest
citizen, whose home is a log-cabin and whose sole patrimony consists of less than a dozen acres of land, how
must it be intensified in the bosoms of those whose
plantations spread out into all the magnificence of old-
country manors!

As it is our desire to present the reader faithful pictures of the home life of the Southern States, we wish
we could fitly paint to his mind's eye how the Southern
Gentleman appears when reclining under his own vine
and fig-tree.   Much has been said of his generous hospitality, but this to be fully appreciated should be enjoyed.   We doubt if there is any where on the globe

its parallel. Certainly, in some portions of the South the Southern Gentleman does not live in very grand style—his house is not always showy, nor his furniture elegant, nor his pleasure-grounds in the best keeping— but he is always hospitable, gentlemanly, courteous, and more anxious to please than to be pleased. A city-bred gentleman from the North will not always find in the planter's home "the rich curtains, the sumptuous sofas, the gorgeous picture-frames, or the thousand and one other dainty household gods, so carefully gathered and treasured in his own house;" but he will ever find a much heartier welcome, a warmer shake of the hand, a greater desire to please, and less frigidity of deport-ment, than will be found in any walled town upon the earth's circumference. And, to quote the words of one of his class: "As he begins to feel at home, to discover the new pleasures at his command, and to fall into the way and spirit of the life around him, he will feel that the wants of one social condition and climate may not be the wants of another and very opposite one; that on the Southern plantations the people '*live out of doors;*' that their very houses, ever wide open, are themselves 'out of doors,' and consequently but little more cared for than are the self-caring lawns and woods around them.

"When the few cold days come, and the stormy days, this provision for summer and sunshine only may prove for the moment inadequate. But then books, though not showily exposed, are forthcoming for in-door enter-tainment, and the best of pianos may be opened to good purpose, while your hosts, old and young, are at leisure

3*

and command to talk with you intelligently and heartily upon any theme, from the state of the Union to the
state of the crops, or to fight over again bold encoun-
ters with bear and alligator, or with the quiet adversa-
ries of the chess and the backgammon-boards. To revive
the flagging interest in these and other resources there
is, as at all times, the cordial relief of the well-supplied
side-board, and the very model of generous and hospitable tables."

This writer also proceeds further, in the following
very truthful and pertinent remarks:

"It would seem, and so indeed it is, as a rule, that
the Southern Gentleman, even the most assiduous in
business, labors only for occupation, or *pour passer le
temps*, his daily toil being his daily pleasure; and not,
as in busier and mere money-getting communities, a
painful drudgery, submitted to but for the sake of a
scarcely understood good beyond. He never buries
the man in the business, but makes of his business itself his social enjoyment and his true life. Thus, whatever may be his engagements, he seems never to have
any thing to do but to amuse himself and his family
and the stranger within his gates. It is to these habits
of life, in a great measure, that may be traced the certain air of gentlemanly and chivalrous character and
manner which is so characteristic even of the humbler,
of the most rude and unlettered—the rough diamonds
of the race. Some of this result may possibly be laid
also to the circumstance of the distinction between their
class and that of the blacks by whom they are surrounded, and which makes them all of a certain neces-

sity brothers and peers, and also to the habits of command, with the consciousness of *noblesse* and its incident obligations.

"Loving and accustomed to equestrian exercise, the ladies have enough of pleasant and profitable out-door life, while their large households furnish ample employment, even without the generally great cares of hospitality. It is much the custom, at least on the smaller plantations, for the mistress to charge herself with the labors and responsibility of supplying the wants of the blacks as well as the whites of the family, providing them with their rations of food and their stock of clothing, and ministering to them in hours of sickness."

"Immense stores of material have every season to be cut up for coats, and gowns, and trowsers, and shirts. Little quarrels have to be arbitrated at one moment, and little chastisements inflicted at another. Now Hannibal has broken his head, and vinegar and brown paper must be hunted up ; or Lucy is going to be married, and white dresses and white cakes must, according to custom, be prepared ; so that, on the whole, one way or another, black and white together, a Southern matron has no necessity, and but little opportunity, to be an idle woman. The gentlemen are equally well provided with occupation in the care of their plantations, the entertainment of their guests, and with studies in the library and sports in the field. The swamps are full of deer, which beguile them to the chase, and the peopled waters tempt them to wander forth with hook and line. Sometimes a bear has to be looked for, and now and then the alligators require some setting down. These last uncouth gentry are by means pleasant folk to encounter unexpectedly, though they are more apt to avoid than to seek you. Still they are given to the offensive when they dare, and often do they make short work of the unlucky hounds who stray within their precincts."

Thus far a discriminating Northerner.

Nor need you, philanthropic Madam, envy our Southerner because his eye may happen to sparkle with a natural pride, as he scans his broad acres stretching away many a rood in the shimmering sunshine; or because he gazes with delight upon his blooded horses prancing and pirouetting in their green pastures, and his countless herds of cattle lazily browsing the succulent twigs of sassafras growing here and there in the midst of the grassy meadows. Do not, we pray you, disturb that equanimity which has always been such a charming characteristic of your ladyship, by dwelling too intently upon supposititious pictures of the awful contrast between the sunshine that pervades the parlor, and the terrible gloom which always enshrouds the cabin. For, hark! do you not hear those sounds of revelry and mirth? the ceaseless tum tum of de ole banjo, and the merry twang of de fiddle and de bow? as well as the noisy shuffling of not very nimble feet, accompanied by that full-voiced chorus which bursts so merrily, ay, and musically too, upon the midnight air, telling of the free heart and the contented mind? Not even the lark, "singing at heaven's gate," trills his matin song with more of unaffected joyousness, than do these simple Africans shout their evening choruses, until the very rafters of their humble cabins vibrate with the sound! And tell us, honestly; have you ever witnessed in the miserable tenant-houses of your own toiling poor, after the day's weary labors are done, such evidences of unaffected light-heartedness and phy· sical comfort? And do you suppose, O noble cham pion of Equal Rights; you, sir, who turn aside with a curse from the ragged starveling on your own door-steps to clamor that the poor slave shall be freed, but afterwards refuse to sit with the freedman in the house of God, or in the theatres, or in public conveyances, or any where else, indeed, save at Dawson's; do you sup-pose that your love for the sooty African equals that of his vilified master? If you do so delude yourself, the more's the pity; for, despite what you or any other person may think to the contrary, the Southern Gentle-man entertains more real love for his "human chattels," than all the hair-brained abolitionists the world ever saw. His love is not theoretical but practical. He has tried theory and found it would not do. Formerly he was theoretically an abolitionist, but he has long since got rid of such puerile sentimentality.

He remembers that, when the negroes were first sold to his ancestors by the Puritans of both New and Old England, they were nothing but naked, gibbering sav-ages, heathenish and beastly; being but a single re-move above the brutes that perish. He sees now, that a century and a half of slavery has changed them into intelligent human beings, compared with what they originally were, being elevated as high above their kindred, who still remain in Africa, as he is above themselves. He sees, moreover, that wherever the wholesome restraint and intelligent guidance of the master have been taken away, as in Jamaica and else-

where, the poor blacks have invariably lapsed into a
state of semi-barbarism, dragging with them also the
white races with whom they have been permitted to
associate on equal terms. With such undeniable facts
before him, he would be the most jolter-headed fool
alive, did he allow himself to be seduced by any spirit
of a maudlin sentimentality or pseudo-philanthropy, to
destroy by a misdirected benevolence all the good results which it has taken nearly two centuries to accomplish. Hence, the ceaseless clamor of the so-called
civilized world—of those peoples whose bread comes
through the sweat of the African's brow, and whose
commercial prosperity is mainly due to the products of
slave-labor—passes by the Southern Gentleman as the
idle wind which he heeds not. Yea, let them clamor, let
them denounce, let them misrepresent and vilify to their
heart's content, although they may succeed in putting to
the rack many good republican souls in the Free States,
who are so ridiculously sensitive to the opinions entertained of America by the hoary old European tyrants,
still never will one single Southern Gentleman be influenced by the very disinterested outcry. He knows
that this is not the first time a successful burglar has
joined in the general shout, "Stop thief!" "Stop thief!"
bawling louder than all the rest, indeed, the more self-
interest prompts him to direct public attention to some
other sinner, or at least to some other head than his
own. Of a truth, there is nothing pleasanter in the
world, than to live up to the popular standard of morality; and there is no avocation in life more easy to
master than that of a trimmer—one who sails always
with the current, whose rudder is public opinion, whose

right bower is *vox populi*, and whose left bower is *populi vox*. The Southern Gentleman is as well aware of all this as you, sir, or we; but he chooses to have an honest opinion of his own, and would rather stand in the shoes of the meanest slave on his plantation, of the laziest and most ignorant gumbo whose back was ever made to bleed under the overseer's lash, than to become that *thing*—that most emasculate and miserable mockery of a man—the SLAVE OF PUBLIC OPINION. For the negro, although he may, as the Scriptures enjoin, serve faithfully his "master according to the flesh with fear and trembling, in singleness of heart, as unto Christ," can still maintain his own self-respect, and be accounted by the Master of us all, a MAN; but the poor slave of public opinion—the shifting human weathercock, who is "every thing by starts and nothing long"—must in the very nature of things always loathe and abhor himself, and when he gets his deserts in the future life, will, if such things be, officiate as lickspittle and boot-black to the devil himself, being accounted unworthy to receive even respectable torment.

Do not wonder, therefore, that the Southern Gentleman has never been, and is not now, influenced by the popular and world-wide denunciation of the "peculiar institution." For he is a man every inch, bold, self-reliant, conscientious; knowing his own convictions of duty, and daring to heed them. What that duty is, the Divine Teacher has inculcated in the well-known precept: "Masters, give unto your servants (δουλοις) that which is just and impartial; knowing that you also have a Master in heaven." This the Southern Gentle-

man delights to do. It is almost impossible for a citizen of the North to realize the strong ties which bind
the Southern Gentleman to his bond-servants, and *vice
versa*. In most instances the slaves of gentlemen are
all "family negroes," who have been in their master's
family for several generations, and their family pride
is equal, if not superior, to that of the master himself.
We do not deny that there are estates in the South,
the negroes belonging to which are badly treated : the
South is no second paradise, but has its evils like the
rest of the world. But it is for the most part on the
plantations of parvenues, or the children of such, that
one witnesses those scenes of barbarity which so shock
our humaner feelings ; for on these estates are agglomerated a promiscuous rabble, bought here and there,
without regard to any thing else than their capacity to
hoe tobacco, or pick cotton ; and the consequence is,
they have to be controlled by brute force—just as those
poor bachelor coolies, whom philanthropic England
yearly sells to the Cubans for a term of years, have to
be controlled, or those more savage and heathenish Africans, whom such men as Captain Townsend and other
slaver captains are selling to the same people for a *little longer term of years*, have to be controlled.

We apprehend, however, that as a general thing the
negroes on all the Southern plantations fare much better than the people of the North desire to believe. It
is so very pleasant, you know, to pick splinters out of
the eyes of one's neighbors! And to pull the beam
out of one's own eyes, is such a deal of trouble! We
should think though, that "mad Old Brown" must have
helped to open the eyes of some of the blind leaders of

the blind in the Free States. That poor old monomaniac imagined the slaves to be so oppressed, that they only waited a deliverer, when they would immediately throw off their shackles, and rally as one man under the flag of the Provisional government, trusting in the " sword of the Lord and of Gideon." Vain delusion! He brought his own neck to the gallows, but did not liberate a single slave.

No wonder the failure of the attempted Harper's Ferry insurrection has puzzled the abolitionists. It controverts all their theories, and falsifies all their assertions. And in this connection we beg the reader will indulge our introducing the following editorial remarks of the *New-York Herald*, on the Harper's Ferry raid, published at the time. They are very sensible, as well as truthful.

" Many of the country journals, either from a want of wit or a want of honesty, insist upon calling the invasion of Harper's Ferry by a score of black and white abolitionists from the North, a slave insurrection.

" If there is any one point in the late proceedings of Osawatomie Brown, of Kansas notoriety, that is more prominent than any other, it is the singular fact that none of the Southern slaves were mixed up in the affair, nor did a single one of them voluntarily come forward to accept the great advantages which Brown and his fellow fanatics in the North held out to them. Within a circuit of a few hours' ride of Harper's Ferry fully five thousand slaves reside; but not a sign of disturbance or discontent was exhibited. Yet Brown had been busy for months round there, his means of com-

munication were established, the underground railroad
has its stations all along to the Canada frontier, and
J. R. G. was a willing contributor from Ashtabula,
Gerrit Smith applauded the 'Kansas work' from Pe-
terboro, F. B. S. sympathized in Concord, and many a
scattering abolitionist all through the Northern States,
no doubt wrestled in prayer that the slave might be
freed from his bonds.

"But the deportment of the slaves has shown that
they possess a very correct appreciation of the mis-
named advantages of Northern freedom.   They know
very well that all this mock philanthropy exerts itself
merely to run them off from their comfortable Southern homes to leave them to starve in the cold and in-
hospitable wilderness of Canada.   When we compare
the condition of the free negro at the North with that
of the slave at the South, we can not be surprised that
Cuffee should prefer to remain in slavery.   In the
North, every where, the negro ceases to awaken the
least sympathy for his sufferings in the hearts of the
abolitionists; they cease to care in any way for his necessities, they refuse to admit him to their houses or
churches, they will not sit by his side in the cars or at
table, they reject him as a mechanic, a servant, or laborer, and persecute him with neglect till he sinks to
the very dregs of society, and dies in misery.

"In the South his condition is widely different.   It
is true, he is held in slavery, but negro slavery is a
condition of patriarchal servitude.   From birth the
negro is in close and intimate contact with the white
man.   His childhood is cared for, his youth is instructed in some useful labor, and all through the maturity

and decline of manhood, his master and himself work for the same family interest, until, in old age, he is a family pensioner secure from want. In this life-long intercourse between the white and the black, between the master and the slave, the inferior has the benefit of the control and guidance of the superior intellect. Through this stimulus and this example his morals are improved, his industry is increased, and in every way he is a better member of society than the vicious free negro of the North or the liberated barbarian of the tropics. Eloquent proof of this fact is found in the advice of one of the Presidents of Liberia to the Colonization Society : ' Send us slaves from the South, liberated after they have attained to manhood, for they make better citizens and more industrious people than the negroes from the North.'

"The close intercourse between the two races that exists under the patriarchal institutions of the South can never be obtained under any other system of society. No where else will the white lend his efforts to teach the black, no where else will the black unite his physical labor with the intellectual effort of the white for their common benefit, no where else will the superior admit the inferior race to the advantage of close family contact, as nurses, housekeepers, handmaidens, and not seldom as foster-brothers. No where else will the white labor side by side with the negro in the open field, guiding his ignorance, bearing with his incapacity, and rectifying his errors or neglect. It would be well for the fanatics who wish to dissolve this great social tie in Southern society, through the shedding of blood or the cheat of Northern freedom for the negro, to learn a lesson from the refusal of the slaves in and around Harper's Ferry to accept the boon held out to them through the abolition invasion of Old John Brown of Osawatomie."

The above remarks are so full of truth, so acceptable to one's common-sense, that it is hard to believe there are in these States many men possessing a sound mind in a sound body, who can conscientiously disapprove of them. Indeed, from an extensive personal acquaintance among the so called Republicans of the North, we are persuaded that the best informed of those regard the matter of Negro Slavery from the same stand-point with the editor of the New York *Herald.* Many of them even concede that they do not consider slavery a sin *per se,* since the Bible has sanctioned it. Why, then, the reader is ready to inquire, do they oppose the farther spread of the "peculiar institution?" Well, if their public and private declarations are to be believed, it is because they think it fosters and builds up a kind of privileged aristocracy—which they have denominated the Southern Oligarchy, and which they hate with a cordial hatred. They pretend that the Southern slaveholders are an exclusive class, who have somehow managed to control the government ever since the adoption of the Federal Constitution; and although the country has continued to prosper under the rule of these so-called Oligarchs, they yet seem to entertain the most direful forebodings relative to our future progress, unless the Oligarchs can be deprived of all their political influence. Hence many honorable and conservative men have been brought to affiliate with abolitionists even, in their intense zeal to witness the overthrow of the Slave Power.

These men do not consider that this same Oligarchy existed in the days of the Revolution—and that at that time the distinctions of *caste*, were even more nicely drawn than at present. They fail to note also, that it is not an *exclusive* aristocracy, as they seem to imagine, (except in regard to color,) but that every free white man in the whole Union has just as much right to become an Oligarch as the most ultra fire-eater. In truth, there are thousands of Southern slaveholders more democratic in their instincts than these very ultra Republicans; for while the former wear homespun every day and work side by side with their slaves, the latter are the very pinks of propriety, array themselves in the most unexceptionable silks and broadcloth, and turn up their nose at the "vulgar herd" with as much disdain as the most aristocratic Oligarch in the whole land.

Now, we shall not deny that the Southern Gentleman is exclusive in his tastes and associations, and sometimes possesses strong and deep-seated prejudices of caste : but to no greater extent than usually prevails amongst all other gentlemen the world over. Of the nature of those prejudices, we presume the intelligent reader needs not to be informed. That they are blemishes in any man's character, can not be successfully controverted ; viewing them from an elevated moral stand-point, and regarding with calm philosophic eye the vanity of all those titles and social distinctions which the narrow intellects. of men have magnified into matters of first importance. But pray let us inquire, what class of our fellow-men,

whether high or low, has not its peculiar prejudices of
one sort or another? And shall we blame the favorites
of fortune for entertaining their "peculiar wanities" more
than we blame the street beggars for their love of filth
and vagabondage, or Jack Tar because of his peculiar
predilection for salt water? Dearly beloved, we are
told by the inspired writer that charity covereth up a
multitude of faults; and God knows, there are human
wickednesses enough of a deadly and damning character in the world, to keep us all praying till the crack
of doom, without our wasting a single moment to observe every little mote which may happen to obscure
in part the vision of a frail fellow-being. In truth, it
seems to have been wisely ordained of the Creator, that
our finite minds should never reach beyond the narrow
horizon which bounds our destinies; and that each individual man should be rendered superlatively happy
in the harmless conceit, that his own country, his own
religion, his own home, wife and children, friends and
neighbors, even his horse and his dog, are better than
any other person's. For, even as it is, we have envy-
ings, and jealousies, and heart-burnings without number; and few are they in any age or any country who
are possessed of a truly cosmopolitan spirit, a world-
wide Christian philanthropy, or that even-balanced
understanding which separates the good from the evil,
the solid grain from the chaff, or immortal Truth from
the many idle fancies and childish superstitions which
have in every age more or less dwarfed the human
mind.

But to return.

The natural dignity of manner peculiar to the Southern Gentlemen, is doubtless owing to his habitual use of authority from his earliest years; for while coarser natures are ever rendered more savage and brutal by being allowed the control of others, refined natures on the contrary are invariably perfected by the same means, their sense of the responsibility and its incident obligations teaching them first to control themselves before attempting to exact obedience from the inferior natures placed under their charge. This is a fact which it were worth while to ponder thoughtfully, for herein lies the secret of the good breeding of the Gentlemen of the South, and the chief reason why they seldom evince that flurry of manner so peculiar to many of our countrymen; and why, also, they manifest on all occasions the utmost self-possession—that much coveted *savoir faire*, which causes a man to appear perfectly at home, whether it be in a hut or a palace. Hence in manners the Southern Gentleman is remarkably easy and natural, never haughty in appearance, or loud of speech—even when angry rarely raising his voice above the ordinary tone of gentlemanly conversation. Those boisterous good fellows, whom one meets constantly in the South, and sometimes even so far from home as New-York or Philadelphia, and whose wont is to monopolize all the talking, interlarding their speech with Southern provincialisms and Africanisms, are not in the remotest degree allied or akin to the real Southern Gentleman. He is ever well educated, and. draws his language from the "well of pure English undefiled." Even though he may be poor, (which is neither an impossible nor improbable supposition,) he always manages to give his children the best opportunities for education the country affords : for it is one of his prejudices to detest boorishness and vulgarity—two inseparable companions of ignorance—and he would as heartily detest them in the persons of his own offspring, or other members of his family, as in the person of the most besotted drunkard that ever reeled into a gutter. His sons he sends to the University, but prefers to educate his daughters at home; to please mamma, he may be induced, perhaps, to send the latter for a year or two to some Finishing School, just previous to their debut in life; but he stoutly maintains all the while, that the old-fashioned plan of educating one's daughters at home is the best.

And if in nothing else, in this at least is the Southern Gentleman to be commended—*he educates his daughters at home.* Hence the well-bred and well-educated daughters of the Summer Land, are the model women of the age in which we live. How different are they from your hotel-boarding matrons, who know so well how to ogle and to stare, or your flippant butterflies of fashion, who spread their gaudy plumage so industriously, ambitious alone to win the plaudits of simpering coxcombs and *blasé* libertines! Ah! thou true-hearted daughter of the sunny South, simple and unaffected in thy manners, pure in speech as thou art in soul, and ever blessed with an inborn grace and gentleness of spirit lovely to look upon, fitly art thou named:

> " A perfect woman, nobly planned,
>   To warm, to comfort, and command;
>   And yet a spirit still, and bright
>   With something of angelic light."

Such a woman can well leave to the strong-minded of her sex all political twaddle and senseless disputes about the " Rights of Woman," alienable or inalienable : for she will always be loved and admired the wide world over. The men are not all fools yet, and they know that woman's one sole Inalienable Right, is to be a Teacher; for whatever may be said in praise of Public, or Free, or High, or Select schools, or any other kind of school, we maintain there is one greater and more praiseworthy than these all, for it is God's school, and is called THE FAMILY. And it is in this school that woman finds her proper sphere and mission. This is her God-given privilege and honor, which the tyranny of man can never deprive her of; for it is hers by right and by nature, and hers must it ever remain *in sæculum sæculi.* Besides, in this her proper sphere woman wields a power, compared to which the lever of Archimedes was nothing more than a flexible blade of grass. She it is who rules the destinies of the world, not man. The raging tornado treads with the tramp of an army along the mountain's sides, uprooting loftiest cedars in its fury, but there its power ends; while the silent night dews, stealing without noise or bluster into the heart of the solidest rock, rend the very mountain itself asunder. So man, although he shall march with banners flying and to the music of fife and drum to the world's end, will always find that there is a power behind the throne greater than the throne itself. We of the sterner sex, indeed, may be not inaptly compared to the cold hard iron of the telegraphic wires which span the surface of the civilized parts of our earth; the electric flashes that vivify and move us, are the heart-

4

throbs and transmitted thoughts of our mothers. Hence, when the Apostle commanded that women should not be suffered to speak in public, but on the contrary to content themselves with their humble household duties, he not only spoke as the inspired servant of God, but also as a man possessed of uncommon common-sense. For since to the family belongs the education and gradual elevation of the race, it is most important that mothers should be pure, peaceable, gentle, long-suffering and godly—which they never can be, if permitted or inclined to enter the lists and compete with selfish and lustful man for the prizes of place and public emolument. And that society, we care not how great may be its virtues in other respects, which tends to force woman out of her proper sphere, and to lay on her frailer shoulders the burdens which ought to be borne by man only, is not a natural condition of society, and for this reason is blameworthy. We will not say that, in the Free States, such a state of society already exists; but this we do say, in the South the family is a much more powerful institution than in other portions of the Republic. It may be owing in part to the sparse population of the South, but the fact is indisputable: as a general rule, family ties are much stronger there than in the North, while the parental discipline is more rigid, and Young America is rarely met with, save in the large towns and villages; for these are much the same all over the country, except that the Southern villages have a more wo-begone look, and smell stronger of mean whisky and hogs than the trim villages of New-England.

Now, as we all know, in most American villages and towns, the family has long since ceased to be an institution at all. Boys and girls are things unknown in their streets, and politeness and good-breeding ditto. We have seen it remarked somewhere, that there are thousands of boys in free America, not one of whom has ever made a bow, unless when he had occasion to dodge a snow-ball, a brickbat, or a boulder. A few years ago, ex-Governor Everett, of Massachusetts, with the late Amos Lawrence, was in a sleigh, riding into Boston. As they approached a school-house, a score of young boys rushed into the street to enjoy their afternoon recess. Said the Governor to his friend, "Let us observe whether these boys make obeisance to us, as we were taught fifty years ago;" expressing a fear at the same time that habits of civility were less practised than formerly. As they passed the school-house, however, all question and doubt upon the subject received a speedy if not a very satisfactory settlement, for each one of those twenty juvenile New-Englanders did his best at snow-balling the way-faring dignitaries. It is possible, nay probable, that in some localities in the South the same rudeness would have been manifested; but we incline to think such localities would be found, like angels' visits, few and far between. The better portion of Southern boys are taught to consider themselves boys so long as they remain in their teens, and the valuable advice of Hebrew Solomon is followed to the letter, in case they seek to imitate the vices or to ape the manners of their elders before the down has ripened on their boyish cheeks. Nothing, indeed, so annoys a well-bred Southerner as the impertinent speech and coxcombical behavior of the *youths* of the present day, (they would be offended did we call them *boys*.) Such an youth, however, was never our great Washington, or Calhoun, or Webster. These giants were willing to be looked upon as boys until they grew to be men; but our modern youths will not consent to be boys at any time, and by the general consent of all thoughtful minds they never get to be men at all—at least in any emphatic sense. They may succeed in becoming pretty fair pocket editions of a Brummell or a D'Orsay—wondrously clever at smoking a colored meerschaum and drinking champagne, as well as apt at sucking ivory-headed canes (when they were babies and more natural, they sucked their thumbs)—and in all things else the proper individuals to wed those *ladies* whose lives are devoted to nursing poodle-dogs and reading trashy novels: but *men?*

> " What is a man,
> If his chief good and market of his time
> Be but to sleep and feed? *a beast—no more.*"

CHAPTER II.

THE MIDDLE CLASSES.

" HE that holds fast the golden mean,
  And lives contentedly between
    The little and the great,
Feels not the wants that pinch the poor,
Nor plagues that haunt the rich man's door,
    Embittering all his state."

COWPER'S Horace.

As in all other civilized communities, the middle classes of the South constitute the greater proportion of her citizens, and are likewise the most useful members of her society. In treating of these classes, however, we shall have to tread rather gingerly, for fear we squelch some neighbor's corns, owing to the false and ridiculous notions of respectability, which unfor tunately prevail throughout the whole extent of the United States. In this country every man considers himself a gentleman, no matter what may be his social status; nor shall we find fault with this national trait, perhaps not altogether peculiar to our happy republic; but we must beseech of the honest citizen who reads these pages, to look upon us for the time being as a Hottentot, or other outside barbarian—a citizen of the world, if it please you—one who can afford to look at the people of this great country with unprejudiced eyes—regarding matters as they are and not as they should be, and calling things by their real names, and not by such as have been rendered familiar from long use, and, we might aver, abuse.

We know very well that it would be highly improper to step into the office of Col. Wall Bankstreet, or to stalk into his marble mansion—his brown-stone front, at all events—to sit down in his elaborate parlor in the midst of his splendid furniture, his ormolu, his rosewood, his velvet, and brocade, and say to him plainly: "Sir, you are only a successful tradesman, and when you try hardest to play the rôle of a gentleman only a more successful snob!" We know equally well that it would never do to march boldly up to C. Eyland Bayles, Esq., who owns two thousand acres of land in Georgia, or Alabama, or Mississippi, and a hundred negroes to till them, with cattle, and sheep, hogs and horses to match—and say to Mr. C. Eyland Bayles, Esq.: "Sir, you have neither the birth, nor the manners, nor the education of a gentleman—you are only a successful planter, nothing more!" We should probably be caned out of hand in both instances, for so great a display of ill-breeding and impertinence, as we would richly deserve to be ; but in five out of ten such cases, we should only be telling the truth, nevertheless, for there can be little doubt that many individuals, both in the North and the South, occupy just such positions as Messrs. Bayles and Bankstreet, who are not entitled to be considered gentlemen in the rightful and proper use of the term, though useful and intelligent citizens, and in many respects honester, perhaps, than one half the gentlemen that are in the world.   In other countries, such individuals, together with the great mass of well-to-do citizens of less note and wealth, constitute what are called the middle classes; and why, in the name of common-sense, do we pursue a different course in the United States? Why shall we not call a stone a stone? Does the calling of it a fish make it any the less a stone? Does the buying a picture of Sir Launcelot Grimlook clad in complete armor make Sir Launcelot Grimlook one of your paternal ancestors? Can you make a delicate scented posy out of a Massachusetts codfish by simply naming the latter's head a rose, its tail a camelia, each one of its fins a japonica, and its odorous intestines cape jessamines? Away, say we, with all such snobbery, and let us stand by the honest old English names and customs of our homely Saxon ancestors.

But understand us, our democratic fellow-countrymen. We do not respect Messrs. Bayles and Bankstreet any the less *because* they belong to the middle class, nor young Augustus Fitz Herbert any more *because* he is of the upper crust, to quote a cant phrase. That there are those who do, 'tis true, and pity 'tis 'tis true. Speaking for ourself, permit us to assure you, however, we respect a man for his virtues, his talents, or his goodness alone, wholly regardless what his pedigree may be, or whether each morning he purchases a fresh pair of kids, or proceeds to labor humbly with toil-worn hands for his daily bread. And we will also add, that we despise as heartily the pampered knave (we care not how sleek his coat, or if he possess all the blood of all the Howards) who uses his gold merely to gild his vices, as we do the most poverty-stricken wretch ever put into the stocks; notwithstanding, too, the world may fawn upon the former and crouch to do him reverence, while the tattered rags that barely hang upon the latter's back, but serve to magnify his guilt in the eyes of a virtuous public, which sees in every separate tag and patch only accumulative evidence of the wearer's villainy. Wherefore, O democratic citizen! we rail against no class of men *as a class* —not even princes, dukes, or lords—and we believe the king on his throne can be just as honest and virtuous as the humblest laborer in this great Republic; while we are equally persuaded the poorest citizen can, if he so will, make himself a "king o' men for a' that;" yes,

> "For a' that, and a' that,
> His toils obscure and a' that;
> The rank is but the guinea's stamp,
> *The man's the gowd for a' that!*"

Coming, then, understandingly, to the subject of the middle classes of the South, we trust the reader will not be offended at the liberties we shall take while speaking of them, who as we said in the outset, are very numerous, very useful, and we will now add, in many respects very worthy. They belong to many different callings, professions, and trades; and we propose to speak of them according to their several pursuits. There are among them farmers, planters, traders, storekeepers, artisans, mechanics, a few manufacturers, a goodly number of country school-teachers, and a host of half-fledged country lawyers and doctors, parsons, and the like. Since the South is mainly agricultural, however, perhaps the larger proportion of her middle classes are to be found among the tillers of the soil; of these, therefore, we shall endeavor to speak first. And, as we think it always best to begin at the beginning, we crave the reader's indulgence while we say a single word about the ancestors of the middle class farmers and planters in our Southern States.

In the remote times of English history, their ancestors were, doubtless, sturdy Saxon thanes and franklins, freemen and landholders, but boasting no alliance with baronial or ducal houses; plain men, indeed, ignorant of courts and bearing no knightly insignia, but famous for skill with the cross-bow and the old English pike. So long as they were permitted to live in peace in England, Scotland, or Ireland, and had no better place to fly to for refuge, they bore in patience, first with the oppressions of their Norman masters, and next with the persecutions and exactions of the Cavaliers and the Church of England: but when America held out to them an asylum in which they might rest secure from the further molestation of enemies, like nearly all who sought the New World, they hastened to its then savage shores, seeking liberty of conscience as well as freedom from a galling political thraldom. Now, in view of these undeniable facts of history, is it not a little curious, that windy Northern demagogues have endeavored so industriously to mislead the mass of our Free State citizens, swearing roundly that in the South, aside from the negro slaves, there exist but two other classes—Poor Whites and Cavaliers? Do you presume, gentlemen, that the honest English frank-

4*

lins have left no descendants in the Southern States?
Have the Scotch-Irish Presbyterians, the daring Covenanters of Auld Reekie, and the English Baptists who
settled in Virginia, Georgia, and the Carolinas, as well
as the humbler classes of Huguenots—have none of
these hardy and intelligent races left representatives?
According to the popular Northern view of the existing
relations in the society of the South, they could not have
done so; but the real facts show that they have left a
numerous posterity, far outnumbering the descendants
of the Cavaliers, and greater in numbers indeed, than
any other one class of whites in the whole South. They
have added as much, too, to the material progress and
advancement of the Slave States, as all the other
classes combined, owing to their industrious and frugal
habits, the general pureness of their morals, and their
strict religious principles. Like their forefathers, they
are chiefly small farmers or planters, though sometimes
possessed of much wealth, which has been acquired by
steady industry and economy; and not infrequently
they are both cultivated and refined, and perfect gentlemen in every sense, as we have already shown in
the last chapter: particularly is such the case, when
they possess a little admixture of Norman blood,
brought about by intermarriages with the descendants
of the Cavaliers and Huguenots. From such connections, indeed, have sprung some of the proudest names
in our country's history. Jefferson, for one, was of
such a race. Jackson was nearly full-blood Scotch-
Irish, and Calhoun was the son of a middle-class
planter; while the well-beloved and eloquent Harry

of the West, as is well known, came of English Baptist parentage, and noble-hearted Patrick Henry sprung
directly from the bosom of the people.

But not only have the Middle Classes of the South
helped to furnish these great leaders, as well as many
others of less note; they have always exercised a healthy
and sensible influence upon both national and state politics from the adoption of our Federal Constitution till
the present day. Had it not been for them, the law of
descent never would have been changed in Virginia,
or materially in any of the other Southern States.
For the old Law of Primogeniture was pretty generally
upheld by the Cavaliers, and besides these were no
other voters at that time but the respectable Middle Classes. So, also, was the extension of the elective
franchise bitterly opposed by the major part of the
gentry, who were opposed, indeed, to all innovations
whatever upon the old English Common Law, or any
other interference with the established order of things.
Being out-voted, however, by the more whole-hearted,
and less exclusive, though humbler freeholders, they
yielded quietly to the change at length, applauded it
after a few years, and thus became again reïnstated in
the favor of the public as well as in political power.
But for a long time, in some of the poorer districts of
Virginia, so strong did popular prejudice rage against
fair-tops and ruffled shirts, almost any ruffian who
would ply the rabble strong enough with flattery, could
be elected to the Virginia Assembly over the heads of
the most able and refined of the First Families. We
remember to have heard a Virginian tell once of such
an election, in which the contest was between one of

the oldest of Virginia statesmen and—well, a dirty fellow, whose chief delight and occupation was to groom a stallion! This worthy was elected by a handsome majority. After that, who will pretend to disbelieve in the divinity of the oracle, *vox populi, vox Dei!*

So far as physical appearance is concerned, the middle-class planter differs very materially from the Southern Gentleman. The former does not possess that lithe, airy, and graceful carriage, that compactness and delicacy of muscle, for all which the latter is distinguished. The former is, moreover, of all sizes, from the most diminutive and bandy-legged runt, to the coarse, large-featured, awkward, and bony seven-footer; but most usually is above medium size, with broad shoulders, and angular outline in general. Though not so polished as the Southern Gentleman, and even, perhaps, a little blunt in manners, sometimes to rudeness, the middle-class planter is still no boor, but whole-souled, generous to a fault, and extremely hospitable, entertaining freely all strangers who neither look suspicious nor affect to put on airs of superiority. For, mark you, he is a man of the stoutest independence, always carries a bold and open front; asks no favors of either friend or foe, and would no sooner doff his hat to the Autocrat of the Russias, than to his poor neighbor, Tom Jones, who owns not a darkey in the world, and barely makes a shift to live by the cultivation of a sorry patch of five acres or so of sandy soil, which scarcely possesses enough strength to sprout peas: nor would he, let it also be said in his praise, insult the one any sooner than the other.

He is usually a slaveholder, owning from five to

fifty negroes, (sometimes more,) and generally looks after their management himself. If he does employ an overseer, the latter habitually eats at the table of his employer, and in many cases it is difficult to distinguish employer from employé, so similar are they in every respect—dress, manners, speech, and *tout en-semble.*

In regard to his dwelling-house, out-houses, yard, etc., he is sometimes extremely negligent and careless; but is just as frequently the opposite, is anxious to have every thing look neat and comfortable, and keeps the whole in thorough repair and good condition. But he will persist in eating hog and hominy; believes bacon to be better than any other kind of meat, or a corn hoe-cake or well-cooked ash-cake superior to the finest flour bread that ever was baked. Our Yankee readers, however, need not blame him so much for this predilection; for we have never eaten any good bacon yet out of the South, unless it came from there originally; and corn, hoe, and johnny cakes, are very·different in Kentucky or Virginia from what they are in Massachusetts or Illinois—which is partly owing to the better quality of the Southern corn, and partly to the difference between the old-fashioned *cuisine* of the South and the modern cooking-stove of the Free States. In the Southern States, generally, the kitchen is disconnected wholly with the dwelling-house—is a house apart to itself, indeed, and is appropriated to nothing beside. At one end rises a magnificent (in proportions, we mean) chimney of brick or stone, with a fire-place about ten feet across, more or less, well supplied with pot-hangers, cranks, ovens, pots, skillets, griddles, pans, and the like. Every thing is cooked in the old-fashioned way, and, to our liking, is much more palatable than food cooked in smothering stoves or furnaces, ranges or any thing of the kind. Perhaps we could not give the reader a better idea of the *real corn bread* of the South, than by quoting the following practical remarks on the subject from Dr. Hall's *Journal of Health*, to which they were contributed by a gentleman of Kentucky:

" A corn-dodger is not now what it used to be. Originally it was a corn-meal dumpling. In very early Kentucky times, the universal dinner, winter and spring, at every farm-house in the State, was a piece of middling bacon, boiled with cabbage, turnips, greens, collards or sprouts—cabbage-sprouts—according to the season. The pot, if the family was a large one, contained about ten gallons, and was nearly filled with clean pure water: the middling and the greens were put in at the proper time, to give them a sufficient cooking. Almost always the cook would make with water and corn-meal and a little salt, dough-balls, throw them into the pot, and boil them thoroughly with the rest. These were called *dodgers*, from the motion giving them by the boiling water in the pot. They eat very well, and give a considerable variety to a dinner of bacon and collards. A dodger in modern times is corn-bread baked in a roll about the size of your hand, and about three times as thick, and in my judgment is not a veritable first-rate dodger, unless when on the table it bears the impress of the cook's fingers on it, in placing it in the oven to bake.

" A pone of bread is corn-bread baked in a skillet or

small oven. The skillet or oven when at the proper heat is filled with corn dough, which when baked and turned out, is a pone of bread.

"A hoe-cake is not now what it used to be. I do not believe there will ever be any more good hoe-cakes baked. I have an unextinguishable longing for hoe-cake—real hoe-cake, such as the black woman Jinny, my mother's cook, always baked. It gets its name from the mode of baking. It was originally baked upon a hoe. An old hoe, which had been worn bright, was placed upon live coals of fire, with the eye down, and on it the cake was baked. Now, hoe-cake is baked upon a griddle, or was before cooking-stoves came into use. It just occurs to me, may not the cooking-stove militate against the griddle ?

"Corn-dodger, corn-pone, and hoe-cake are different only in the baking. The meal is prepared for each precisely in the same way. Take as much meal as you want, some salt, and enough pure water to knead the mass. Mix it well, let it stand some fifteen or twenty minutes, not longer, as this will be long enough to saturate perfectly every particle of meal; bake on the griddle for hoe-cake, and in the skillet or oven for dodger or pone. The griddle or oven must be made hot enough to bake, but not to *burn*, but with a quick heat. The lid must be heated also before putting it on the skillet or oven, and that heat must be kept up with coals of fire placed on it, as there must be around and under the oven. The griddle must be well supplied with live coals under it. The hoe-cake must be put on thin, not more than or quite as thick as your forefinger; when brown, it must be turned and both sides baked to a rich brown color. There must be no burning—baking is the idea. Yet the baking must be done with a quick lively heat, the quicker the better. Saleratus and soda, *procul, O procul!* Let there be nothing but water and salt."

In a majority of cases the middle-class planter is a kind master, works not unfrequently in company with his slaves, and always personally attends to their wants in sickness or their necessities in old age. Like the Southern Gentleman, he usually owns one or two very old "family negroes"— heirlooms which have come down from a past generation—and to these he pays the utmost deference. They are the plantation oracles, in fact, without consulting whom the plantation machinery and every thing else would go to wreck and ruin. They are respectfully called *Uncle* by black and white, old and young, and usually possess a very sage, sober look, shake their heads with the utmost gravity, and are equally remarkable for their piety and their love of a wee drop too much of the "critter" on all holiday occasions. They think they know much more than their master, whom they always look upon as *young*, and continue all their lives to call him Marse Josheway, or Marse Peter, or whatever else his name may be. They are always giving him advice too, in consequence ; and tell him with all oracular dignity whether the moon is just right to plant the different kinds of grain, or how to hoe tobacco to best advantage, or when to give the corn the last ploughing, or to harrow the cotton, or to kill the pork-hogs, or to shear the sheep, *ou chatrer les truies*, or how "they" shall resort to some new and untried expedient to keep "dem debbelish pigs from gettin in dat ar tater patch, and rootin up de taters"—all of which the master listens to good-humoredly, and in most cases to profit.

When the master is inclined to be religious, these old Africans receive double honor. They are usually pious members of the Church in full fellowship, are great on quotations from "scripter," and oftentimes aspire to become preachers or exhorters. Some of them are allowed to preach off their own plantation, both by the consent of their master and a license from the Church; and they are often very sensible and practical in their remarks, though sometimes in their manner and mode of expressing their thoughts a little ludicrous, thus giving rise to many amusing anecdotes.

A characteristic instance of the kind we will furnish the reader by way of example. A sable "Brudder," whom we will call Brudder Jones, being deeply impressed with the story of Zaccheus, conceived the idea of employing the same, in illustration of the way in which the "bredderen" ought to "use de means of grace," and lay hold on "de tree of life" in time, "for, my bredderen," he exclaimed triumphantly, "little Zacch'us was boun' to see de Lord for shure, dough he had to clomb up de tree to do it. And how did he got up der tree? Ah! how did he got up der tree, my bredderen? Did he wait for some lazy nigger to brung him a ladder? Ah! no, my bredderen. Did he wait to be boosted? Ah! no, my bredderen; not a boost, ah! He clumbed right straight up de tree hisseff, like de possum, by his own hands and feet and de grace of God, ah!"

Many of them, while not ambitious of filling the sa-

cred desk, do yet delight to shout with Mars'r, and sing
and pray and exhort at home; for very frequently the
master meets with them in their prayer-meetings, and
reads to them out of the Bible, afterwards calling on
the most venerable of the colored patriarchs to pray.
And, O Rev. Creamcheese, you should hear the aged
African's prayer! Unlike yourself, he flourishes no
perfumed cambric before proceeding, nor does he fold
together two soft, white hands with languid ease and
grace; but humbly kneeling upon the bare, uncarpet-
ed floor, instead of lispingly reciting a few chaste sen-
tences to win the applause of fashionable ladies and
attar-scented dilettanti, he prays to Our Father in
Heaven, with whom is no respect of persons! Rough
indeed may be the old man's speech, unpolished and
full of Africanism, but gushing fresh from an overflow-
ing heart, simple as the undoubted lispings of childhood, and rolling forth from the trembling lips in that
full, musical richness of voice and enunciation so peculiar to the negro race: his must be a very callous and
worldly heart, that could listen unmoved to the simple
and fervent petition. And on all such occasions, in
truth, it is rare that a shout does not rise from some
sympathetic African present, long before the prayer
has been brought to a close; while hearty amens respond from every side, and "glory! glory! glory to
God!" is unceasingly ejaculated by the most aged ne-
gress in the assemblage, down whose furrowed cheek
stream big tears of joy, and whose whole body sways
constantly from side to side in the intensity of her religious enthusiasm. And when the prayer is ended,
with what an outburst of heartfelt religious fervor do

master and slaves strike up some familiar old-fashioned camp-meeting hymn, full of simple but plaintive sweetness; and sing with melody in their hearts to a common Lord! Verily the old Covenanters, driven to the glens and caves of canny Scotland by the myrmidons of kingly and priestly power never evinced in their most secret conventicles away off in the heart of the inaccessible highlands, more of spiritual exaltation than is almost every day to be witnessed in some portion of our Southern States, among the descendants of those same Covenanters and their Christian Slaves.

Indeed, take them all in all, and there is a striking similarity between the middle - class planters of the South, and the more well-to-do and intelligent farmers of New-England. They have all undoubtedly sprung from the same original stock. Differences in climate, in outward circumstances, as well as their lifelong rivalry and antagonism have rendered them dissimilar in some particulars, but in the main features of their character there is a very strong similitude. That stern devotion to principle, that religious enthusiasm, that spirit of dogmatism, that practical wisdom which teaches to keep one's powder dry while trusting in the Lord, united to an unquenchable love of independence, which characterized the rebellious Roundheads and Covenanters of the days of Cromwell and Hampden, Cameron and Knox; still survive in their descendants, no matter whether these live among the granite-boulders of New-England, or plant cotton and tobacco on the sunny savannas of the South. Besides, they strongly resemble in that spirit of bigotry and intolerance which always characterizes the middle classes of all communities, but in particular the middle-class Englishman, from whose stout loins most of our own middle classes in all parts of the Union are descended.

The fanaticism and bigotry of the early Puritans, which led them to persecute Quakers and Baptists, to burn witches and broomsticks, and to pass blue laws which forbade a man's kissing his wife on the Sabbath; is still visible in that intense and bitter hatred with which their descendants regard all slaveholders, and which leads them to canonize John Brown and his fellow murderers; while the religious enthusiasm of the offspring of the Pilgrim Fathers now finds vent in Spiritualism, Free Thinkerism, Political Priesthoodism, Free Loveism, and the like. On the other hand, the hereditary dogmatism of their Southern kinsmen, is manifested in the summary disposition these make of all vagabond Yankees—tinkers and peddlers—found strolling about without any "local habitation," whenever they suspect them of being abolition emmissaries: for they incontinently ride the poor fellows on rails, and ornament their backs with a coat of tar and feathers, and sometimes administer to them hydropathically, giving them a succession of gentle douses in the nearest mill-pond, or oftener perhaps, in the pond attached to the nearest farmer's goosery. Their religious fanaticism, however, has hardly yet led them into that miserable chaos of absurdities and crude isms, which at the present time disgraces the Free States. Camp-meetings are about the only bane of the Southern religionists. Certainly, there are many good people, pious, God-fearing people, who attend camp-meetings; and so we doubt not there are good and virtuous abolitionists, who entertain their peculiar convictions from the honestest motives. But because a man is honest in his convictions, is no argument that his convictions are right.

But camp-meetings are not wholly confined to our Southern States; in certain parts of the North they flourish as greatly as they do in the South. Although the writer never could see any fitness in such a mode of conducting the worship of God, (who commands us to do all things "decently and in order," while camp-meetings are often any thing else than decent or orderly,) still he knows that many wise and good men view the subject in a very different light. And it is possible that there are certain classes of the community, whose emotional instincts are predominant, who can be influenced religiously more easily by means of the exciting appeals addressed to them by camp-meeting orators than by any other. But it is unquestionably true, nevertheless, that such appeals more often partake of the ridiculous than the sublime, and we have ourself seen an intelligent audience convulsed with laughter, while a weak brother occupied the "stand" and labored with "might and main" (sobbing convulsively all the time himself) to produce a different result. Hence camp-meetings are rapidly falling into disrepute of late years, and we trust they will disappear altogether in time; for true religion consists much more in deeds of charity and works of love than in bodily shivers, or nervous shrieks, or sepulchral groans, or any kind of dreaming whatever, whether of devils, hell-flames, spirit-circles, broomsticks, or shovels and tongs.

However, despite his periodical furor at camp-meetings, the middle-class farmer of the South (when religious) is practically pious and God-fearing; just as the mass of Down-Easters are virtuous and sensible, despite an occasional Kalloch in their pulpits, and spiritual mediums and circles without number every where. He keeps away from race-courses, cock-pits, groggeries, brothels, and the like; makes no bets; plays no cards; shuns profane company as much as possible; attends to his own business diligently, and so finds but little time to trouble his brain about the affairs of his neighbors; but above all, endeavors to raise up his children "in the nurture and admonition of the Lord." The old family Bible is always to be found on the centre-table in the quiet unostentatious parlor, with its neat curtains and nicely sanded floor, or, of late years, more frequently ornamented, perhaps, with a good substantial three-ply carpet. The venerable Book, with its dark leather-back and sometimes dog-eared leaves, gives evidence of having seen much service; and opening it, you discover in the family register, at the end of the Old Testament and the beginning of the New, the births and deaths, as well as the dates of the marriages which are of recent occurrence, of both the living and translated members of the little household. And if you tarry all night, when the evening shades begin to appear, you will observe the pater familias, so soon as the candles are lighted, call mother and sons and daughters, and domestics also, into the "big room;" after which the lids of the good Book are reverently opened, a lesson is read and commented on, then a hymn of praise and thanksgiving is sung, and all finally bow down humbly in the presence of the Infinite Father, and without pomp, or form, or ceremony, present their devout supplications at the Throne of Grace. The same religious observance takes place on the morrow morning, while the dew is still fresh on the jessamine that overhangs the window-lintel, filling the room with sweetest fragrance, and before yet the laggard sun has fully emerged from the mists upon the neighboring hills: and thus, morning and evening, the whole year round, is the Creator worshipped—the ever blessed God of Abraham, Isaac, and Jacob.

Occupying a middle position between the Southern Yeoman and the Southern Gentleman, the children of the middle classes associate with the children of the one or the other of those, according as their several inclinations may lead them. When given a polite education, they usually prefer the company of gentlemen, as is natural, being truly gentlemen themselves; but ordinarily their education is deficient in many particulars, from which cause, feeling hampered and ill at ease when permitted to mingle with their superiors in refinement and culture, they usually prefer in such cases to mix with more congenial associates; and do sometimes, from sheer envy and jealousy, entertain a most cordial hatred of those whose attainments and good-breeding they despair of ever being able to emulate. This miserable boorishness is manifested in divers ways, but in especial by the dislike they evince to being brought into contact with the sons of gentlemen in any of those many rollicking out-door sports, so common among all classes in the South. For you must know, our readers, that in the South hunting is an universal pastime, and the sons of the poorest farmer are often as good shots as Viscount Palmerston, and in many instances are as fond of fox-hunting as the sons of the gentry; instead, however, of selecting refined associates on such occasions, they much more prefer to hunt in company with rowdy characters and people of that description—preferring to be hale fellows with those beneath them, rather than to enjoy an equality with their superiors, which is due to no matter how graceful a condescension on the part of the latter: a very natural human weakness, by the way, and let us not judge them too harshly.

As a general thing, however, the sons of the middle classes, whether farmer, artisan, tradesman, or what not, are quite provincial in manners, speech, and opinions. Educated, when educated at all, at third and fourth-rate seminaries, where they imbibe a smattering knowledge of Greek and Latin, with the slenderest possible amount of the humanities, they yet fancy that they are cultivated in the highest degree, and strut and attitudinize equal to our Western Congressmen, evincing as much pride and self-importance as any English Oxonian of seven years' standing. And these are the fellows who make what in the outset we called middle-class lawyers, doctors, school-teachers, parsons, and the like. Happy, jovial, well-contented blades! Each one fancies he carries the world in a little private sling of his own, somewhat as David carried the pebble with which he slew the giant; with this difference only, that each flatters himself he is a veritable Goliah of Gath, instead of a very, very small David, indeed! Hence, when invited to make a Fourth of July speech before some village lyceum, they imagine the applause which greets their sophomorical rhodomontade to be as lasting and full as merited as that which used to greet the old Grecian masters of oratory in the famous Athenian Areopagus. And when they devote themselves to law or medicine, and succeed in becoming only fifth or sixth-rate proficients in these professions, verily they would not yield their own opinions a hair's breadth to Hippocrates in the one or to Sir Mathew Hale in the other. If we may be indulged to use a vulgar saying, *they just think they know it all.* Thus they very often render themselves quite ridiculous in the eyes of persons who have seen more of the world; particularly so when, while entertaining the pleasant conviction that they are the most notable individuals in the society in which they move, they solemnly and seriously declare to you that said society is the most refined, the purest, and the perfectest every way in the whole world! O ye pretty fellows, what a nice set of country cockneys you are, indeed!

Now, we always did abhor a cockney—we can't help it. A New-York cockney is a terrible bore enough in all good conscience, and a Paris or London specimen of the genus is no better, but a country cockney! Truly, we had almost as soon get some deft-handed mechanic to auger a hole straight through us at once. Even the Sacred Screw of inquisitive Yan-keedom, is almost tolerable in comparison. Whenever we come in contact with individuals of such meagre capacity, but overweening self-esteem, we do not fail to call to mind the words of Burns:

> "Ah! wad some power the giftie gie us,
> To see oursels' as others see us,
> It wad frae mony a blunder free us,
>   And foolish notion !"

But let us turn to more agreeable themes. We do not believe we have said any thing as yet touching the women of the middle class. These, almost without exception, are worthy of our admiration and respect. Modest and virtuous, chaste in speech and manners; they are, besides, very industrious house-keepers, kind-hearted mistresses, and the most devoted of wives and mothers; although, we are free to confess, they are not unfrequently quite simple and unsophisticated, easily gulled or deceived, knowing at best but little of the world and its manifold follies, and caring even less for its empty vanities and trumpery shows. The labors, indeed, of such a Southern matron are onerous in the extreme. Besides the cares of a mother, the anxieties of a house-keeper, and the wants of her husband, she has also to look after the wants of the blacks. She nearly always superintends the cutting and making of every garment worn by the latter; makes daily visits to the " smoke-house" in company with the cook, in order to see that they are bountifully supplied with provisions; visits their humble cabins when they are sick, or infirm through age; with her own delicate hands administers the healing medicine left by the doctor; and when all medicines have become alike unavailing, sits down beside the lowly couch of the dying African, and tenderly consoles his last moments with all those unwearying assiduities and kind utterances of Christian gentleness, which make the women, God bless them! our better angels and our ministering spirits, all the wide-world over. No wonder, therefore, that such a Southern matron is ever idolized and almost worshipped by her dependents, and beloved by her children, to whom no word ever sounds half so sweet as *mother*, and for whom no place possesses one half the charms of *home*. She lives indeed only to make home happy. She literally knows nothing of " woman's rights," " or free love," or " free thinking;" but faithfully labors on in the humble sphere allotted her of heaven—never wearying, never doubting, but looking steadfastly to the Giver of all good for her reward ; and she is to-day the most genuine pattern and representative of the mothers of our Revolutionary history, to be found any where in the land. 'Tis true she wears no costly silks, and instead of fine linen every day, is simply arrayed in homely calico; nor can she boast an expensive crinoline ; nor many gold rings on her fingers, or jewels in her hair ; yet, believe us, O ye spoiled children of Fashion, in all the superabundance of your flounces and furbelows, your sparkling diamonds, your topaz broaches, and necklaces of pearl, never once can you claim to be apparelled like unto her ! For, as the Lady Countess of Godiva was " clothed on with chastity," so is she, as well as with unassuming modesty and Christian meekness, the peerless raiment of the daughters of heaven—without which, though McFlimsey may count her silks by the hundred and her flounces by the score, she yet has truly " nothing to wear," but walks the earth in nakedness and shame. Neither has this Southern matron ever visited the Opera—never hung entranced on the warbles of a Strakosch or a Piccolomini—never heard of *andante, allegro ma non troppo,* or *prestissimo ;* and only is acquaint with such òld-fashioned songs as " John Anderson my Joe," and the psalms of David versified by good Dr. Watts: but, ah! Mesdames and Mademoiselles, we think, in the Great Day when we shall every one positively appear for the very last time on this earthly stage, you will sing quite small by the side of her whose heart is ever in perfect accord with the mind of the Great Master Symphonist, who, with immortal finger and a voice whose echoes are the echoes of Eternity, leads and directs the Grand Orchestra of the Universe.

In most instances the daughters of such a Southern matron resemble their mother, save that they possess a little more modern polish and culture, and hanker more eagerly after the vanities of the world; but even the daughters are often quite uneducated in the current literature of the times, and in all things else evince a simplicity of mind and character altogether refreshing. Sometimes, 'tis true, they are sent to Boarding-Schools, (which are becoming more common in the South of late years,) are there exposed to a false and shallow system of hot-bed culture for a few sessions; and emerging therefrom in due time make their debût in life, possessed of full as much pride and affectation, as well as conceit and vanity, as of artificial graces of person and manner; and boasting a superficial knowledge of twenty different branches of learning, but in reality having a perfect mastery and comprehension of none. Southern young ladies of this character, however, are usually the daughters of tradesmen, village store-keepers, and the like, who constitute a pretty fair proportion of the Southern Middle Classes, and of whom we shall next come to speak.

Almost every village and hamlet in the United

States can boast one or more storekeepers, so-called in our American vernacular : in England called shopmen. These storekeepers generally keep on their shelves a miscellaneous assortment of goods, groceries, hardware, cutlery, hats, caps, shoes, agricultural implements, and, in fine, almost any thing you can name "in their line." While many of them are gentlemanly and honest, the major portion (as we all *think*, if we don't say so) are shrewd, sharp, cunning fellows ; glib of tongue, full of their own conceit, but prodigal of bows and compliments, and always smiling of countenance, yet, did one credit their own most solemn asseverations, always selling every thing at a "most tremendous sacrifice." How often do they remind one of Dryden's translation · of a poem of Persius :

> " Be sure to turn the penny : lie and swear,
>   'Tis wholesome sin : but Jove, thou say'st, will hear.
>   Swear, fool, or starve, for the dilemma's even ;
>   A tradesman thou ! and hope to go to heaven ?"

Alas ! how true is that saying of some modern moralist, that formerly, " when great fortunes were made only in war, war was a business ; but now, when great fortunes are made only by business, business is war." In the old times, the weapons used were swords and battle-axes, and the fighting was mostly done in broad open day and aboveboard : but now, the most efficient weapons are lies and cunning, and the fighting is all done in darkness and in secret. If this be true of our merchant princes and largest wholesale dealers, how much more true must it be of the little retail-dealer who peddles his wares by the shilling's worth : for the small

hucksterer, particularly the country haberdasher of
either a New-England village or Southern cross-roads,
is sure to be jewed and worried past endurance any
how, by his fourpenny customers, who will never consent to purchase any thing save at a reduction from
the price first demanded; and hence the seller has to
swear that he paid fabulous sums for his goods, but
" as it's you" he will part with them for once " at a sacrifice." Certainly, all country store-keepers are not of
this stamp, but we apprehend that a majority of them
are not overburdened with conscientious scruples; we
do not care what their parentage may be, or in what
climes they may have their local habitation. Lying
and cheating, as well as jewing down a seller and disparaging that which one wishes to buy, are neither
sectional nor national peculiarities—they are human
and world-wide.

The reader will understand us, therefore, when we
tell him that Southern Store-keepers (we do not speak
now of the city merchants) are pretty much like all
other shopmen the world over. They certainly do
possess some marked peculiarities, but aside from
those which are mainly due to local surroundings, they
differ but little from any ordinary shop-keeper in New-
England or the North-West. They generally, in all
the States, spring from the thrifty middle classes; and
their heads are much more constantly occupied with
how they may turn an honest penny, than with politics, or science, or religion. Mark, however, we say
generally; for there are two classes of storekeepers, as
we trust there are of lawyers, since the writer belongs
to the latter very pious and honest fraternity. We

wish the reader to bear this fact in mind; and while we proceed first to describe the larger and less honest class of storekeepers—those, in reality, who ought to figure under the caption of " Southern Yankee"—let him not forget that we will yet have a good word to say, by and by, of those honest and straightforward tradespeople, who happen, we regret to believe, to be in a minority so far as mere numbers are concerned.

If a respectable farmer of the middle class in the South, has a son who early evinces a fondness for trade, by eternally swapping jack-knives with his school-companions, or exchanging marbles, or fish-hooks, or puppies, or any thing else, and always making a " good thing" by the operation, even if it be at the expense of a few white lies; this hopeful juvenile is very soon installed behind some merchant's counter, and the doting parents consider that their youthful prodigy's fortune is already made. And the youthful prodigy entertains the like conviction, and determines that the old folks shall one day see him the owner of a store ; and dressed in broadcloth every day, and a black satin vest, and big gold watch with a heavy gold chain; and owning a white painted house " in town," with an immense portico in front, and making semi-annual visits to New-York or Philadelphia after goods ; and coming in a carriage with servants in livery, to see the old homestead every Christmas; and having the seat of honor awarded him on such occasions, while he makes the eyes of all to stare in awe and wonder at the marvellous yarns he spins out concerning the sights to be seen in the metropolis ; until even burly Andy, as he pretends to be piling the wood high up in the old-fash-

ioned chimney, grins as a darkey only knows how to
grin, and fumbles about his work unusually long, pok-
ing and punching the big back-log and stirring up the
coals, impatient to hear the conclusion of the last magnificent story about Dead Rabbits and Rip Raps.
These are the pleasant dreams Young Hopeful indulges
in while he is learning to split skeins of silk, selling a
half-skein for a whole one, as well as to lie genteelly,
to look at all times smooth and insinuating, to be obsequious to the rich, and condescendingly affable and
confidential to those of mean condition.

Young Hopeful's preceptor is usually a shrewd Yankee from Down East; and here a word about this Yankee; for the Yankees who have gone South with their
descendants, form no inconsiderable share of the Southern Middle Classes.   Of course we are speaking of the
great mass of them, who have been by no means the
flowers of the New-England parterre, allow us to hint to
our Southern friends.   When not school-teachers, they
have usually been trading people, who started out in
life with their all tied up in a bundle on their backs,
which said bundle is presumed to have contained wooden
nutmegs, jewsharps, rat-traps, patent corkscrews, and
other Yankee notions; but so soon as they get the
means, they set up for merchants or storekeepers.
They then profess to be intensely pro-slavery, though
they seldom own slaves, unless acquired by marriage,
preferring otherwise to "hire;" either because they find
it impossible to overcome their early anti-slavery prejudices, or else owing to a fixed resolve to return to the
land of their nativity at some future period of their
lives. For, aside from the natural and inborn love of one's

birth-place which remaineth ever in the human heart, few Yankees have the tact to feel comfortable and perfectly at home in a Slave State. Oftentimes they have evidently seen more of the world than the people with whom they select to live — particularly more of city life—still they appear to find it almost impossible to acquire that easy, unaffected simplicity of manners, which is the charming characteristic of all classes in the South, the slaves not excepted. Without intending it, they yet appear either too pert and consequential, or else too fawning and sycophantic. They are too frequently patronizingly good-fellowish, with the bluff yeomanry, and at the same time most torturingly polite to the wealthy planter. They manage, however, to fleece most of those who deal with them; or else become bankrupt and run away from their creditors, having previously mortgaged all their stock of goods and other property to some friend or relation in the North; who quietly comes and takes possession of the same, sells every thing to the highest and best bidder for cash, pockets the money—for *whose* use, deponent saith not—and returns whence he came, leaving the poor creditors minus their funds as well as their tempers. But the honest and prosperous Yankee usually associates himself with a Southern partner who is well known and possessed of influence in the community— the union proving beneficial to both parties. The firm soon gets a large run of custom, owing to the popularity of the Southern partner; and the familiarity of the Northern partner with the quality and prices of goods in the large cities, enables him to buy to better advantage than could a raw Southerner who visits the Me-

5*

tropolis for the first time; and in consequence to make better bargains with his customers. For the Yankee knows all those places where "old goods are sold for Southern and Western trade"—all the large auction establishments—all the second-hand dealers, and the pleasant den of My Uncle of the Three Balls. He buys most of his invoice from these people, and the "likes of them," and only enough new and fashionable articles to supply a few of his wealthy patrons, well knowing that these alone would ever be able to detect the fraud of his endeavoring to palm off goods two or three years old as the "latest styles." Even if he must lose on the few rich and fashionable articles he does "lay in," he is bound nevertheless to make fully one hundred per cent on all the rest. Certainly it will require considerable lying to "effect sales"—no doubt of that; and is no better than downright swindling, to use the mildest epithet: but our Yankee consoles himself with the reflection, that in a few more years he will grow rich, when it will be plenty soon to enjoy telling the truth and being conscientious along with the other luxuries of life. And besides, the honest farmers and mechanics, and calico-loving negroes, will never entertain a doubt but what they have received their money's worth any how; and then, too, if he did not swindle them somebody else would; and you must not forget, you know, the good old English maxim—"Every body for himself, and devil take the hindmost," and the Scripture declaration, that whoso provideth not for his own household, has denied the faith and become worse than an infidel; and—a hundred other plausible excuses and pretexts, all of a kindred character.

Such is a hasty sketch of the usual preceptor of our Young Hopeful. Being both a willing and apt pupil, under such tuition he makes the most wonderful progress, and soon acquires the sobriquet of Model Clerk, and is promoted accordingly. And a Model Clerk is he, in truth—one that will swear black is white, or white is black, nor wince once while he does it either, but preserve all the time such a severe look of gravity and injured innocence, as rarely fails of disarming even the shrewdest of all their doubt or suspicion. In a little while, too, he learns to read a customer the moment he or she enters the store, and mentally soliloquizes, "Here's a country greenhorn to be plucked," or, "This lady is of the *haut ton;* I must win her favor." In the former case he puts on a gracious patronizing air, looks very pleasant and affable, and speaks with an affectation of frank heartiness: " How are ye, Tom, ole fell'—give us your paw ! Haven't seen you in a coon's age—why haven't you been round to see a feller, eh ? And how's the old folks, and *craps*, and that blamnation pretty sweetheart of yours, ha, ha ?" By this time he has made verdant feel at his ease, for the latter was a little shy when he first came into the presence of so much unaccustomed finery, and rubbed his mouth and nose confusedly with the sleeve of his "jeans" coat, and stammered, and blushed, and looked sheepish ; but now he says, with a broad grin, " As how he wants to buy *her* a nice dress, been's they' re gwine to have some mighty fine doin's down to Aunt Sally Dubbin's fore long." And the simple fellow blushes again to hear himself talk, and grins somewhat bewilderedly : and the Model Clerk grins too, but he doesn't blush, not

he! But he takes his *friend*, Tom, confidentially by
the sleeve, and leads him around the counter to where
are stowed away some worthless old goods, which
have lain on the shelves of the New-York importer
until they are fit for moths only; and picking them up
daintily, he thrusts them into the face of the admiring
countryman; grins again; winks; elevates his eye-
brows knowingly; chucks poor Tom under the short-
ribs in a playful manner; then softly whispers in his
ear: "Times are hard, old fell'—and so we have put
these *splendid goods* down to *cost for cash.*" And he
immediately proceeds to ask just one hundred and fifty
per cent more than the miserable stuff cost at auction.
Verdant is delighted, charmed, but hesitates—sizes his
pile, and says ruefully, "he haint got the rhino." "Is
it for *her?*" asks the Model Clerk, with a sly wink.
"Yes, 'taint for nobody shorter." "Then, confound my
buttons, Tom, you shall have it *at a sacrifice!*" He
offers it then at a large deduction, but still fully one
hundred per cent above prime cost; and sells it of
course. Verdant marches off with the prize, grinning
audibly as he does so, well-pleased with his "bargain;"
while the Model Clerk trips quietly smiling to his
ledger, *well pleased with himself.*

But let us suppose the customer to be a lady of ton
and wealth—how humble is the Model Clerk! How
affable, how polite, how cringing, how nimble of feet,
how full of smirks and grimaces! With happiness
divine beaming in his glowing face, he tumbles down
silks, brocades, velvets, laces, ribbons, etc., etc., piling
the counter with the costly fabrics until he is almost
hid from view behind the same; and yet, after all his

toil and flatteries, his bows and smirks, he is in the
end most humbly thankful to sell madam a simple
yard of *ruban de fil !* When she has left him, floating
in all her crinoline and flounces out at the street door,
reminding one of a ship's cargo passing through the
vessel's narrow hatchway; he does feel somewhat hu-
miliated, but then she will call again. "Ah! yes,
you will come again, madam, and *then !*" Well, the
deep significancy of that *and then,* is best interpreted
by looking ahead a few years, for we will surely find
that the Model Clerk has become the Model Storekeeper; the urchin who erewhile swapped jack-knives
so deftly, at last realizes his early ambition, and is
the owner of a "town house," and a "brick store,"
rides in his own carriage, drinks his weak wines every
day, or his stronger brandy and water; visits New-
York and other seaboard cities twice a year, and,
proudest of all his honors, goes to the old country
homestead during the holidays, takes the seat of honor,
none disputing, and proceeds to spin his Christmas
yarns to the delectation of old folks and young folks,
as well as to the utter bewilderment of the open-
mouthed Andy and his fellow blacks. So wags the
world, our readers, so wags the world.

When the Model Storekeeper goes abroad, (which is
to say, when he visits the land of the Northerners,)
despite his everlasting satin waistcoat, he assumes to
be a Southern gentleman, and so tries very hard to free
himself of certain little tell-tale habits, which trades-
people sometimes unfortunately contract in the "shop."
But not knowing precisely how the "thing" should be
done, and possessing besides somewhat original and

peculiar ideas on the subject, he endeavors to convey some notion of his importance to strangers by looking eminently grave and consequential, and picks his teeth along with those flashy *chevaliers d'industrie* who are wont to assemble in front of the St. Nicholas or the Girard, in the rather ludicrous conviction that such a dirty and ill-becoming practice makes him appear non-chalant and "up to snuff"—a vulgar phrase, this last, but significant of our meaning. He is very proud, too, when you inform him that you could have taken your Bible oath he was a Southerner the moment you laid eyes on him; and if he does not tell you so, he yet secretly congratulates himself that there is some-thing in his *air*—in his *bearing*—peculiarly *distingué*, and peculiarly Southern also. And, although often not pecuniarily interested in slave property, save that his largest patrons are slave-owners, he is ever a valiant champion of the peculiar institution, and takes every opportunity to discuss the merits of the question, just as some New-England men are always sure to run every topic of conversation into a denunciation of the South, if you do not tell them plainly, "you'll none of it."

At home, in his own little village, the Model Store-keeper prides himself upon his superiority to the other members of the middle class, partly because he thinks the life of a farmer or mechanic quite degrading, and that of a storekeeper the *ne plus ultra* of ton and re-spectability; partly because he has cheated and swin-dled them all so long, that he very naturally concludes they are but dull common sort of people as compared to a person of his own wonderful 'cuteness; partly, also, because he really is better informed than they about most subjects which are discussed in the journals of the time ; and partly and mainly, too, because he is ambitious to be considered aristocratic. This last is his greatest weakness, in truth, for his sole ambition becomes, later in life, centred in a desire to move in the select society of the landed proprietors of wealth and refinement. Filled with this "one idea," he rushes into all sorts of vulgar display, pretty much like his brother Potiphars of the Free States, and not unfrequently educates his children in such an unwise and senseless fashion, that they almost invariably grow up to be nothing better than dawdling fops and par_venues, instead of refined and well-bred ladies and gentlemen, who know how to be courteous to even the poorest beggar in the streets, and to whom sneers and all other modern genteel vulgarities are as wholly unknown as servile crookings of the "supple hinges of the knee, where thrift may follow fawning."

But the Model Store keeper—the successful and money accumulating shopman, whose gains are chiefly gotten by reason of his adroit cozenage and subtlety—though the most prominent of his class in the South, as elsewhere, is not the exemplar and archetype of all Southern storekeepers—not by a great odds. Neither would we have the reader to believe, that the cozening knave is always successful, for roguery more often than otherwise overreaches itself in the end ; and there are many scores, yea, and hundreds and tens of hundreds, too, we dare say, of poor shop-keepers in the South, as in the North, who do not remain poor through any lack of cunning or dishonesty, but simply because the fates are not propitious, and they themselves have not the abilities requisite to command success, even in swind-lers and cheats.

There are, indeed, many different kinds of store-keepers, and we are almost at a loss for a classification of them. Some of them are gentlemen of wealth and the first social position, who, in a majority of instances, were never educated to the business, nor passed through any previous store-keeping novitiate or apprenticeship, and who are not therefore to be considered as properly belonging to the class of store-keepers. For which reason we shall not attempt any description of them or their families, but proceed to speak of that class of gen-uine tradesmen, who are the antipodes of the Model Storekeeper, and hence deserving of both our consid-erance and respect.

At the time the Model Storekeeper was serving out his indentures as the Model Clerk, he had many fellow clerks, may be, all of whom were fashioned after very different models from himself as well as from each other. There were delicate, simpering, weak-voiced, soft-handed, be-oiled, and be-curled clerks, with pretty mustaches, and whose brains seemed to have all melted and run down into their shirt-collars. These charming little fellows knew no higher ambition than to be valiant knights of the yard-stick, and of course never rose any higher in the scale of being; unless, perchance, by some very easily imagined process of metempsychosis, they finally were transformed into old women, after that the halcyon days of youth had been wasted, and when, through the infirmities of age, they could no longer successfully mimic the simpering smiles and mincing steps of the younger feminines—which seemed to be the sole aim and study of their earlier years. So, too, there were fast clerks, who gave oyster-suppers to their friends after work-hours; who played the flute and old sledge every night, till near upon "day-break in the morning;" who drank oceans of champagne, and old Bourbon, and brandy and water; who kept a pretty negro wench for a mistress, or may be some poor milliner's apprentice; who bet on horse-races and the elections, and loved fast driving, and to talk about "such a splendid rig," and their "two-forty," and all that; and who, as a natural consequence of the foregoing, sometimes took money out of the till of their employers which did not belong to them—got discharged for their pains—lost caste thereupon—took to drink and cards harder than ever before, and finally died of *delirium tremens*, or degenerated into the Southern bully— of whom, more anon.

But (and we now crave the reader's attention, particularly if he be a young man of humble position) behind the same counter with all these worthless fellows, and side by side with the Model Clerk himself, there stood an honest, homely lad, possessing a sad but thoughtful face; a lad whose parents had placed him in that servile position (bowing his manly nature down to the hard necessity of doing a woman's labor; for what else is it, good faith?)—because one sturdy father's arm could afford to give at best no more than one or two of his offspring the means to enable them to acquire any thing like a liberal education. Religiously trained at home, and naturally full of all generous impulses, this honest young fellow continues to be honest despite the lessons and examples of dishonesty all around him; continues to be frugal and economical, despite the continuous jeers and sarcasms of the sleek-coated coxcombs, who every day thrust their scented locks between him and the more wealthy patrons of the establishment, with a contemptuous smirk dispatching their more plain and homely fellow-clerk to attend to the wants of the οἱ πολλοί—the bluff, straightforward old farmers, the independent yeomanry, the drawling and gawky hoddy-doddies from the "hill country," and the grinning, good-natured, thick-lipped, and woolly-headed Africans.

But mark, young gentlemen, honesty, frugality, and unwearied faithfulness, always, sooner or later, bring their own reward. In time, and by slow degrees, it may be, our honest lad emerges from his obscurity, and, as a young man, is noted among all classes for trustworthiness and fair dealing, for a courteous affability which knows no respect of persons, and a conscious pride of demeanor, which declares that he is not ashamed of honest poverty, feeling and knowing that " a man's a man for a' that." By and by he has saved enough to go into business for himself; else some wealthy gentleman kindly furnishes him the capital, taking for security the *honest fellow's reputation;* and now, although he may not accumulate riches as rapidly as the Model Store-keeper, he yet steadily advances in the way to prosperity, winning all the while, what is worth a deal sight more than money, the respect and confidence of his fellow-citizens. Neither does his prosperity ever elate him any more than did his poverty render him servile and sycophantic; for it is a painful truth, that your domineering and overbearing rich men who have risen from obscurity, were equally servile and truckling while they remained poor, crawling ever on their bellies at the beck of their employers, and eating dirt with as much apparent zest as the vulgar gourmand manifests while discussing a flavorous *pot pourri*. Though not much read in books, the Honest Storekeeper is remarkable for hard common sense— what the country people vulgarly call *horse-sense*—and this prevents his aping the manners of those whose superior advantages have rendered them more elegant and refined than himself. Hence he is truly a gentleman at heart, and is rarely given to any kind of vulgar ostentation ; but, instead of a showy house, luxurious furniture, liveried domestics, and extravagance in dress, so soon as he finds himself possesor of more cash capital than his business requires, he invests it in a suburban farm—small at first, but enlarged and added to from year to year, until after a while it assumes the stately proportions of a plantation, to which the thrifty owner retires in his old age, seeking that *otium cum dignitate*, to which we all look forward as the reward of honest industry; and leaving his sons or sons-in-law to carry on his former business. Such storekeepers are always deservedly respectable and well thought of; and their children in most cases being properly educated and well-bred, have the *entree* of the best society, and usually conduct themselves worthily in every relation of life, whether civic or social.

'Tis most true, however, that the Honest Storekeeper does not always succeed in acquiring a fortune, but in a majority of cases dies with the harness on, and goes to receive, in a better country than this, the rewards due a life of honest toil and unflinching integrity. Ah! how few of us who are blessed with abundance of this world's goods, ever consider what trials and temptations always beset the path of the struggling tradesman! What doubts and fears! What hopes deferred which make the heart sick! He always presents to us a pleasant face, but who can paint the unutterable grief which lies hid behind that smiling mask? There is a note in bank due on the morrow, and he has not the money to take it up. There are grocers' bills, and butchers' bills, whose owners are clamorous to be paid, but he can not raise a "red." Must his note go to protest? and must the families dependent upon the grocer and the butcher be turned into the street by their landlord, because *he* is delinquent in paying them their honest dues? In the first case his honor is at stake and his good name, and in the other his manhood and all the kindly instincts of his heart. No wonder his head is prematurely gray, and his quiet subdued manner even sometimes borders on humility, not to say servility. Wait until we have been similarly tried! After all, despite the world's blind worship of its mighty men, the most praiseworthy heroes are those whose walks are the common ones of every day life, whose names perish and whose memories are buried with their bodies—but who, having received only one talent from the good Master, wrapped it not up in a napkin, but used it honestly and faithfully, and at last, when called upon to give an account of their stewardship, returned it with interest compounded to the Benevolent Donor.

For who could not bear patiently the buffetings of

the world and the cold neglect of mankind, when per
suaded that aftertimes will honor his memory with that
reverence which he feels is due, though denied to him
by his contemporaries? But to have to run the gauntlet of life alone, only to find neglect and oblivion at the
end of the race—buffeted at every turn by adversity
and misfortune, kicked about, thumped about, worried
and wearied by the struggles and cares of poverty, and
above all disheartened by reason of the sneers and contempt of an unfeeling world : the man who runs such
a gauntlet contentedly and in peace, never complaining
of the hardness of his lot nor envying the riches of his
neighbor, though he should faint by the way before his
race is ended, and fall wounded and sore under the feet
of the groundlings to be trampled in the dust, is yet
the moral hero of the universe. Ah! yes, and there are
thousands of such in the world, although the world
may never know them, and no trump of fame shall ever
with brazen tongue proclaim their worthiness in camps
or courts, in the presence of kings or peoples. They
are the rough diamonds of our race, discarded and set
at naught by ignorant men, only to be translated to a
more princely kingdom, there to become the crown diamonds of its majestic Sovereign.

> " So, gentlemen,
> With all my love I do commend me to you :
> And what so poor a man as Hamlet is
> May do, to express his love and friending to you,
> God willing, shall not lack."

We come next to speak of the Southern manufacturers. These bear a strong family resemblance to the

various classes of storekeepers, and even sometimes to the more refined and intelligent city merchants, who are pretty much the same in the South that they are in the North. The manufacturing interest is rapidly advancing in the South, particularly the manufacture of cotton and woollen stuffs of a coarse grade. Manufactories of this kind are springing up every where in the cotton States of late years; but they are most numerous in the State of Georgia, which has been appropriately called the Empire State of the South, and in this State they are owned not infrequently, at least in part, by persons from the North: what is more, these manufactories are generally profitable investments—more so, in truth, than those of Massachusetts or other Northern States. We do not see any reason, indeed, why cotton or woollen manufactories in any of our Gulf States could not be made to pay handsomely, if in the hands of enterprising and intelligent capitalists. They can certainly compete successfully with Lowell or Manchester in supplying the wants of the South, as well as our Pacific States, Mexico, Central and South-America, and, in time, China and Japan — the trade with these latter countries being destined ere a great while to pass inevitably through or over either the Isthmus of Darien or Tehuantepec. Even discarding slave labor altogether, the Poor Whites alone of the South, to say nothing of the Yeomen, are numerous enough to work more spindles than are in the whole of New-England at present. And we are disposed to believe that they could be induced to forsake their usual idle and profitless manner of living, and to devote themselves to the labor of factory operatives; although there are those who think their blood has so long flowed through lazy channels—first in the veins of their remote English ancestors who lived and died in the poorhouses of England, and latterly through the veins of their immediate progenitors, who seem to have vegetated among the Southern sandhills something like the native mullein-stalks, which neither toil nor yet do spin —until there is no longer any possible method by which they can be weaned from leading the lives of vagrom-men, idlers, and squatters, useless alike to themselves and the rest of mankind. But we should like to see the experiment tried, notwithstanding.

From a late digest of the statistics of manufactures, which has just been completed in accordance with an act of Congress, and transmitted to that body by the President, we learn that the total value of manufactures in the South for the year ending June 1, 1858, amounted to one hundred and sixty-two millions one hundred and twelve thousand three hundred and twenty-four dollars. The number of establishments is about thirty thousand; the number of hands employed about one hundred and sixty thousand; the amount of capital invested ninety-one millions two hundred and eighty thousand nine hundred and sixty-four dollars. This is certainly no mean showing for what has been considered an almost exclusively agricultural community. Of course, however, in the present embryo state of cotton and woollen manufactures in the South, the greater proportion of her present manufactures is the product of more intelligent labor than what is ordinarily performed by factory operatives. It is the product indeed of mechanical skill—the value of the labor of Southern mechanics, even those " greasy mechanics," about whom certain Northern dema-gogues have been so much exercised of late.   It is the value of the labor of carriage-makers, leather-dressers, harness-makers, hatters, cabinet-makers, cobblers, iron-workers, engine-builders, trunk-manufacturers, and the like.   And yet it has been asserted in the North time and again, and the assertion is still reïterated every day, that Southern mechanics are put upon a level with the negroes, and are not respected because they labor with their own hands for a livelihood!   You, Reverend Sir, have, in the hotness of your political zeal, doubtless aided in the circulation of the charge; and if only to prevent your again desecrating the pul-pit with such utterances of falsehood and calumny, al-low us to inform you implicitly that all such cock-and-bull stories are the sheerest fabrications, concocted by those political tricksters who, to serve their own sel-fish purposes, seek to inflame the breasts of the honest sons of toil in the Free States against the landed pro-prietors of the South.   Did not these latter afford them a safe and shining mark at which to spit their venom, the hollow-hearted knaves would soon begin to agitate with viperous tongue agrarian sentiments at home, hoping to thrust themselves into power by ex-citing the rabblement and riffraff of the community against all citizens of affluence and respectability.

Now, the mechanics in the Slave States constitute a very worthy portion of the Southern middle classes, and, when moral and upright, are fully as much re-spected as they are any where else in the world; though they are not at the same time any more admitted to a social equality with the Southern *élite*, or the family of the high-bred Southern Gentleman, than they are to the fashionable and exclusive society of the solid men of Boston, or to the gilded and luxurious drawing-rooms of a New-York millionaire. As we view it, respectability is one thing and gentility or fashion is quite another. It is respectable to labor— to acquire an honest livelihood by one's own industry —all the world over; but where, we should like to know, is it considered genteel or fashionable? Besides, respectability may be of different degrees, sometimes graduated according to a man's pecuniary circumstances, but much oftener according to his mental capacity and largeness of soul; but fashion, on the contrary, never allows of but one standard, whether of dress, of manners, or equipage, or birth, or wealth— and to this standard must conform all those devotees who would fain bask in the smiles of the uncompromising goddess, who in all things else allows the very largest liberty, not to say license. Hence men may be, and often are, both fashionable and genteel, who still remain any thing else than respectable, and *vice versa*. Thus the code of fashion and modern gentility demands that poor Mrs. Sickles shall become an outcast, while a noble Briton, said to be as guilty, is feted and his society courted by the very *quality* who turn their backs upon the helpless girl-adulteress, *upon principle*, too! and who would still smile upon the greater sinner, who doubtless lured the poor victimized wife to her ruin, had his life only been spared by the dishonored husband. Yea, load even an ass down with jewels and broadcloth, give him a long pedigree, and the

6

entrée of "our best society," and in a very little while
it would be looked upon as "flat burglary" not to cry
bravo! every time the quadruped might bray, and
hear! hear! if he so much as flapped one of his lovely
auricles; but who is such a born fool as to imagine
once that Long Ears is the recipient personally of such
tokens of distinguished regard! Strip the poor fellow
of his costly trappings, and you will soon perceive
what a sorry ass he becomes indeed, with none so poor
as to do him reverence. So is it with many persons
of ton and fashion; strip them of their trumpery gew-
gaws, of the glitter and glamour in which their wealth
and surroundings envelop them, or effectually remove
the gilded mask which hides from the world's eyes
their black and viperine natures, and verily not a wild
ass that brays among the sandy wastes of Judea but
would more deserve our respect and esteem. While,
on the other hand, every where, in all ages and climes,
and no oftener in the Slave States than in the Free
North, men are to be met with of sterling integrity, of
noble natures, of generous impulses and the purest
moral character, who would find themselves completely
at a loss how to behave in a fashionable drawing-room,
would never be able to dine in any peace of body or
mind at a rich man's table, and whose life-long friendships and associations wholly unfit them to mingle on
terms of social equality with the educated and refined,
the high-bred and aristocratic. And none but a fool
or a knave, or a philosopher of the school of Robes-
pierre, or a demagogue of the family of the Gracchi,
would ever advocate such an impossible social mon-
strosity as the fraternization of natures so dissimilar;

or, failing in the accomplishment of their quixotic emprise, would begin to rail, with rancorous malice and spite, against riches and refinement, against culture and pride of station, one or all of them. For the discerning eye of the truly wise and thoughtful man will ever pierce through no matter what sort of outward disguise, be it of poverty or wealth, of rags or purple raiment, until he shall be enabled to measure the spiritual stature of every one of his fellow-creatures; and when he has done this, he will then predicate his esteem of each individual upon what he finds written upon the tablets of his heart, and upon nothing beside. This is the true Christian philosophy, and it is founded upon that immutable and eternal Rock of Ages, which will remain firm and unshaken when all mutable and perishable things shall have passed away.

Those doughty individuals who bawl loudest and fiercest against (not the abuses of wealth, but) wealth, are the very fellows, if the truth were known, who in their hearts honor riches most, and who run thereafter with greatest greed, until they find that the coveted treasure still continues to elude their grasp; when, out of pure envy, they resolve not to permit those who do possess the coveted prize to enjoy the same in any peace or comfort. Such honest worthies always remind one of those leathery blue-stocking damsels who, (after having baited their man-traps for full thirty years or more with every delicate morceau known to female ingenuity, but all in vain,) finding themselves in the autumn of their days shrivelled and hideous, rail so indignantly against matrimony, and sneer so virtuously at the buxom charms of a blooming girl of sixteen, whose fresh young life and healthy heart-beats *will* make her the cynosure and idol of all her gentleman friends, who are neither *blasé* nor misanthropical. So, also, your factious demagogues, whose oily tongues are always appealing *to* the PEOPLE and *for* the PEOPLE, are ten to one the greatest knaves alive, and in their hearts care no more for the dear people than the purring tom-cat cares for the mouse he tenderly fondles before eating, or the dirty swine for the reeking draff in which it wallows before taking thereof its swill. And when we reflect that the disclosures of the shameful practices of our Forty Congressional Thieves have so fully demonstrated the truth of this charge, we are inexpressibly astonished and confounded, that the citizens of our Free States will not open their eyes to the necessarily demoralizing tendency of that miserable politicalism of the hour, which appeals to nothing higher than base passion or baser prejudice. O beguiled fellow-countrymen, why will you not be instructed by the warning voice of all past history? Without considering the multiple revolutions and periodical massacres which have stained Europe with blood during the last half-century, when was it, let us ask, in the history of the Republics of Greece and Rome, that the most fervid and intemperate appeals were addressed to the fickle populace in favor of an universal brotherhood? It was when the tyrant Scylla was liberating convicts and slaves to rape and debauch the patrician dames of the Imperial City: and when Aristides was being ostracized by the Athenians, because he dared to be juster and honester than the servile demagogues who, by flatteries and wire-pulling, had wormed themselves into the hearts of the unthinking rabble. Believe us, gentlemen, the sway of passion, if long indulged, leads inevitably to mob-law in the end; and thence to despotism is a *facile descensus*, from which the *revocare gradum* is only to be accomplished at the expense of oceans of blood and treasure. But in our excessive zeal we are fast losing sight of the Southern mechanics; so, *revenons à nos moutons*, our readers.

As a general thing, the mechanics of our Slave States are much better conditioned, so far as worldly goods are concerned, than their brother-craftsmen of the North; and for three very good reasons. First, there is in the South less competition; and in the second place, higher wages; and thirdly and lastly, the Southern mechanics get work all the year round, and do not have to lie idle all winter, sucking their paws like the grizzly bears of the Rocky Mountains, eating up in the mean time all the little store they may have accumulated during the summer months. And particularly is this true when slack times prevail, and labor is not in demand. This, indeed, is the great curse of the life of a mechanic in the North, and keeps just about one half of them always dodging from pillar to post, uncertain to-day where to-morrow's dinner shall be eaten.

Why, at the present time, we do not entertain the least doubt but there are fully *one hundred thousand respectable families* in the North who are out of employment, and who in consequence will have to live for the next three months (we write this about the beginning of December) in a state of semi-starvation! What a commentary may we here read on the boasts of the Northern press only two short years ago. Then the South was every where decried as poor and bankrupt, as on the eve of beggary and starvation, while in the Free North all was progress and reform! But the hard times came—the winds blew and the rains beat; and now we all know who has been the wise man, building his house upon a sure foundation. The great Northern house of sand has been overwhelmed in the storm, leaving nothing but a wreck behind; but the South stands firm as a rock, and her financial condition never was better. And in the general prosperity her mechanics have shared in the good fortune of her other citizens; they have suffered no reduction from their usual wages, and have had pretty constant work all the time.

Indeed, our abolition parsons who have been praying so devoutly for God to heap coals of fire upon the heads of the Southerners, are now beholding their own flocks subjected to the ordeal, and to save themselves from destruction are forced to rely upon foreign gold—to beg alms of the enemies of their country! Have their maledictions come home to roost? Why, if this be not true, does one meet so constantly in the Free States haggard, care-worn faces, which are seldom lighted up with a smile of contentment, or the broad grin of a hearty and wholesome good humor? In the streets, on the cars, on the ferry and river steamboats, in the churches, in the theatres, in the workshops—every where you meet continually the dull restless eye of the weary brain, or the wistful, longing look of the wearier heart, in sad contrast to that smiling, rollicking spirit, which seems to pervade the entire South. If any of our readers doubt the truth of the assertion, only let them travel for one month in one section and then one month next succeeding in the other, and they will have their skepticism removed beyond a peradventure.

So much for the Middle Classes.

Whatever else we shall have to say concerning them will be found in the two next succeeding chapters, which treat respectively of the "Southern Yankee" and "Cotton Snobs;" only we will here remark, what should have been adverted to before now, that most of the classes treated of in this chapter are much given to a love of military titles, bestowed without regard to any sort of military service and upon all sorts of people. The young men, also, very much affect blue coats with brass buttons, and even sometimes sport veritable stripes down the legs of their pantaloons. To such an extent does the military fever rage in some localities, a stranger would conclude at least every other male citizen to be either "Captain, or Co-lo-nel, or Knight at arms." Nor would he greatly err, so far as the title goes, for, we verily believe, in some favored districts, he would find more than every other man a military chieftain of some sort or other. Illustrative of this weakness for sounding handles to one's name, (an American peculiarity, by the by, and by no means confined to the South,) a well-known gentleman of Winchester, in the State of Virginia, is in the habit of telling something like the following anecdote. Crossing the Potomac on a certain occasion into Virginia, with his horse, in a ferry-boat, the ferryman said:

"Major, I wish you would lead your horse a little forward!"

He immediately did so, observing to the man :

" I am not a Major, and you must not call me one."

To this the ferryman replied :

" Wall, Kurnel, I ax your pardon, and I won't call you so no more."

Having arrived at the landing-place, he led his horse out of the boat, and said :

" My good friend, I am a very plain man ; I am neither a Colonel nor a Major—I have no title at all, and I don't like them. How much have I to pay you ?"

The ferryman gazed at him a while in astonishment and silence, but at last exclaimed :

" By jinkers ! you ar' the fust white man that I ever crossed this ferry with who warn't jist nobody at all ; an' I swar, Kur—a—Cap—O dangnation ! Wall, dod seize me, *Squire*, you shan't pay not a red cent—you allers can go over this ferry scot free—if you shan't, hang old Jake Wiggins !"

CHAPTER III.

"How many a man, from love of pelf,
  To stuff his coffers starves himself;
Labors, accumulates, and spares,
  To lay up ruin for his heirs:
Grudges the poor their scanty dole;
  Saves every thing except his soul:
And always anxious, always vexed,
  Loses both this world and the next!"

                        OLD SATIRIST.

THE name Yankee was originally bestowed upon
New-Englanders alone, but for what reason it would
be difficult perhaps to determine at this time. At
present, however, with all foreigners it is used to designate the natives of any of the Anglo-American States
of our Republic. Thus Mr. Paul Morphy, though a
Louisianian, is always spoken of abroad as the Yankee
Champion of Chess. At home, matters are somewhat
different. In our Southern States all Northerners are
regarded as Yankees, while the Southerners will not
consent to have the name applied to themselves. But
even in the North there are those who still disclaim
the appropriateness of the cognomen, when applied to
any persons other than the natives of New-England;
hence, the New-Yorker becomes quite indignant if you
call him a *Yankee*, and so do the Keystoners, and the

6*

people who live in our Western States. Yankee with all these is looked upon usually as a term of reproach —signifying a shrewd, sharp, chaffering, oily-tongued, soft-sawdering, inquisitive, money-making, money-saving, and money-worshipping individual, who hails from Down East, and who is presumed to have no where else on the Globe a permanent local habitation, however ubiquitous he may be in his travels and pursuits. In this sense of the word, however, we are disposed to opine that, while New-England may possibly produce more Yankees than other portions of the Republic, owing to the sterile nature of her soil and the consequent necessity of hoarding up and husbanding every thing, even to stinginess, on the part of her teeming population; still, any numbers of the close-fisted race are to be met with all the way from the banks of the Hudson to the deltas of the Mississippi—all to the manor born too, and through whose veins courses not a drop of New-England blood.

Of these all the Southern Yankee is, without dispute or cavil, the meanest. He has nothing whatever to plead in excuse or even extenuation of his selfishness; for all around him is a boundless hospitality, and even the very air he breathes excites to warm-heartedness, relaxing the closed fist of more Northern latitudes into the proverbially open palm of the generous-hearted South. Time was, indeed, when the Southern Yankee had neither a local habitation nor a name. During the grand old Colonial days, as well as the happy period which immediately succeeded the Revolution, Southerners did not dream of devoting their whole lives—all their time and talents—to the base pursuit of riches—

the mere acquisition of dollars and dimes, regardless of family ties, or the duties one owes to society, and the much higher duties also one owes to his God. There is, in truth, only a single instance on record of such a Southerner existing in those days; and he was that scurvy fellow, who, according to Patrick Henry, at the very time our Revolutionary fathers were rejoicing over their hard-won victory and independence, ran about frantically from camp to camp, bawling hoarsely at the top of his voice, *beef! beef! beef!* But alas! this famous beefman must have been no less than a second Grand Turk, to have left so many descendants after him! At the present time, the Southern Yankee is quite an institution in the South. Although he has sprung up in the last fifty years, he has thriven faster than Jonah's gourd, has waxed fat exceedingly, and already elevates his horn amazingly high in the land. He flourishes like a green bay-tree in every Southern State. Whether this has been owing to the influence and example of his Northern brother, or to the sudden wealth bestowed upon the South by the invention of the cotton-gin and the purchase of Louisiana, or to some other undefined and indefinable cause, we are not prepared to say. We simply record the fact, as in duty bound to do, and leave to more inquisitive minds the labor of tracing out the cause.

The Southern Yankee comes of no particular lineage, but springs from all manner of forefathers, though in most cases from persons of the middle class. No matter whence he derives his origin, however, he invariably boasts but one 'armorial motto, and that is, *vincit omnia* AURUM. These are the words he emblazons is letters of gold upon the silken gonfalon which he flings so bravely to the breeze, and such is the inspiriting ensign under which he fights: and he proves no recreant soldier, we can assure you, but fights the good fight to the death, and verily he hath his reward: For,

> "—— Satan now is wiser than of yore,
> And tempts by making rich—not making poor."

' Indeed, were we disposed to imitate the style of our political parsons, (which is no difficult thing, O reader!) we should declaim somewhat on the following wise: Like his Northern brother, the Southern Yankee is deterred by no obstacle whatever from his tireless pursuit of riches. In the tobacco-fields of Virginia, in the rice-fields of Carolina, in the cotton-fields of Alabama, or among the sugar-canes of Louisiana, when a farmer or planter, he is in all things similar and equally bent on the accumulation of the sordid pelf: and the crack of his whip is heard early, and the crack of the same is heard late, and the weary backs of his bondmen and his bondwomen are bowed to the ground with over-tasking and over-toil, and yet his heart is still unsatisfied; for he grasps after more and more, and cries to the fainting slave: "Another pound of money, dog, or I take a pound of flesh!" And the lash is never staid, save by one single consideration only— *will it pay?* Will it pay to press the poor African beyond what he can endure, and thereby shorten his life, or is it better to drive him just so far as his health and continued usefulness will justify? this is the great and the only question with every Southern Yankee:

Conscience? *Basta!* he knows no such a thing as conscience: he cares only to get gain, and get it he will, and let conscience go to the dogs. Religion? Kiss your grandmother! Go talk to the women and the parsons about religion: a man who has uncounted treasures visible and tangible, will not be such a fool as to give them up for those which can be neither seen nor felt, and the enjoyment of which is postponed to the Hereafter. Humanity? The devil! what care I for your humanity? Don't I see every body else trying to cheat every body, and to get the upper hand; and shall I remain such a milksop as to let every body get ahead of me? So he reasons; and he acts accordingly. Who of us, dear friends, shall cast the first stone at him? Will you, Sir, regular church communicant, negrophilist too, and all that, who gamble in stocks, in railway shares, bank shares, and mortgage bonds? in grain, in whisky, in lands? who blow your great financial bubbles in a venal public press, until you have pocketed the savings of the widow and the orphan, when you suddenly collapse, suspend, fail, or abscond, leaving your poor victims a prey to want, and beggary, and starvation? Will you, our gentlemanly manufacturers, who live in your brown-stone fronts and fare luxuriously every day, while in your establishments "down-town" thousands of weak, hollow-eyed women and sickly-hued men, are every day dying by inches for lack of proper nourishment, and proper rest, and freedom from corroding cares, and a mouthful now and then of pure country air, and an occasional scent of the clover-blooms or the sweet perfume of the new-mown hay? Or will you, ye swearing, libidinous

Free Thinkers, who labor to undermine public virtue and public morals by denying the authority of Revelation and the existence of a God, hoping in the universal corruption which would ensue upon the success of your doctrines, to gratify more easily your beastly and lustful natures? Which one of you all, we repeat, will cast the first stone at the Southern Yankee? Come now, gentlemen, do not all throw at once: one at a time, if you please—one at a time!

The farming class of Southern Yankees abounds more in the Gulf States, than in those which border on the Free States. This is owing to the greater richness of the soil in the former States, as well as to the greater profitableness of cotton-raising or sugar-planting as compared to the production of tobacco, wheat, or hemp. Besides, in the extreme South, the Southern Yankee puts himself to very little expense about any sort of improvements on his plantation, and his gin-house not unfrequently costs twice as much as his mansion. Sometimes, indeed, he lives in a log-cabin similar to those furnished his negroes, and even when he possesses a better and more pretentious dwelling, he rarely keeps it painted, but lets it rot down over his head, being too penurious to spend the money necessary to keep it in repairs. Usually there is only a "worm fence" of rails around his yard, in which pigs, poultry, cows, sheep, horses, and the like are allowed to roam at will; and his stables, barns, negro cabins, and other out-houses, are, in most cases, not more than a stone's throw from his own domicil. Under such circumstances, is it at all wonderful that the Southern Yankee is fully as restless as the Yankees of the North

—always on the move, or ready to sell out at any time if settled? Home to be loved must be made attractive, but he who is so wedded to filthy lucre as to despise all ornament that costs money, is not capable of entertaining in his selfish and narrow bosom so refining a passion as the love of home, or the love of any thing else, indeed, that is pure and beautiful. In the words of the poet,

> "A river or a sea
>   Is to him a dish of tea,
>   And a kingdom, bread and butter."

In regard, however, to the dwellings, or log cabins rather, of those persons who have just moved into any of the new States of the South-west, the reader will please observe, that there is a great difference between the man who lives in a log cabin from necessity and because nothing better is to be had, and the individual who does so from choice, and because he is too penurious to own a better dwelling. For you will find in many a log cabin in all the South-western States as perfect gentlemen—gentlemen of the first breeding and education—as in most of the mansions on Fifth Avenue.

However, though often a farmer or planter, the Southern Yankee is much more frequently a trader or speculator. The slow but sure gains of agricultural pursuits are not swift enough to satisfy his inordinate craving for money; hence he speculates, either in merchandise, or stocks, or tobacco, or cotton, or sugar, or rice, or grain, or lands, or horses, or *men*. In all which he is but a type of the Wall Street prototype. He will lie or cheat if need be, and scruples at no dirty trick provided it enables him to make a "good thing of it"—such is the chaste vernacular of these sharp-witted fellows. Of course there are those who speculate in most of the things we have enumerated, both in the North and the South, who are yet honorable and trustworthy citizens. We are by no means disposed to confound the innocent with the guilty in any of the affairs of life. But the Southern Yankee, as well as the simon-pure Northern Yankee, is unscrupulous in his speculations, as in every thing else almost which is not put down in black and white as a penitentiary offence. Neither of them has any principles he could swear by, unless you except the principle of making money and saving it when it is made. When the former goes to live in the North he is sure to turn abolitionist, although he may have been a negro-trader up to that time; and so, too, when the latter directs his steps Southwards, notwithstanding he may have been previously a constant employé on the Underground Railroad, he immediately discovers a sweet divinity in the peculiar institution, and no Southern overseer could expatiate more eloquently on its manifold beauties than he.

We have had the good fortune or the bad fortune (whichever the reader prefers) to meet with many of these knavish, unprincipled turn-coats, both in the North and the South. The most striking instance we ever knew of a Southern Yankee turned abolitionist, was that of a Marylander, who had left his country for his country's good no doubt, and had gone to live in a Northern State. We met him by accident on one of the many leading lines of railway in the Free States—when or where does not matter; and since we two occupied the same seat, so soon as we became aware that each of us was Southern born, we very naturally began to discuss the subject of slavery. We do not know why it was, unless the fellow desired to curry favor with the Northerners all around us; but he certainly did extol the North with undue lavishness, abusing the South at the same time in as scurrilous a manner, as that preëminently virtuous and sweet-spoken paper, the New-York *Tribune*, is wont to do every day. At first we were exceedingly shocked, but recovering from our surprise and mortification, we answered with some bitterness the aspersions of our fellow - Southerner, which so confused him, he seemed completely at a loss what to say, but wriggled like a crushed worm upon his seat, shaking his head the while in a manner so doleful and wretched, that a New-Yorker present and the amiable Conductor (this was the label on the latter's hat) volunteered to back him; and so at it we went again more spirited than before. Luckily for the writer, an intelligent Englishman and a gallant son of the Old Dominion came to the rescue, seeing the odds against us; and right soon we had routed the enemy horse, foot, and dragoons. But being all of us young and somewhat heady, and our blood being up, we determined, so soon as we reached our hotel in the Southern city we were bound to, that a diligent inquiry should be instituted concerning the antecedents of this person, who could be so mean and ungrateful as to strike at the mother who brought him into the world. Old Dominion undertook the task of smoking out the cunning fox, and he soon had Master Reynard unearthed to our entire satisfaction. We learned that the fellow had formerly lived in a little country village in

Maryland; was there the cashier of the village bank; was withal a miser of the straitest sect, *and so cruel a master to his servants as to be universally detested.* Such, O reader, are some of the recruits to the great Army of Freedom!

The Southern Yankee is very often a village store-keeper or country merchant, as he delights in styling himself, and is always pretty much of the like pattern with the Model Storekeeper, only he is even less scrupulous than that worthy. For, besides the practice of selling auction-bought goods as the "latest styles," and general lying and swindling, he is also given to one other practice much more reprehensible and blame-worthy, though equally if not more profitable. In all parts of the South, it is the custom of village storekeepers to sell goods on a credit of twelve months, at the expiration of which time, if you are rich and influential, you are seldom asked to pay up, but simply to give your note for the amount due. If you are in only moderate circumstances, however, and so "short" that you can not meet your yearly bills promptly when pay-day arrives, the Southern Yankee is very kind; does not wish to distress an old patron and friend; all he asks is, that you too shall give him your note, but secured by *good collaterals*—which means a trust-deed of your land and negroes. These may be worth ten thousand dollars, while your note does not exceed five hundred; but, no matter, the whole of your property is demanded as security. Then you are permitted to buy on credit again; and again at the end of another year your note is taken as before; and thus from year to year, until your indebtedness amounts to about one

half what your property is worth. Hitherto the Southern Yankee has been to you the very best friend in the
world. He has fawned on you in public, invited you
to dine with him whenever you have been in the village to remain all day; and has so completely obfus-
cated your wits by means of his adroit flatteries, that
you are absolutely fool enough to believe him, when
he tells you in a confidential whisper, that he *loves you
like a brother.* But now his aspect suddenly changes—
the cat which has been lying so demurely in the meal-
tub this long time, throws off all disguise at last: your
advances are met with coldness; your stale jokes are
not laughed at so furiously as formerly; you are no
longer asked to dinner, but are snubbed on all occasions; and next you are forbidden to buy any longer
on credit, but are sternly called upon to "pay that
thou owest." And wo be unto you if you fail to meet
the demand of your unjust creditor, promptly! for he
will immediately proceed to put your whole property
under the hammer of the sheriff; will buy it in himself for one half its value, and then in the coolest manner possible return to you your notes, telling you im-
pudently: "Now, Sir, *we are square,* and I trust we
shall remain so!"

But the most utterly detestable of all Southern Yankees is the Negro Trader—Speculator he delights to
call himself of late years. The unmerciful master is
bad enough in all conscience; the swindling storekeeper is no better, while the unprincipled knave who
is all things to all men if by any means he may make
money, is equally to be abhorred with the rest; but,
above all these, preëminent in villainy and a greedy

love of filthy lucre, stands the hard-hearted Negro Trader, who is in every respect as unconscionable a dog of a Southern Shylock as ever drank raw brandy by the glassful, or chewed Virginia tobacco, or used New-England cowskins to lacerate the back of a slave. Of course, when we thus characterize the Negro Trader, we allude to the worst class of them; for they are not all corrupt, or ignorant, or ill-bred. Some of them, we doubt not, are conscientious men, but the number is few. Although honest and honorable when they first go into the business, the natural result of their calling seems to be to corrupt them; for they have usually to deal with the most refractory and brutal of the slave population, since good and honest slaves are rarely permitted to fall into the unscrupulous clutches of the speculator. And we all know how soon familiarity with ignorance and a vicious brutality tarnishes even the characters of good men: for example, who does not know that our city police are nearly always rendered corrupt from a long familiarity with vice?

The miserly Negro Trader, then—once more to speak in the language of the tabernacles—is, outwardly, a coarse ill-bred person, provincial in speech and manners, with a cross-looking phiz, a whiskey-tinctured nose, cold hard-looking eyes, a dirty tobacco-stained mouth, and shabby dress. But what he is inwardly can not be so well arrived at or determined. He is not troubled evidently with a conscience, for, although he habitually separates parent from child, brother from sister, and husband from wife, he is yet one of the jolliest dogs alive, and never evinces the least sign of remorse. Neither has he any religion; for almost every sentence he utters is accompanied by an oath, and as for downright blasphemy, he is in this particular almost as gifted as those infidel socialists, free-lovers, and abolitionists, who annually assemble in some one of the Free States for the purpose of resolving the Bible a humbug, and our Federal Constitution a compact with the devil. His heart, indeed, is full of all villainies and corruptions. It is never warmed by a single generous impulse, but is all blackness and barrenness— black with guilty thoughts and wicked machinations how he may increase his gains, and barren of all good deeds or virtuous resolves. But his greatest wickedness, Reverend friend, does not consist alone in his cruelty to the African. He has other sins to answer for fully as heinous; for nearly nine tenths of the slaves he buys and sells are vicious ones sold for crimes or misdemeanors, or otherwise diseased ones sold because of their worthlessness as property. These he purchases for about one half what healthy and honest slaves would cost him; but he sells them as both honest and healthy, mark you! So soon as he has completed his "gang," he dresses them up in good clothes, makes them comb their kinky heads into some appearance of neatness, rubs oil on their dusky faces to give them a sleek healthy color, gives them a dram occasionally to make them sprightly, and teaches each one the part he or she has to play; and then he sets out for the extreme South, taking with him a complete company of low comedians—for low comedy is usually the *role* in which he prefers they should appear. At every village of importance he sojourns a day or two, each day ranging his "gang" in a line on the most business street; and whenever a customer makes his appearance, the oily speculator button-holes him immediately, and begins to descant in the most highfalutin fashion upon the virtuous lot of darkeys he has for sale. Mrs. Stowe's Uncle Tom was not a circumstance to any one of the dozens he points out. So honest! so truthful! so dear to the hearts of their former masters and mistresses! Ah! Messrs. stock-brokers of Wall street—you who are wont to cry up your rotten railroad, mining, steamboat, and other worthless stocks—for ingenious lying you should take lessons from the Southern Negro Trader!

Do you observe that sour-faced, broad-shouldered negro man, leaning so lazily there in the sunshine against the garden fence, his blood-shotten eyes roving restlessly from place to place, while ever and anon there is an uneasy twitching of the muscles about the corners of his mouth when he forces out a grin? Well, he was bought in Ole Virginny. He is a cold-blooded murderer — a sneaking, cowardly assassin. For this reason and no other was he sold. He poisoned a fellow-slave with whom he fell out about a game at cards, and because he owed him ten dollars more than he could pay. To save the paltry debt he poisoned his fellow-bondman. The evidence was strong to convict him, but his master loved money better than justice, and thought the loss of the murdered slave was enough, without having to lose the murderer as well. So he sold the latter to the shrewd Negro Trader, who was knowing to all the circumstances, and who therefore drove the sharpest bargain the nature of the case would allow It was a dark transaction all round, and what the Trader actually paid for his honest chattel perhaps will never be known; but one condition of the bargain was, that the murderer must be removed beyond the limits of the State. These are the plain, unvarnished facts. But let us hear our oily-tongued Negro Speculator when he comes to sell this capital boy—to sell him, too, into a virtuous and unsuspecting household:

"Well, Gin'ral, look o' here now. Thar's a trick for you—A No. 1. Tell you what, Sir, he's worth his weight in gold. Cost me adzactly fifteen hundred dollars, and cheap as dirt! His master wanted two thousand; but debt, Gin'ral, *debt*. His master was one o' them raal ole fashion' Virginny high-flyers—proud, Sir, proud! kept mighty fine liquors, played high, bet high —and, Gin'ral, you know how hit all ends. He broke! was laid out flatter'n a stewpan. But d—n my buttons if he warn't a honerubble gentleman as ever lived. You see, he was a pertickler friend o' mine, and so he says to me when he broke, says he: 'Dick'—(he allers call' me Dick)—'Dick,' says he, 'I want you to take Alf— the cleverest boy in the world, a little stiff in the upper lip mebbe, family pride, Dick, you know—and I want you to sell him to some gentleman as knows *how* to treat a high-bred Virginny nigger. Do you take, Dick?' says he. 'And so I do,' says I. 'I'm got my eye on Gin'ral Blank of Alabama right now, the very man for Alf.' 'Well,' says he then, 'what sort o' feller is the Gin'ral?' And says I, 'The most perfectest gentleman in seven States—rich as the Jews, lives like a prince, and wants jist sich a boy as Alf to look arter his blooded horses.' Them's the very identical words I tole him, Gin'ral, if I didn't, d—n me! And so he says, says he, 'Take him, Dick; I'll give him to you, bein's hit's you, for *fifteen hundred*, but ary nother white man wouldn't a toch him with a dime less n'r *two thousand;* for I know you, Dick, of old—you can be relied on for doin' what you say, and sayin' what you do. You is honest, Dick, and I hope you will give the Gin'-ral my 'espects, and tell him to treat Alf kindly.' Now you see, Gin'ral, that's the way I come by Alf. D—n your woolly head, Alf! don't you look so down in the mouth, you old aristocrat, you! Here's a gentleman jist like your ole master, boy! the raal quality, regular grit, none o' your flams nor shams, but who'll keep you in the same style you's fotched up to. What's the word, Gin'ral? shall we say two thousand? and worth his weight in gold, Sir!"

The "Gin'ral" is completely taken in, and agrees to pay the "two thousand."

This will serve as an imperfect specimen of the manner in which some of the Negro Speculators impose upon honorable men, selling them criminals whose hands are red with murder for honest Uncle Toms, and palming off for sound and healthy servants diseased ones, to keep whom is sometimes a dead expense. You can fancy, gentle Miss, who weep so sorrowfully over the wrongs done the poor blacks, and contribute so freely in behalf of John Brown, how pleasant it must be to live on the same plantation with a sneaking, cowardly poisoner—one who does his wickedness in darkness and in secret, and when no eye but the Eternal's sees the damning iniquity. Nor need you fancy the sketch over-drawn; but if you do, only turn to the last chapter of this book and read the same attentively through, and we opine you will have your skepticism

removed. You will there learn that Mrs. Stowe knows
no more about the real negro character than does Queen
Victoria, who, we dare say, never heard a negro speak
a dozen words together.

Although it is true the Negro Trader proper sometimes presents the disgusting figure we have represented, there is yet another and a very different class of
negro-traders, confined mostly to the cities of the South,
and who are never suspected of trading in slaves. You
must know, our readers, the Consul-General of Cuba,
and the Emperor Napoleon, and the British Naval officers, and the solid men of Boston, are all ostensibly the
greatest enemies in the world to the much-decried slave-
trade. But the Consul-General, we are told, realizes
thousands every year from the traffic; the Emperor
Napoleon, we know, openly buys the colonists sent out
to Liberia from Virginia and sells them again at a magnificent profit to his own colonies, just as the British
cruisers sell their prizes to her Christian Majesty, who
has them sent to Jamaica and there disposed of as her
virtuous subjects usually dispose of the poor coolies;
while even some of the solid men of Boston, though
pillars in the anti-slavery church, are said to be the secret partners of Captain Townsend and his piratical
crew! So, too, at the South many men, who are both
rich and respectable—commission merchants chiefly,
whose legitimate business is to sell sugar, cotton, tobacco, etc., for the planters of the interior—and who are
bold as the boldest in denouncing the common, vulgar,
ignorant Negro Trader, do yet privily advance the
funds necessary to enable the latter to carry on his business, and usually take the lion's share of the profits.

7

These are the respectable well-to-do Southern Yankees, who have a position in society to maintain, and who would as soon be considered guilty of highway robbery as of participating in the vulgar traffic of buying and selling slaves. Still they do not scruple to sell a man from his wife, provided they can do so on any plausible pretext, and have reason to believe that they will at the same time make a few pennies more by such heartlessness. We remember seeing one of these conscientious individuals once offer at auction a large number of negroes, belonging to an estate of which he had been left the administrator. Although himself reported to be worth hundreds of thousands, and though the commissions he would receive would have amounted to nearly as much by an honest course, still, so great was his thirst for gain, he told the auctioneer to offer the youngest married couples in separate lots, thinking the humanity of the purchasers would lead them to give higher prices for the husband, having previously bought the wife, or for the wife, having previously bought the husband. When this fact became known to the crowd, a cry of *shame!* rose from the lips of many; and the disgust of every person was so great and so apparent, the bloated rich man was fain at last to get up and publicly state, that he had been influenced to pursue the course he did, *from an honorable regard for the interest of the heirs!* Wonderfully conscientious fellow, wasn't he?

We hear your objection, Reverend Clergyman, and will briefly pause to answer the same. You say, *He is not to blame; it is the blame of the institution.* You came near to saying *blamed institution*, and would have used a still more expressive adjective yet, had it not been for your cloth. Now, with all due deference to the latter, we beg to inform your reverence that you reason like a sophist or a suckling. Do you not know, that if the blame were in the institution, every slaveholder would be equally cruel and corrupt? But was not there Abraham, and Philemon, and Roger Williams, and the early Puritans, and George Washington, as well as hosts of others, all of whom lived and died in favor with both God and man? Suppose we were to cast your reverence into a pond of water, and you should be drowned, (which Heaven forbid,) would you blame the water for your drowning? Of course not. The fault would rest solely with yourself; you ought not to allow yourself to be drowned, but should keep your head above water by swimming. So, too, when you suffer strong drink to overcome you, you are the sinner, not the brandy-and-water; or when you allow lust to seduce you into the sin charged upon Kalloch, you alone are blameworthy, and not your Maker for creating you with a passionate nature; or when you permit mercenary motives to influence your course in the pulpit, your own heart is the corrupting evil, not your five thousand a year; or when you abuse your wife and children beyond what is lawful and just, the sin rests on your own shoulders, and "marriage is still honorable in all;" or when you preach politics and make the name of Jesus a reproach among men, it is not Christianity which is to blame, but the old Adam that has given you an "itching ear" for vulgar applause.

What would you think of the writer, were he to portray a Christian Inquisitor-General of the middle ages,

in the torture-room of the Spanish Inquisition, surrounded by his familiars, engaged in all those devilish
atrocities so common at that time, or a Pilgrim Father
in the act of burning a witch or a Baptist, and bid you
behold the legitimate fruit of Christianity? You would
be quite indignant, wouldn't you? *What*, you would
exclaim, *do you pretend to argue against the use of an institution because of its abuse?* Well, that is just the
very question, dear Sir. You argue against slavery as
a domestic institution simply because it is abused, and
for just the same very logical reason the infidel argues
against Christianity. And so likewise do the socialists
and free-lovers argue against the marriage relation, because married people are always quarrelling, and running off to Indiana to be divorced. They have not the
good sense to discriminate between the legitimate uses
of an institution and the illegitimate abuses to which it
can be subjected. Hence they cry out, Do away with
marriage-vows—leave us all to choose our "affinities"
at will—and there will soon be no divorces or causes
for divorce. Sagacious philosophers! you do not reflect, that evils of much more portentous magnitude
would in that event succeed to family quarrels, and
even to divorces. The experience of the French Age
of Reason, or of such institutions as the Love-Cure at
Berlin Heights, weighs not so much as the softest down
with such preëminently sage political economists. And
yet it is just in the same spirit, our Reverend friend,
that you are all the time proclaiming, Do away with
slavery, and my humane nature will not be any more
shocked with such exhibitions of mediæval barbarity as
the public sale of man and wife to separate masters.

Venerable Rabbin! You do not consider, that the evils resulting from emancipation would be far greater than those which now accompany the peculiar institution, even when in its worst degradation. The sad experience of Jamaica, and Hayti, and barbarous Africa, weighs not a feather with you and those of your friends who entertain similar convictions. Why not, O learned savan, come out boldly and declare, Do away with all cities, and then we shall have no more Dead Rabbits, no more Plug Uglies, no more tenant-houses, no more brothels, no more liquor hells, no more gambling hells, no more thieving outcasts who live by pilfering or even murder? For you will never see any where on the face of the earth, so long as time endures, any large city, but you will find it filled with just such characters and institutions as these. Believe us, Sir, the fault is not in cities, nor yet in slavery, nor in marriage, nor religion; it is in MAN. The old Adam is large as life to this day, and boasts a roomy and well-swept apartment in every human heart, until through faith in Christ and practical godliness we all learn to "put off the old man and his deeds;" hence, although you were to abolish every institution under the sun, so long as the human race continues mortal and frail as at present there will be no lack of sin and shame, sorrow and suffering. Moreover, though the writer is but a layman, still he takes the liberty of telling your Reverence, that the true and only mission of Christianity is, not to abolish institutions or to set up dynasties, but to make every *individual man*, whether bond or free, rich or poor, high or low, a *new creature in Christ Jesus;* and whoever endeavors to pervert the Gospel to any other pur-

pose, using it for secular or political ends, will assuredly
find his efforts prove abortive in every instance.   In
proof whereof, a word in your private ears, ye friends
of abolition.

We know (what you could get very few Southerners
to believe) that many of you are amiable people, refined, highly cultivated, full of all gentle emotions,
charitable and godly.   We are convinced that many
of you honestly desire the good of the African, but
would scorn at the same time to exhort him to mingle
poison with his master's food or drink, and do not allow
your sympathy for the slave to overcome your charity
for the slaveholder.   So, too, the society in Paris, *Les
Amis des Noirs*, (which without doubt caused the massacre of San Domingo,) was composed of some of the
purest as well as wickedest of men: Lafayette and the
Abbe Gregoire, for example, both genuine philanthropists; and on the other hand Anacharsis Cloots
and Marat, demons in human shape.   In the case of
Les Amis des Noirs, however, so soon as the good men
in its confidence became aware of the evil of its influence and tendency, they immediately cut loose from its
communion, and let it run its bloody course in its own
wicked way; and we doubt not but the really good
men in the abolition ranks of to-day, could they only
awake to a consciousness of the evil they are doing,
(and if John Brown has not awakened them we know
not what can,) would turn aside with loathing from the
viperine natures of some of their leading and trusted
associates.   For up to this time, notwithstanding fifty
years of agitation, according to their own confessions,
they have gained nothing—*absolutely nothing*—while

slavery has strengthened itself an hundred fold. We know they do claim some merit for the abolition of slavery in Jamaica, but, alas, with how poor a show of reason! After twenty years' experience of the blessings of free labor, Great Britain has at last been forced to introduce into that Island a *new species of slavery*, which we boldly assert to be a thousand-fold more heartless and cruel than the patriarchal institution. Even while we write, there is before the two Houses of the English Parliament the Jamaica Immigration Act, recently passed by the Jamaica Legislature, and which only awaits the approval of the Home Government to become a Law—an Act to legalize corporal punishment to be inflicted upon refractory Coolies and other *free apprentices!* What the provisions of this Act are, we are unprepared to state in detail, having never seen a full copy of it; but we know that the members of the British Anti-Slavery Society are up in arms against it, denouncing it as a virtual return to slavery, and are using all their influence to prevent its becoming a Law by the sanction of the British Government. So great a bobbery have they kicked up about it, in fact, the London *Times* has felt called upon to defend the Act; and in order to pave the way for its smooth reception by the English people, uses the following language, which we find in its issue of February 10, 1859:

"When the slaves were emancipated, first from actual thraldom, and ultimately from even the modified restrictions of agricultural apprenticeship, *they went the way which it was prophesied they would go.* They certainly did not become riotous, turbulent, or disloyal, but neither did they become industrious or enlightened, nor could such progress be well expected of them. They were under no valid inducements to work, and they were surrounded by every temptation to idleness. Their wants were confined to the simplest necessities of life, and the number of estates thrown out of culture supplied them with squatting grounds, on which they might vegetate with the indolence and apathy natural to their race. In the mean time, *the planters went to ruin*, until at length they took heart and cast about for labor to serve as a supplement or substitute for that which the liberated blacks so grudgingly and insufficiently gave."

The labor here spoken of is the Coolie or free-apprentice system of labor, to render which more useful and effective is the intent of the afore-mentioned Immigration Act; and to render which latter more palatable to the honest Britishers, the Thunderer proceeds, in the same article from which we have quoted above to hold forth as follows:

"The truth is, that on both sides of these bargains the conditions are peculiar. The immigrants who come (?) [what cool impudence hath this honest Englishman, to be sure!] to the West-Indies for work are either negroes or creatures as helpless as negroes, utterly incapable of that discrimination which would be exercised by English laborers in forming an engagement, *and absolutely dependent upon the care of others for obtaining equitable terms.* The planters, however, are also critically situated, for the character of agriculture in these countries requires that work shall be steadily performed; and that, in particular, at certain seasons of the year the cultivator may be able to reckon with confidence upon an unceasing supply of good effective labor. *For this purpose it is necessary that the bargain between master and man should be stringent*, and that the negro, while duly secured in all his own rights of good wages, good treatment, and terminable hire, should nevertheless, for the fair term of his actual engagement, be bound under penalty to give fair work. *Were it otherwise, the indolence and instability of the negro charac- ter, stimulated by the possesssion af a little money and the prospect of immediate ease, would infallibly operate to the destruction of the planter's hopes as harvest time came round.*"

After which and in conclusion, the *Times* proceeds to rap the heads of the Anti-Slavery Society's men foɪ their intermeddling officiousness and fanatical zeal, in the following words :

"For the sake of interests which, if not imaginary, are certainly insignificant, they have overlooked the broad contest between slavery and freedom, and the result has been *that Cuba has thriven, and Jamaica has suffered under the auspices of those whose objects and wishes lay in exactly the opposite direction.*"

Now, Messrs. abolitionists, ought not such a retrospect as this to induce you to pause in your present tactics, at least long enough to ask yourselves, Why is this ? A skillful commander does not persist in battering always at the same gate of a besieged fortress, after he once discovers that nothing is to be gained by the pro- cess. And, seriously, do you not sometimes suspect that you yourselves have aided in riveting the manacles of the slave more securely by your dogged persistence

7*

in the fanatical attempt to liberate him? We think so, and we are supported in our opinion by many others wiser and better than ourself. The reason too is very plain, and can be stated in a breath. For you have only to consider, gentlemen, that you have never yet endeavored to make the condition of the slave any better *as a slave.* Your efforts have been directed all the time against the master, with the end in view of ultimate freedom to the bondman, but not a dollar have you expended for the purpose of bettering the latter's condition without any disruption of the ties binding him to his owner. Hence, the sole result of all your lavish expenditure of time, and money, and breath, and brains, has been to band together all the slave-owners, both the humane and the heartless, and to lead them to resist every encroachment upon their rights of property in their negroes; and while you have thus succeeded in strengthening the South politically, you have indubitably rendered the slave's condition much worse than it otherwise would have been.

What is more, we are persuaded that the Southern people, if left to themselves, and freed from all apprehension of intermeddling from outsiders, would soon establish their domestic institution of slavery upon a more humane basis than it rests upon at present. None but Southern Yankees, and persons of like kidney, would then uphold any laws which allowed families to be broken up and sold to separate masters; or the numerous other undoubted hardships under which slaves, when in the possession of unscrupulous men, labor at the present time. The great mass of the people of our Southern States, are fully as philanthropic, evangelical, and freedom-loving, as the descendants of the Puritans. They do not desire to oppress the dusky children of Africa to any greater extent than is demanded by a proper regard for their mutual safety and wellbeing : and should the negro ever evince a capability for self-government, (which he never yet has done,) they would be as ready as the citizens of the Free States to put the peculiar institution "in course of ultimate extinction." But so long as the British and Northern abolitionists endeavor to force them into measures—measures fraught with most disastrous consequences to both themselves and their slaves, not to mention the inevitable overthrow of the commercial prosperity of the rest of the world—so long will they resist to the death all such impertinent officiousness ; and so long, too, will the Southern Yankee continue to wield his merciless lash, while the debauched Negro Trader will continue to sunder at his pleasure, the most sacred of human ties, laughing the while at every precept of religion and all the teachings of humanity. The anti-slavery men of the North may close their eyes to these unpalatable facts, and may, if they choose, continue to wage their relentless and unscrupulous war upon the South ; but even if they ultimately succeed by mere brute violence and the force of numbers in freeing the slave against the will of his master, it will be through such scenes of carnage and devastation as the world never saw before, and the effects of which will be to throw the wheels of civilization back fully a century. And after all, it will only be to try an experiment ! an experiment which, on a much smaller scale in Jamaica, has already cost the English hundreds of millions of pounds sterling, only now in the end to be pronounced by the leading statesmen of Great Britain, a most magnificent humbug and failure !

But to return once more to our subject.

Having said so many hard things about the Southern Yankee, perhaps we had better now say a good word in his favor; for he is not altogether without redeeming qualities. Although swallowed up completely in selfishness, which prevents his ever undertaking any object or enterprise unless well assured beforehand that it "will pay," he is still of very great advantage to the community at large, and in most cases is a useful citizen. The Northern Yankee proper (for all New England men even are not Yankees, by great odds) has been the main instrument in advancing the North to her present proud position, as a great manufacturing, inventive, and commercial community. So, on the other hand, the Southern Yankee, aided by the thrifty Middle Classes, has contributed no little to the present unprecedented prosperity of the Slave States: for, aside from his own labors and industry, he has also stimulated the Southern Gentleman to activity and enterprise. Certainly there is a vast difference between the motives which have instigated the two, the latter being influenced by public spirit and patriotic pride, while the former has only sought to make money and to advance his private interests; yet the result of their labors has been the same. Thus the worn-out lands of Virginia and the Carolinas, which ten years ago went a-begging at five dollars per acre, by judicious culture and scientific manuring have been so improved that they now readily command from twenty to fifty dollars per acre. So, also, the vast savannas and heavily-timbered forests of the Gulf and South-western States, have been brought under cultivation, until the lands on which fifty years ago stood one grand and primeval forest, now produce annually more than two hundred millions of dollars' worth of *surplus* agricultural products. In the achievement of these wonderful results, the Southern Yankee has played no mean part; but he has ever been foremost among the pioneers, clearing up the "new grounds," and draining the swamps, preparatory to introducing the virgin soil to the close embraces of "de shovel and de hoe." Neither has he been backward in assisting the South to build her great lines of railway, most of which are profitable investments ; and the Southern Yankee troubles himself about nothing else, if satisfied that the investment will prove pecuniarily profitable.

The best specimens of the genuine Southern Yankee, are to be met with in Georgia. In this State they grow to enormous sizes, and seldom stand under six feet in their stockings, often, indeed, reaching six feet and a half. Muscular, heavy-jawed, beetle-browed, and possessed of indomitable energy, they are well calculated to command respect almost any where, did one only have it in his nature to forget that SELF is the only god they worship, and MONEY the only incense that ever ascends as a sweet-smelling savor to the nostrils of their idol. But persons of a certain cast of mind, and possessing certain unfashionable properties of heart, (and the writer must plead guilty to such a weakness,) will not, and can not be blinded to their real characters, and instead of respect entertain for such Shylocks only pity and disgust. Now, do not understand us to find fault with any man for diligence in business, or for the skill and enterprise which enable him to provide bountifully for the members of his own household; but there are reasonable bounds to every thing. There is a happy mean betwixt business and pleasure, betwixt idleness and ceaseless toil, which only a mind of philosophic mould can ever hope to comprehend or appreciate. The Southern Yankee does not possess such a mind, no more than does his restless, craving, ever-pushing brother of the North. Neither of them knows when he has enough of this world's goods, or when is the fit season to leave off the tireless chase after riches which satisfy not, but must perish with the using. They both die usually with the harness on, and, if old, go out of the world reluctant and despairing, clutching even in their last hours after the poor gilded baubles they have wasted their lives to accumulate. So true are the words of the learned Dr. Johnson :

> " Unnumbered maladies man's joints invade,
>   Lay siege to life, and press the dire blockade ;
>   But unextinguished Avarice still remains,
>   And dreaded losses agravate his pains ;
>   He turns, with anxious heart and crippled hands,
>   His bonds of debt, and mortgages of lands ;
>   Or views his coffers with suspicious eyes,
>   Unlocks his gold, and counts it till he dies."

Indeed, to a well-balanced mind, there can be no more painful spectacle than the death of a rich and avaricious old man. Other sinners, while they can look forward to no bright prospects " beyond the river," still feel that in death they will at least get rid of a present load of crime and shame—that at the worst they will but exchange a world of vice and wretchedness for one of merited punishment. But the miser's heart, his hopes, his very life—all centre in the glittering heaps of yellow metal he has wasted so many precious hours in accumulating. The terrors of the unknown world bring no terrors to him; the upbraidings of conscience he never hears, or heeds not if he hears; friends and wife and weeping children he could part from without a pang; the bright sunlight, the starry night, balmy morning and dewy eve, the velvety green of spring, the rich hues of summer, and ripened sheafs of autumn, and frosty but kindly breath of old winter—all that is in Nature to bless and brighten the life of man, he could cheerfully give up: but oh! to have to part from his GOLD! Ah! any thing but this! Willingly at such an hour would he remain content to roast in Tophet all his days, could he only take his treasure with him. But alas! he can not. He must die like other men, and like the poorest beggar he must go out of the world as naked and destitute as he came into it. Already the film of fast approaching dissolution gathers upon his hard and cruel old eyes, deepsunken in their sockets and nearly hid beneath the shaggy brow; already the air thickens, and the room darkens, and the muffled drum of life beats slowly, slowly, the dead march; but in the gloom the miser still views his hoards, and fancies the bags of precious dust are vanishing out of his sight. Thieves! robbery! help! He stretches out his bony arms and clutches with his skinny fingers at the coveted treasures. 'Tis his last effort. In the wildness of despair the bleared and leaden-slumbering eyes for one moment stare with a stony stare — then there is a contortion, horrible, ghastly, of the thin face; a quiver of the sunken limbs; a death-rattle; and the untenanted clay lies stiff and grim in the cold embrace of Death.

Alas! how true is that saying of Him who spake as never man spake: "The LOVE OF MONEY is the root of all evil." And yet in this respect how few of us are guiltless? How many of us, think you, are free from a prejudice in favor of riches? How many of us ever let the bloated worshippers of Mammon know how utterly despicable they are, or how honestly we abhor their selfish natures? That is the question which concerns us all. Does any one doubt but the avaricious old curmudgeons who now disgrace the world by having a foothold on it, would speedily amend their ways, if they knew in what abhorrence they are held by the whole community? Does any one believe that Mr. Augustus Thorndike ever would have made the unjust will he did, had he known that the drawing up, signing and sealing of the same, would cause himself to be *damned to everlasting fame?* We tell you honestly, our noble fellow-countrymen, we that throw stones so virtuously at the dead old misers who can no longer repay us in the same (if not a little better) coin, are no better than they if we cringe, and fawn, and "crook the supple hinges of the knee" to the plethoric misers who still remain above ground. And yet we all do it more or less. Even gowned clergymen are moved by the sight of a sleek millionaire, however bloated he may be with sin and selfishness, more than by the vision of honest worth struggling with poverty. And shall we wonder that the rich mistake the nature of our adulation, and only go on in consequence from bad to worse, letting the gangrene gold eat up their hearts, until no place is left for natural affection—no love of home, or wife, or children? We say, let us not be so uncharitable. We assist the poor souls to delude themselves into a belief that whatever they do is proper, and we have no right to throw stones at them when they turn upon their own offspring, as did the unfortunate Thorndike, and seek to carry their bloody revenges even beyond the grave. Let us be consistent at least.

So far as regards family affection, or rather the want of it, the Southern Yankee is no better than other mammonites the world over. He is cold and repulsive in his intercourse with his wife and children, and regards the latter with somewhat the same feeling of envy and jealousy which British Peers are said to entertain for their eldest sons, who are presumed to be impatient to stand in their fathers' shoes. Indeed, when he comes to die, the Southern Yankee nearly always seeks by some species of testamentary Thorndikeism, to prevent his children from coming into a fee simple possession of his estates. If the truth must be spoken, however, in most cases the Southern Yankee does a very wise thing by depriving his children of the free use of his property after he is dead: for as the toiling grub always produces the thoughtless butterfly, so does your genuine mammonite nearly always give birth to thriftless snobs, or drunken debauchees, or idle spendthrifts. And for this the fathers are chiefly to blame. Children learn a great deal more from example than precept;

and while the Southern Yankee devotes himself almost wholly to the sordid acquisition of wealth, his children are left to devote themselves as wholly to dissipation and a senseless love of pleasure: else, they are unreasonably stinted and too harshly dealt with while their father is alive, and on his death coming suddenly into the possession of wealth which they know not how to *use wisely*, they proceed immediately to *abuse* the same most *unwisely*.   Hence, from the loins of the Southern Yankee have sprung in the main our Cotton Snobs and rich Southern Bullies; of both whom we shall speak more at large in the proper place.

CHAPTER IV.

> "A barren spirited fellow, one that feeds
> On objects, arts, and imitations;
> Which, out of use, and stalled by other men,
> Begin his fashion: do not talk of him,
> But as a property."
>
> SHAKSPEARE.

MR. MICHAEL ANGELO TITMARSH has discoursed to us very entertainingly upon the character, attainments, etc. etc., of Snobs in the Old World, while Mr. Geo. W. Curtis has in an equally pleasant manner sketched for our delectation, the family portraits of the Potiphars of the North. But the South has had as yet no chronicler to note down the distinguishing peculiarities of her own Cotton Snobs, who indeed, either through ignorance or malice on the part of the enemies of the South, have been pretty generally confounded with the Southern Gentleman—than which a more egregious blunder could hardly be committed. For although the Cotton Snob may possess many Southern characteristics, and thus differ materially from the New-York or English Snob, he is yet not a whit more respectable than these, and never once is a gentleman. Let the reader not forget it—to be a Cotton Snob is one thing, and to be a Southern Gentleman is quite another.

By the term *Cotton*, used to designate the class of Snobs peculiar to the South, do not understand us to mean a person who must of necessity hail from the cotton-growing States. By the expression we wish to embrace the entire class of agricultural snobs—so to speak—without reference to whether they raise cotton, or tobacco, or rice, or sugar, or wheat, or hemp, or Indian corn. We have already spoken of your store-keeping snobs, who are the same in the South that they are in the North ; while nearly all classes of residents in the Southern cities, differ in no essential particulars from the same classes in other cities any where else in the Union. But the Cotton Snob does not hail from the city originally, though he may later in life go to the city to live, and when he does so becomes invariably the most disgusting cockney one can find any where in the four quarters of the globe. He is always of country breeding, and his manners more often than otherwise lack that *quasi* polish which the city snob sometimes possesses, despite his toadying mannerisms and want of native manliness of character.

Owing sometimes to the penuriousness and ignorance of his parents, and almost always to his own distaste for and neglect of mental application, the Cotton Snob rarely is well educated, possessing at best the merest smattering of learning, and is as ignorant of the rules of grammar, as of the rules of good breeding. Nevertheless he ever entertains a happy, not to say flattering conceit of himself, and imagines that he is capable of solving all knotty questions, whether in Law, Medicine, or Politics : but as for Religion, early in life, he prides himself on knowing nothing about *that*, boasting that he is a Free Thinker ; and when he is a little too deep in his cups he is apt to allude to the " demned parsons," as the greatest rogues in the world. More particularly is this true of those Cotton Snobs who have, for a wonder, come of pious parents of the middle class, and have even been members of the Church themselves at some former period of their lives. If the reader has ever been a little " fast" himself, and hails from New-England, we need not to inform him where one can every day meet the counterpart of these last-named Cotton Snobs. Of course, as we all know, there is no sort of deviltry or other sinfulness ever carried on in a New-England college — that is to say, *publicly*. But when fellahs get a good lot of fellahs in rooms of fellahs—why, they know how to kill time in an amazingly orthodox fashion ; especially those degenerate sons of the Puritans, who carry their mother's Bibles on one side of their hearts, *and a good stout brandy-flask on the other.* Ah ! ye gentle dames of Massachusetts, " it gars me greet" to tell you how often, even while may be you have on your bended knees been petitioning the ever-blessed God in behalf of your dear, pious boys, these have been hobnobbing with b'hoys of another class entirely, and with drunken gravity have essayed to sing the " sweet songs of Zion" in the midst of ribald and most ungodly companie ! But, alas ! such is the unpalatable truth.

But the Cotton Snob rarely comes of parents who are pious or strictly temperate : in nine cases out of ten he is the son of the Southern Yankee. If sent to college at all, it is without the previous preparation requisite to enable him to take an honorable position ;

and having been accustomed at home to be flattered by his father's negroes, as well as by many poor wretches in the shape of white men, who have a most worshipful reverence for any person owning wealth; and finding now that the studious and refined of his new associates avoid his company as much as possible; even if he has remained temperate and virtuous hitherto, he very soon yields to the blandishments and cajoleries of those sharpers who hang about every college in the world—regular Deuceaces and Blewitts—and so proceeds immediately to dress extravagantly, to give wine-suppers, to get drunk, to play cards, and just as certainly to lose his father's money. But the more he loses, the higher are his bets and the deeper his potations. In a very little while he becomes a confirmed tippler—unless, as sometimes does happen, drink disagrees with him, producing only nausea and headache instead of the much-coveted "good feeling." He thinks indeed it is very *distingue* to get drunk. He reads how that the old Cavaliers were wont in ancient times never to rise from the dinner-table sober, and damme, Sir, he intends to live like the *bloods* did in the good old times. Egad, he would hang your temperance folks, Sir, and send all your cold-water fools to the devil! Particularly is the Cotton Snob valiant and chivalrous, when under the influence of two or three Brandy Straights and as many Cocktails. You should hear him talk on such occasions. "I'll tell you what, Boys, Pa makes lots o' cotton—bags on top o' bags"—or, "lots o' tobacco, hogsheads and hogsheads, the world and all— but it's all for me. Blamenation, won't I make it fly? Wine and women, women and wine, fast nags, splendid trotters, New-York buggies—hurrah! You must all come to see a fellow, then—you shall live like princes of the blood." Ah! the subtle, invisible spirit of wine, how does it loosen one's tongue, and let out even the closest secrets of the heart!

But though never so bold when closeted with his roystering fellows in their college dormitory, the Cotton Snob is at great pains to conceal his drunken debaucheries from the Old Man, (as he affectionately calls his father,) well knowing that the Southern Yankee would never tolerate the miserable waste of time and money such riotous proceedings occasion. So our Cotton Snob resorts to all manner of lies and brobdignagian stories to melt the heart of his stern " parient," so that the latter shall still afford him the means to purchase his flash apparel—to sport his heavy rings, watch-chains and seals, and other showy jewelry—to give his wine-suppers—to play his little games of Euchre and Seven-up—and to supply the cormorant demands of that terrible leech which drains of their freshest blood the youths of all lands, the *Strange Woman.* Sometimes he professes to have had a long spell of sickness, and in addition to the heavy doctor's bill, etc., etc., he spins out a pitiable story about having been robbed of his clothes and money, by the servants, during his illness. At other times he falls among thieves, and so has his pocket picked on board the steamboat, or the cars, or at the theatre, or even while attending church. Or not unfrequently he professes to have loaned a hundred or so to a fellow-student who seemed to be " hard up" but honest, yet who did run away with the same, not so much as leaving with his creditor an *I. O. U.*

By such cunning fables the Old Man is deluded, despite his lynx-eyed wariness in regard to whatever affects his purse. And when our Cotton Snob does at last return to the paternal roof, he dissimulates so well, pretends to love money so devoutly, gets drunk so slyly, and flatters the Southern Yankee so unceasingly, the latter is totally blinded, at least for a time. But if by any chance he should linger on this mortal stage a little too long, the impatient heir wearies of playing the part of supernumerary, and by some ill-advised utterance, or downright open defiance of authority, shows to his astonished sire that he is impatient to enact the part of principal himself, and chafes that the only opposing obstacle to his wishes is so long a time being knocked by the friendly hand of Death out of the way: upon which unfortunate discovery there is *some* swearing in Flanders you may be assured, but all to no purpose. In the end, and in the course of nature, the gray head sinks into its unhonored grave, and the eager heir steps with hot haste into his father's shoes, and proceeds to hobornob with his boon companions over their brandy and cigars, almost before the paternal dust is cold.

> "*For this* the foolish, over-careful fathers
> Have broke their sleep with thoughts, their brain with care,
> Their bones with industry!"

And now, if our young Snob be unmarried, what a life of drinking, gambling, horse-racing, fox-hunting, and vulgar display of one kind and another, he immediately rushes into! *Vivimus dum vivamus* is his motto, and what he calls enjoying life is comprehended in the above excesses; for he knows of no rational pleasure, but passes from one beastly gratification to another, thinking all the while, poor imbecile! that he is one of the favored children of Fortune. If he does not go to Cuba, or Europe, or attend the sessions of Congress, or visit some of the Southern cities, he spends his winters on his plantation, in company with an equally moral and gentlemanly set of bachelor companions, whose nightly carousals end only with the morning, and whose jolly fox-hunts and other out-door sports are conducted with such a reckless disregard of the rights and feelings of the neighbors, as at once to point out the difference between the Cotton Snob and the Southern Gentleman. For when the latter desires to hunt off his own broad acres, he invariably asks permission of the owners of adjacent estates before proceeding to trespass on their lands with his retinue of horses, dogs, and darkeys—and, in particular, in the Cotton States, wherein the planters dislike exceedingly for the fox-hunters to overrun their unpicked fields with their devastating train; but the Cotton Snob imagines it would not be *distingué* enough to ask permission to do any thing, and so dashes right on, regardless of whose property he may be injuring, pulling down fences *ad libitum*, and destroying any quantity of the imperial staple—yelling and shouting meanwhile to his comrades and his dogs at almost every turn, and riding more like a madman just out of a strait-jacket than a sane or sober human being.

In the summer months the Cotton Snob travels—visits all the famous watering-places—flirts with senseless girls, who, like the tortoise, carry their fortunes

8

on their backs, but, unlike the same, ever hold what little of hearts they possess in their hands, ready to exchange the hollow baubles at any moment for *an establishment*, no matter if it be encumbered with either a toothless old simpleton or a simpering and bloated young rake. Hence the Cotton Snob is frequently to be seen in the Free States, and when seen is pretty sure to make himself a "shining mark," for he assumes to be the very tip-top of the first families, and as such considers his individual corporosity a thing too sacred to be touched even by the hands of Northern *canaille*, "greasy mechanics," or what not. He also seeks every opportunity to talk about "my niggers," (observe, a Southern Gentleman rarely if ever says *nigger;*) endeavors to look very haughty and overbearing; sneers at whatever he considers *low*, and "their name is legion;" carries a cane not infrequently; affects a military step and manner, and tries to look daggers, bowie-knives, revolvers, blood and thunder, whenever or wherever he meets an abolitionist or a *nigger*. By such and other similar displays of vulgarity and ill-breeding, the Cotton Snob pretty soon renders himself both ridiculous and contemptible; and, what is more and worse, brings a reproach upon the true Gentlemen of the South, which goes far to increase that bitterness of feeling at present rankling in the breasts of many loyal citizens of each section of our great Republic, against their fellow-citizens of the other. While we know, from a pretty intimate acquaintance with all classes of our fellow-countrymen of the Free States, that they all —with the exception of a few radicals here and there— entertain a very high regard for the genuine Southern

Gentleman such as they imagine him to be, and such as he is in reality, still, we grieve to say, they are too credulous in believing the professions of every little stammering upstart who lays claim to be a gentleman from the South. Hence, when they come in contact with a dirty fellow, who swears roundly, drinks deeply, boasts incessantly of his patrician blood, and is always in a snarl with every body and every thing, instead of setting such an individual down for what he really is, they prefer to believe that he is what he represents himself to be; consequently they lay to the charge of the lion all the dirty mean tricks and senseless braying of the ass that is simply robed in the lion's skin.

So much for the unmarried Cotton Snob.

When he gets him a wife, and afterwards, he takes a little more respectable position in society, leaves off many of his ungentlemanly practices also, but runs into many new extremes of absurdity and bad taste. Like all snobs and parvenues the world over, he seems bent on nothing higher than a foolish display of his wealth, and erroneously imagines his chief honor to lie, not in what he is, but in what the *beau monde* takes him to be; but he differs somewhat from the snobs of the North in his manner of playing the fool.

The Potiphar families seek usually to display their wealth in costly houses, splendid furniture, rich plate, magnificent dresses, dazzling jewelry, and an occasional "perfect jam" of a party when parties are in season, as well as they affect French customs, French morals, and French manners, and consider a little successful intrigue as the very perfection of good breeding. The Southern Snob delights in all these luxuries too, but not to the same extent as the "new rich" of our Free States—remember, we are speaking now of the *agricultural* Snobs of the South, not of those who figure in New-Orleans, or Charleston, or Washington City. The peculiar "wanity" of the Cotton Snob is a weakness for fine horses, fine carriages, and obsequious footmen and outriders. We do not remember ever to have seen a "coach and four" with outriders in any Northern State, but such institutions are much delighted in by all Southern upstarts whose purse-strings are long enough to enable them to support so much state and ceremony. Fifty years ago, indeed, it was customary for most Southern Gentlemen to go in state in their lumbering, old-fashioned coaches, which two horses would hardly have been able to drag along; but, *autres temps, autres mœurs*. While in those old-fashioned times there was nothing at all objectionable to good taste, in the sight of a hearty old Virginian Gentleman bowling leisurely along over the heavy dirt-roads in his great family coach, having of necessity from four to six horses attached, and with outriders and lackeys in any number he might desire; still, in these days of steam-engines, railroads, turnpikes, and telegraphs, there is no longer any fitness in such old-time customs. This the Southern Gentleman has seen and acknowledged for many years, and so confines himself to a modern-built carriage of the best style for country use, and keeps but a single pair of carriage-horses, and never more than a single outrider, whose business is to open gates, etc. etc. Not so, however, the Cotton Snob, who much affects a "coach and four," even on the best turnpike roads, and loves to see the liveried blacks galloping after him, looking as consequential and full of their own importance as though they followed the triumphal chariot of an Emperor. Ah! who does not feel tempted to exclaim, when he sees such a Southerner hobornobbing at Northern watering-places with the Potiphar families of New-York and the Ramrods from Boston, as well as numerous other Free State families of renown—who, we say, does not feel tempted to exclaim, not once but all the time, *par nobile fratrum*—O noble band of brothers!

Alas! how unfortunate is it that true gentility is so little understood or appreciated in this great country. Here we are, not yet a century old, and while in the full enjoyment of all those blessings which are the rich heritage won for us by the struggles of our ancestors, affecting to despise the plain domestic virtues in which those same ancestors excelled, and blindly and madly imitating the lax morals, the effete civilization, the luxuries and the vices of that rotten Old World, with whose rulers and whose traditions we ought to entertain not a single feeling in common. Is there any manliness in this? any virtue? any worthiness? Do you delight in feasting on toads, gentle reader? or are you ambitious to ungirdle the native independence which should encircle every freeman's loins, to wear in its stead the effeminate cest that binds with silken folds the poor slave of courts and princely ceremony? And yet, good faith, what else are we doing when we discard the plain but honest virtues of our sires, to embrace every hollow flam or shallow pretense newly im-ported from Paris or London? 'Tis time indeed Americans should learn to cease from following after strange gods, and to put more trust than they have done of late in straightforward integrity of purpose and a pure genuine morality, and less in corrupting riches and a shallow outward polish, which, like the sleek crust over the smouldering volcano, conceals ever beneath its shining exterior only stifling ashes and treacherous fires.

But let us proceed once more with our subject.

If the Cotton Snob *père* appears so ridiculous in the eyes of common-sense and common manliness, the Cotton Snob, *fils*, appears even more so—for you must know, our readers, our Southern snobs have already reached the second generation. The Cotton Snob, *fils*, lives an idle, worthless life, too lazy even to fox-hunt; and bestows all his time and attention upon his immaculate kids and patent-leathers, upon the culture of his incipient mustachio, and in experimenting with the different kinds of pomatum for his precious locks of hair. He reminds one of that Mendycides of Sybaris, spoken of by Seneca, who was so fatigued at "seeing" a man dig, that he ordered such work never more to be done in his presence; or more aptly still, of those pretty little coxcombs to be seen in all our large cities —those degenerate sons of some old Bullion, who would feel insulted if you were to accuse them of ever doing any useful labor, or even of possessing the manly strength, the brawn and bone necessary to the successful accomplishment of such labor. Hence, however unfortunate the father may be in his attempts to revive the practices and customs of fifty or a hundred years ago, the son is still more unfortunate when he goes back yet another century, and endeavors to revive the

Tournaments of the Middle Ages. For these in the old days of chivalry, were chiefly participated in by war-worn heroes, clad in steel from head to foot, armed with a genuine lance of truest temper, and mounted on spirited steeds, whose fiery natures had never felt the debasing touch of *el castrador*. Placed *vis à vis* to such a Knight of the Past, behold the dwarfish dimensions of our modern Cotton Knight, who ambles daintily forward on the back of a docile gelding, holding a sharpened stick under his arm, and gallantly and gloriously endeavoring to thrust the same through an iron ring, which is suspended by a rope of twine from an horizontal beam! Note well with what a cavalier-like grace the thing is done. How stiffly stands his shirt-collar, how spotless are his patent-leathers, how mildly flaps his lengthened coat tail in the wind, how charmingly glistens his carroty-colored hair underneath his shining beaver! *Plaudite, Romanes, Plaudite, Omnes!* Here is bravery for you, and chivalry and gallant deeds in arms. Tremble, O Cuba, and quake with much fear, O States of Nicarauga and Costa Rica, for the old lions have refreshed themselves, and the young lions are preparing against the day of battle! Stand in awe, O Nations, and hide your little heads, ye Isles of the Sea, for verily Cotton is King, and the New Order of Chivalry is the Cotton Snob!

But alas! our countrymen, we blush even while we smile.

Like his father before him, the Cotton Snob worships money, but in a different sense. The Southern Yankee loves money for its own sake—the Cotton Snob loves it because it supplies him with cigars, and brandy, and fine clothes, and fine horses, and fine houses, yea, and fine women too, my dears, as Mr. Titmarsh would say, as well as a *quasi*-public esteem. In truth, he fancies that money is more potent than the lever of Archimedes—that its glittering dust will blind the eyes of Justice (though proverbially blind any how) as well as hermetically seal up the mouth of Mrs. Grundy; while, on the other hand, he looks upon poverty as a sort of crime, and thinks every poor man is just about good enough to be hanged and nothing more. Hence he shuns the society of the poor man as he would the plague, but clasps every brother Crœsus to his bosom with the most unfeigned delight, asking no questions; as, by what means the latter has come by his riches, or to what base uses his life may be habitually devoted. Wherefore, should you speak to the Cotton Snob admiringly of the charms of some female acquaintance, his very first inquiry would be, *Is she rich?* Or if you tell him of the unsullied honor and manly uprightness of some gentleman friend, his stereotyped interrogatory is, *What's he worth?* And until his vulgar mind has been assured respecting this all-important matter, he never will consent to see any thing estimable or praiseworthy in any individual. Nor does he know of any more satirical or witty remark, than to say of a person praised for his intelligence and his virtues: "Ah! yes, very clever, I dare say, but poor as Job's turkey!"

As is well known, the Southern Gentleman rarely prides himself upon his dress—indeed he is only too negligent in regard thereto; but the Cotton Snob is fully as sensitive on that subject as his Northern bro-

ther, and in every thing which concerns Fashion is
equally as thin-skinned and foolish as the latter. Nothing so mortifies the genuine Southern Snob as to be
considered *out of the fashion;* and he would at any time
rather lose one of his most valuable *niggers* than to be
seen in public with an old coat, or wearing an unfashionable hat, or with hands ungloved and boots un-
blacked. So too would he never be able to survive
the mortification caused by any notorious breach of
etiquette or conventional ceremony. We remember
to have witnessed once a most amusing instance of this
fear of making some such breach of etiquette, in the
person of a Cotton Snob who hailed from Charleston,
South-Carolina. He was a be-oiled and highly be-
scented coxcomb, having a stronger resemblance to the
New York Fifth-Avenoodle than to the Cotton Snob
proper, save that his complexion was sombre, and his
hair long *à la* cavalier. The scene was enacted in the
Exchange Hotel, Richmond. The Charlestonian, it
appears, was just setting out on his summer travels,
but had stopped in Richmond for a few days, and was
desirous in the mean time of giving a dinner party to a
select company of friends. He was discoursing on
this topic to the landlord, at the registry-desk, when
the writer chanced to overhear what in substance is
given below. He spoke in a thick, half-choking, drawling sort of tone, and with a slight imitation of the dialect of Samivel, (an unusual thing with most Cotton
Snobs, by the way, for they much oftener imitate the
dialect of Sambo;) and as he spoke, he turned his head
languidly from side to side, evidently persuaded in his
own mind that he was "cutting a swell."

8*

"Now, you see," said he, "I desire to give a very *select pawty*, ye kno', and I want it to be just the thing. Do you think it would be altogether *recherché*, proper, and *the thing*, to have it in the Ladies' Ordinary? Aw, now? Would that be *distingue* enough, my deah sir? You see, I live a mile or two out of Chawlston, South Cawolina — have a very nice, *recherche*, and elegant Bachelor's Hall there, in which I entertain my friends in the most *distingue* style two or three times every week, when I'm at home, ye kno'; and I would not like to give a pawty here in Wichmond, that was not just *the thing*. We Cawolinians must keep up the weputation of our gallant Commonwealth, ye kno'—the land of the chivalwig, ye kno'."

The land of the chivalwig, indeed! Had this fellow not been a Southerner, and hailing from the most really chivalrous of all the Southern States, we should have laughed outright at the absurd figure he played; but as it was, we felt too much mortification. Not so, however, on another occasion (which we can not resist the temptation of alluding to here, although seemingly out of place) when we fell in with two Northern Snobs of a like kidney, noble sons of York both, who, at the time, were spending their winter travelling through the South. This chance adventure happened in Alabama, at a certain country railroad depot which shall be nameless. It was on a very chilly winter's night, and the railroad passengers were forced to remain in the rather primitive sitting-room of the wooden dépôt, from one till three of the clock in the morning, nearly cooked by the red-hot stove and almost stifled by that horrible stench which always is emitted from burning iron; and all because the rival railroad companies would not agree to make "connections" simultaneously. Had it not been for the entertainment afforded one by the two New-York coxcombs spoken of, we do not see at this late day how we ever should have rendered those mortal two hours tolerable. They were pretty fair specimens of the cultivated dandies of the Sawedwadgeorge earllitunbulwig species, such as Mr. Tennyson describes:

> " Oiled and curled like an Assyrian bull,
> Smelling of musk and insolence."

They were acting as gallants to some female friends, who seemed to be akin to the *New Order of Southern Chivalry*, (pardon us if we refrain from using any more disparaging epithet while speaking of the *ladies ;*) and betwixt their attentions to these, and their conversation between themselves, we managed to kill the time pretty agreeably. There was one other young gentleman in the room, from Nashville, we think, but a stranger to ourself, who seemed to enjoy the sport even more than we did ; else, his organ of mirthfulness was more fully developed, or he had not yet acquired that self-control which is becoming. His efforts to restrain his pent-up laughter were almost as ludicrous as the stilted conversation of our two New-Yorkers, which was one continuous flow of "dictionary words" and "my deah f'la," and "my deah f'la," and "twue," "twue," and " I dessay," "I dessay." In the desperate determination to maintain his composure, our Nashville acquaintance shook like a jelly from his head to his feet ; his cheeks swelled every now and then as if ready to burst, and had not the pent-up wind managed to escape in little short chuckles at the corners of his mouth, (stifled, 'tis true, in his travelling shawl,) we do not know what would have become of him. Although he was evidently an intelligent person, despite a little rudeness, at last he could contain himself no longer, but almost split his sides, and startled the whole company with his unbridled cachinnation, just as our *distingué* fops reached the culminating blunder of the night.

They had for some time been descanting on Dickens, Thackeray, poetry, and the fine arts generally, but the opera in particular, and in a manner too, it must be confessed, which showed that in literary and artistic matters, at least, they were pretty well versed. But, unfortunately for their laurels, from the discussion of the muses they proceeded to discuss politics, of which they knew as little as any Southern Gentleman's *valet* would be presumed to know. Still they talked in the same stilted and consequential manner as before, and seemed to fancy "they knew it all!" To have heard them, one would have thought they dined regularly with Mr. Buchanan and his whole Cabinet, and besides were intimately acquainted with all the leading statesmen in the Union. In particular, did they admire Prentice, of Louisville, and S. S. Prentiss, sometime of Mississippi; the respective merits of whom they discussed with much volubility.

"But, my deah f'la," said one of them during the conversation on this topic, "they tell me that Prentice, of the Louisville *Courier* [here our Nashville friend gave indications of much bodily pain in the epigastric region] has had a stwoke of pawalysis lately."

"Beg your pawdon, my deah fwiend," replied his

companion, " but I am intimately acquainted with Mistaw Pwentice, and saw him not two weeks ago, when he was pweffectly well."

" Ah! twue, I dessay. Then it is Pwentice of Mississippi who is pawalyzed. I knew it was one of them, but did not remember distingly wich."

Considering that Mr. S. S. Prentiss had then been dead and buried for some five years and more, we felt inclined to overlook the rudeness of the young gentleman from Nashville, who, at this juncture, by his unrestrained overflow of merriment first notified our worthy young sparks that they had been making the most consummate asses of themselves. But though in so unwelcome a manner advised of the fact, and while they evidently entertained the opinion that they were " the observed of all observers," they yet did not possess native wit enough to perceive wherein their blunder lay; but blushing, stammering, and in the blankest confusion, continued to make matters worse and worse by their fruitless efforts at explanation, until even the writer, serious and self-possessed as he fancied himself, was constrained finally to join in the general laugh.

*But how does the Cotton snob treat his human chattels?
Come, tell us that!* O dear madam—our very dear and reverend friend—only exercise a little patience, there's a good soul! Can you never think of any thing else than the woolly-heads? One would almost be persuaded to believe that you are more pained to hear of .the servile condition of his dependents than to learn that the Cotton Snob is himself a slave of slaves—not only the slave of passion and vanity, but the slave of Satan also. For we would have you to know, re-

spected mother in Israel, that there are in the world two kinds of slavery, both of which existed as now when our Saviour was on the earth; but the Great Master never mentioned but *one*—never but one, our dear Madam, on our faith as a Christian gentleman; at least he never reprobated but one. Now, can you guess which or what species of bondage that was which fell under his censure? *Why, human bondage, of course; the sum of all villanies.* Indeed? *why, certainly, for don't our preachers always preach about that, and arn't they all called and sent to preach the Gospel?* Yes, Madam, they are called and sent, and do likewise preach *a* gospel—the gospel of "pike and gun," the glorious gallows gospel of John Brown, the thief and murderer; but not THE GOSPEL; for this commands us not to kill, not to steal, not to bear false witness against one's neighbor, not to engender strifes among brethren, and at the same time comdemns only one kind of bondage, and that *is not human bondage.* Jesus declared that he found all men, whether free or bond, under bondage to sin, and his sole mission was to emancipate them from this thraldom. Do not find fault with us, therefore, if, in imitation of the Divine Master, and of his disciples and ministers for the first eighteen hundred years after his crucifixion, we prefer the GOSPEL OF CHRIST to the gospel of John Brown. For this we know, if bodily servitude be a hardship, (as it often is, as well as poverty, or sickness, or even marriage sometimes, or any other human relation whatever, in a certain sense; but how much greater blessings are these all in a higher sense, God only knows!) still there is but one way to do away with it, and that is by first

freeing man from that much more galling servitude—
the Bondage of the Soul. Had there been any other
method Jesus certainly would have made it known to
us, for he was expressly commissioned to do away
with "all sin." Yet in the Primitive Church, slaveholders were admitted to as full fellowship as any of the
poorest saints, and not infrequently, as we learn from
Eusebius, master and slave suffered martyrdom at the
same time. But why will we fall into this prosing
vein, to the disgust of the general reader? Let us return to our "sheeps," impatient sir. You would have
us tell you how the Cotton Snob treats his human chat.
tels. We shall do our utmost to gratify you. But allow
us to insist in a friendly way, that you do not begin to
weep until there is a demand for your sympathetic
tears.

Know, then, O negrophilist, that the Cotton Snob is
a man like yourself; given to like infirmities and possessing the same benevolent emotions. Now we would
like for you to answer; have you ever yet seen a man
so utterly corrupt and abandoned, as not to possess a
single redeeming characteristic? We doubt if you
ever have. Even thieves sometimes evince a sense of
honor, and murderous highwaymen have been known
to be charitable; while that poor degraded wanton,
whom the soulless son of Belial stabbed in Cincinnati
only last year, because she refused his gold, died with
a prayer on her lips for her babe and her husband, totally oblivious of herself! Yea, so true it is, no matter how thickly the human heart may be incrusted
over with sin and shame, we will yet oftentimes catch
a glimpse of some sweet flower of the earlier Eden,

budding and bearing heavenly fruit in the midst of all its loathsome corruption; just as the water-lily with unstained blossom peeps out above the offensive scum of the malarious marsh, telling by its lovely presence of pure, cool waters, far down below the poisonous green spume of the surface. Hence, do not be surprised when we inform you, that some of the kindest masters of the South are to be found among her Snobs; for such is the fact. Some of them are even indulgent to a fault; allowing their slaves to traffic at their pleasure with the groggery keepers; to insult poor white folks with impunity—their masters always maintaining before the courts their servants' innocence; and encouraging them to brow-beat and bully overseers and managers, until it sometimes happens that no honest or capable person can be induced to undertake the superintendence of the estates to which such negroes belong. We have known masters of this character, when not residing on their plantations, but in some neighboring village, ten or twenty miles distant, to encourage their slaves to run off when corrected by the overseer—no matter how deservedly—and present themselves to " Mas'r," giving a doleful account of wounds and contusions without number, of untold hardships and ill-usage—all apocryphal, and when, in reality, the saucy fellows had, in most instances, fared a deal sight better than any poor white man, guilty of similar offenses would have fared in any town or city in the United States, blessed with an honest and faithful Justice of the Peace.

Now, there are two reasons for such conduct on the part of the Cotton Snob—one an honorable and the other a dishonorable motive; for, however paradoxical the proposition may seem, a man can be led by a dishonorable purpose to do an honorable action. The honorable motive alluded to above, is the pure result of a large development of what the phrenologists would call the organ of benevolence. When naturally benevolent and humane, though vain as a peacock, though shallow as Dogberry, though profane of speech as Horace Greeley is said to be, though notoriously unchaste and as notoriously a wine-bibber and a drunkard, though vulgar and coarse in manners, and obscene in conversation, and in every thing else indeed "tolerable and not to endured," still, in kindness to his negroes—a practical benevolence which sees that they are warmly clad, comfortably housed, abundantly fed, and not over-worked—the Cotton Snob is the peer of the most gentlemanly and virtuous person in the whole South. Of a truth, we have known just such characters to be avowed emancipationists in sentiment; even while holding slaves, professing themselves unable to see *any right* by which one man can be privileged to hold a fellow-being in bondage. So true is it, that persons of a single idea, can never perceive the absurd discrepancy between their teachings and their practice, and are always straining out the gnat to swallow the camel.

As for the dishonorable motive which not infrequently leads the Cotton Snob to be a good master, we shall not shoot very far of the mark if we say, that it always grows out of his excessive vanity, and that torturing anxiety—which characterizes all snobs—to be well spoken of by the world, and applauded for every thing he does; the right or wrong of any act never once entering into his thoughts. It is no credit to any man in the South to have the reputation of being a hard master; but if it were, the Cotton Snob would soonest boast of his cruelties; and would doubtless keep a little private torture-room, wherein to entertain his friends with a show of some of his most devilish inventions for producing human agony; something like the pious Priests of the Middle Ages were wont to torture heretics for the delectation of Popes and Cardinals. Nor need you conceive that we exaggerate; for only consider all the wicked things the race of snobs the world over, and in all ages, have committed, merely to be *in the fashion*. Consider the mutilation of the feet in China; the *hari-kari* of Japan, or happy process of disembowelling; the intrigues in the fashionable circles of the Old World, and the ease with which our own patriotic fellow-citizens learn to forget old friends and familiar faces, merely because the wheel of Fortune has, in its blind evolutions, whirled the former *up* and the latter *down*. We tell you plainly, honest reader, the genuine Snob will make wry faces at no toad, however large or disgusting; but will make it a point of honor to swallow the animal whole, the little stump-tail, the big goggle-eyes, the bloated belly, slimy back, toe-nails, gristle, skin and all! And the Cotton Snob verily, if persuaded it was *the thing* to have a juvenile African served up whole on state occasions, stuffed like a young grunter or prepared like a baron of beef, would never once hesitate to have young Sambo served with parsley and egg-sauce, or whatever else might be the taste of the hour; and what is more, he would pretend to enjoy the delicious repast with as much gusto, as he at present evinces while discussing the mysterious compounds served at the St. Charles or the St. Nicholas—not one of which, in most instances, he would be able properly to translate into his own vernacular. For he holds it a sin to cry out against any dish that Fashion and a French cook have pronounced in favor of; and would, in consequence, be totally unable to appreciate at its full value the honest verdancy of a stout Alabamian we once knew; who, visiting New-Orleans for the first time, and having a dish set before him, the contents of which would not go *down* at his bidding, after many contortions of visage and sundry and divers attempts at swallowing the savory mess, at last threw up his hands in alarm, ejecting the sweet morsel from his mouth at the same time, and with his "eyes in a fine frenzy rolling," bawled at the top of a very stentorian pair of the lungs: "Take it away! take it away! *carrion! carrion!*" If every man were as honest as this stout gentleman from Alabama, and, having no fear of Mrs. Grundy before his eyes, dared to call every caprice of Fashion by its proper name, what a flutter would there be in "our best society!"

But, (and we see you grimly smile, worthy Negrophilist!) the Cotton Snob, when he is situated so that he can hide his wickedness from the world, is sometimes as hard a task-master as his father was before him; driving day and night, as the negroes express it, being solely intent on acquiring the means to enable him to fare sumptuously every day, and—speaking in figures—to be every day arrayed in that purple and fine linen which is the peculiar delight of the vain, rich man the world over. He generally employs for managers shrewd New-Englanders, or canny Scotchmen, or native Southern Bullies, who are to be seen at all times astraddle their horses and overlooking the field hands while at work, wearing a big "bull-whip" tied over one shoulder and under the other, scarf-fashion, and rarely addressing a slave without cursing him in the same breath. These very gentlemanly-looking personages are instructed to "drive like h—ll," and make all they can : hence, the more the Cotton Snob sinks at Faro, or at the "races," the harder his negroes are "pushed," and the heavier the lash is laid on their weary backs; and the more his wife and daughters spend in silks and jewelry, or at the fashionable summer resorts, the longer the poor African is forced to labor on into the night, even sometimes till the "wee sma' hours atween the twal;" when he drops down to slumber by the roadside, or wherever he may chance to be when his weary labor is done, tired nature refusing to support him on his legs until he can reach his humble cabin. Of course, Reverend Sir, we are here presenting an extreme, and let us hope an exceptional case ; and, allow us to add, chiefly for your own peculiar delectation. It is better than a play, we assure you, to see with what a righteous unction you roll your weeping eyes to heaven, inwardly thanking God that you live in a "land of Bibles and Freemen, where such villanies are never perpetrated."

But, if your Reverence please, we would beg to remind you of a scene said to have been enacted in the land of Judea. We are told that, upon a certain occasion, two men went up to the Temple to pray. One of them stood afar off, and bowing himself to the ground seemed overwhelmed with the consciousness of his guilt, and kept smiting himself on the breast, crying bitterly all the time: "Lord, have mercy on me a sinner! Lord, have mercy on me a sinner!" But the other straightened himself up, lengthened his phylacteries and spread out the borders of his robe, and folding his hands with an air of the most perfect self-righteous· ness, cried out in a loud and confident voice: "Lord, I thank thee that I am better than other men! Lord, I especially thank thee that I am unlike that publican and sinner, who stands there beating his breast and bemoaning his sins." And the Great Master declared, that the Publican went away more justified than the Pharisee. Now, your Reverence may be unable to perceive the present applicableness of this parable, but it has its application nevertheless. For, while you stand thanking God that you live in a land of Bibles and Freemen, and especially thanking him that you are better than your brethren of the South; your own Northern Snobs and Northern Yankees are daily tram· pling in the dust hundreds of thousands of God's poor all around you, and yet, you miserable Priest of Cant and Hypocrisy, you only wrap your self-righteous robe closer about you, and pass unheeding by on "the other side!" Nay, more; the very gold which clothes your precious person in broadcloth, and which is the hire paid you for introducing politics into the pulpit, comes from the plethoric pockets of those same Snobs and Yankees; and is virtually red with the heart's blood of poor consumptive seamstresses, of pale and

haggard artisans, and of the widow and the fatherless.
For there is this marked difference between the Snobs
and Yankees of the South, and those of the North:
while the former only oppress and render miserable
the bondmen belonging exclusively to themselves; the
latter, by an unholy combination of capital against
labor, oppress the whole working class — reducing
their wages down to the merest pittance — working
them harder than the plough-mules are worked on the
most driving Southern cotton-planter's estate; and giving bread and life only to the strong and the robust,
leaving the weak and helpless, the sick and the infirm,
a prey to want and starvation, as well as to every species of villany and oppression.   Hence, in view of these
facts, we make bold to assert that any man, who ne-
glects to devote himself body and soul to relieving the
burdens of that society in which his lot is cast, preferring idly and profitlessly to carp at the evils of any
other system of society whatever with which he is not
identified; we care not what his profession or his pre-
tensions may be, is at heart a base deceiver and hypocrite; and, although he may receive in this life the
guerdon for which he labors, namely, the applause of his
fellow-men, yet in the life which is to come, he will
receive for his recompense a reward to which he does
not now aspire, but which will be eminently his due.
For we are commanded of God *to do good as we have
opportunity*, and not to neglect our own opportunities
for doing good, to point out to our neighbors wherein
they are remiss in the performance of their duties and
obligations.   In other words, people who live in glass
houses have no right to throw stones.

CHAPTER V.

THE SOUTHERN YEOMAN.

" At length his lonely cot appears in view,
  Beneath the shelter of an aged tree;
  Th' expectant wee things, toddlin stacher through
  To meet their dad, wi' flichtering noise and glee;
  His wee bit ingle blinkin bonnilie,
  His clean hearthstone, his thrifty wifie's smile,
  The lisping infant prattling on his knee,
  Does a' his weary kiaugh and care beguile,
  And makes him quite forget his labor and his toil."

ROBERT BURNS.

WHEN we gaze upon some lofty mountain which
rears its pinnacled and azure summit high up in the
region of mists and eternal snow, lost in admiration of
the sublime spectacle we are prone to forget that, while
its heaven-crowned peaks may dazzle and delight us
with their matchless wealth of grandeur and beauty,
still, deep down in its cavernous base and hidden from
the garish sunlight and the blaze of day, are treasured
up mines of greater wealth and greater splendor, as
well as exhaustless quarries of imperishable marble,
which only waits the hand of genius to be converted
into living forms of beauty, and thus become a " joy
forever." So, too, when we look upon some mighty

and powerful nation, dazzled by the magnificent robes
of state and authority, and by all the splendid pomp
and circumstance of those who move in the upper circles of society, we are very liable to forget that these
all fail to constitute the STATE, and that they owe their
very existence and continued elevation, as well as that
distance from us which lends enchantment to the view,
to the unbedecked and toiling masses, who, like the
unseen but all-powerful forces of Nature, labor on in
secret and unobserved, yet in reality are the producers
of all the real wealth or useful progress and achievements of empires. For while princes, presidents, and
governors may boast of their castles and lands, their
silken gowns and robes of ceremony—all which can
be made the sport of fortune, and do often vanish away
in a moment, leaving their sometime owners poor indeed—the COMMON PEOPLE, as the masses are called,
possess in and of themselves a far richer inheritance,
which is the ability and the will to earn an honest livelihood (not by the tricks of trade and the lying spirit
of barter, nor yet by trampling on any man's rights,
but) by the toilsome sweat of their own brows, delving
patiently and trustingly in old mother earth, who, under the blessing of God, never deceives or disappoints
those who put their trust in her generous bosom. And
of all the hardy sons of toil, in all free lands the Yeomen are most deserving of our esteem. With hearts
of oak and thews of steel, crouching to no man and
fearing no danger, these are equally bold to handle a
musket on the field of battle or to swing their reapers
in times of peace among the waving stalks of yellow
grain. For, in the language of the poet:

" ———— Each boasts his hearth
And field as free as the best lord his barony,
Owing subjection to no human vassalage
Save to their king and law. Hence are they resolute,
Leading the van on every day of battle,
As men who know the blessings they defend.
Hence are they frank and generous in peace,
As men who have their portion in its plenty."

But you have no Yeomen in the South, my dear Sir?
Beg your pardon, our dear Sir, but we have—hosts of
them. *I thought you had only poor White Trash?* Yes,
we dare say as much—and that the moon is made of
green cheese! You have fully as much right or reason
to think the one thing as the other. *Do tell, now;
want to know?* Is that so, our good friend? do you
really desire to learn the truth about this matter? If
so, to the extent of our poor ability, we shall endeavor
to enlighten you upon a subject, which not one Yankee in ten thousand in the least understands.

Know, then, that the Poor Whites of the South constitute a separate class to themselves; the Southern
Yeomen are as distinct from them as the Southern
Gentleman is from the Cotton Snob. Certainly the
Southern Yeomen are nearly always poor, at least so
far as this world's goods are to be taken into the account. As a general thing they own no slaves; and
even in case they do, the wealthiest of them rarely possess more than from ten to fifteen. But even when
they are slaveholders, they seem to exercise but few of
the rights of ownership over their human chattels, making so little distinction between master and man, that
their negroes invariably become spoiled, like so many

9

rude children who have been unwisely spared the rod
by their foolish guardians. Such negroes are lazy as
the day is long, saucy and impertinent, and besides are
nearly as useless members of society as the free blacks
of the North, or Jamaica, or the Central American
States. Indulged from their infancy, never receiving
a stripe unless some one of their young masters is stout
enough to give them a *lamming* in a regular fisticuffs
fight, and in all things treated more like equals than
slaves, it is certainly no cause of wonder that 'they im-
pudently call their masters by their proper names, and,
when permitted, address all other white persons in the
same ill-bred and familiar manner. ' Indeed, Senator
Seward himself could not demand any greater show of
equality, than what is often exhibited by the Yeomen
of the South in the treatment of their negroes; and we
think it would cure even him of nis rabid mania on the
subject of the ultimate extinction of the peculiar institution, could he be brought into personal contact with
some of the free and easy specimens of poor down-
trodden Africans we have had the luck to fall in with
now and then in the Slave States.   If he did not carry
with him to his grave a very unflattering remembrance
of his loutish, lazy, lousy, and foul-scented black "brothers," then he is not the dainty gentleman we have
been accustomed to consider him.   For, after all their
demonstrations in behalf of the Negro, the people of
the Free States are possessed of olfactories like the rest
of mankind, and individually entertain a very wholesome dread of coming personally in contact with their
down-trodden and much-abused *protegé*, however lusti-
ly they may bawl about his being both "a man and

a brother." We know, in some parts of the North, negroes are admitted to the society of a certain class of ·fanatical free-lovers and socialists—dine with them sleep with them, school with them, and even sometimes intermarry with them—while it does occasionally happen, that a big buck African will familiarly slap a white man on the back, with a "How ar' yer, Tom? gib a feller a treat," or, "Harry, my boy, how goes de wedder?" In a majority of cases, however, as we have already declared, decent people in all the Northern States entertain a very wholesome and sensible prejudice against affiliating on terms of equality with persons of color. In this regard, indeed, they are far more scrupulous and sensitive than any class of whites in the South.

Now it is chiefly owing, as we conceive, to this universal prejudice against color in the North, that the citizens of the Free States will insist free labor is degraded by the existence of African slavery, and that the Poor Whites of the South because thereof prefer to starve rather than to labor side by side with slaves. Because they themselves will not consent to work on a level with the free negroes in their own midst, of course (such is their reasoning) any poor Southerner would feel degraded to labor in company with enslaved persons possessing the same objectionable color. Capital logicians! Now, Sirs, what are the facts? Would you believe the declaration, that honest Southern Yeomen (these are the industrious poor whites of the South) always work side by side with their own human chattels in the fields, in the forests, and every where else? Nothing, we assure you, is more common. No man can travel a day through any thickly-settled portion of the South, but he will come up with some sturdy yeoman and his sons working in company of their negroes; sometimes their own property, at other times hirelings whom they have employed by the month or year. In portions of Western Virginia, particularly in the districts settled by the Pennsylvania Dutch, such spectacles are to be witnessed on almost every other farm. Passing by their fields of rich clover, nearly waist-high, and blushing as red in a rich profusion of purple blooms as the cheeks of the plump country maiden who sits singing and knitting under the big apple-tree in front of the neat farm-house, you can not fail of being amused to observe the lazy deliberation with which the broad-shouldered farm-boys, and their equally broad-shouldered sooty companions, lay down their hoes or scythes to gaze at a stranger—gazing long and steadfastly, with hanging lip and open mouth, until you are hidden from their sight by a turn in the green lane, when they all simultaneously burst out a laughing, (at what, Heaven knows!) but in so hearty and boisterous a manner as to wake up the dozing cattle, whose sleek fat sides are scarcely visible about in spots among the clover-leaves, refulgent and glistening in the shimmering rays of the glorious summer sun. So, too, if you leave Virginia and pass down into the Old North State—the State so famous for its tar, pitch, and turpentine—you will hear the axe of master and man falling with alternate strokes in the depth of the whispering forests of dark evergreens, as with redoubled blows they attack the lofty pines, felling them to the ground for lumber, or simply barking them for their resinous sap. Here you will frequently see black and white, slave and freeman, camping out together, living sometimes in the same tent or temporary pine-pole cabin; drinking, the darkeys always after mas'r, out of the same tin dipper or long-handled gourd their home-distilled apple-brandy; dining on the same homely but substantial fare, and sharing one bed in common, *videlicet*, the *cabin floor*.

Again, should you go among the hardy yeomanry of Tennessee, Kentucky, or Missouri, whenever or wherever they own slaves (which in these States is not often the case) you will invariably see the negroes and their masters ploughing side by side in the fields; or bared to the waist, and with old-fashioned scythe vieing with one another who can cut down the broadest swath of yellow wheat, or of the waving timothy; or bearing the tall stalks of maize and packing them into the stout-built barn, with ear and fodder on, ready for the winter's husking. And when the long winter evenings have come, you will see blacks and whites sing, and shout, and husk in company, to the music of Ole Virginny reels played on a greasy fiddle by some aged Uncle Edward, whose frosty pow proclaims that he is no longer fit for any more active duty, and whose long skinny fingers are only useful now to put life and mettle into the fingers of the younger huskers, by the help of de fiddle and de bow.

And yet, notwithstanding the Southern Yeoman allows his slaves so much freedom of speech and action, is not offended when they call him familiarly by his Christian name, and hardly makes them work enough to earn their salt, still he is very proud of being a

slaveholder; and when he is not such, his greatest ambition is to make money enough to buy a negro. We
recall a very amusing anecdote illustrative of this ambition of the Southern Yeoman.

A man named Horne, who was a bachelor, had entered some land at government price, or at all events
at a very small sum. In a few years his land increased
so in value that he sold out at an enormous profit, taking as part payment one negro man, whom we will call
Jeff. The next morning after the bargain had been
closed, the negro was awakened quite early by hearing
his new master bawling at the top of his voice:

"Jeff! you, Jeff! Come here, you big black nigger,
you!"

"Bres God, Mas'r, what's de marter?" said Jeff,
rushing *sans culotte* into his master's room, and nearly
out of breath with alarm.

"O nuthin," replied Horne dryly, "*I only wanted to
see how 'twould sound jist—that's all!*"

In his origin, aside from the German settlers in Western Virginia, the Southern Yeoman is almost purely
English. He nearly always bears some good old
Anglo-Saxon name, and will tell you, if interrogated
about his ancestors, that "grandfather so and so came
over from the Old Country"—by which familiar and
endearing phrase he always designates Great Britain.
He is thorough English in fact, in both physical heartiness and dogged perseverance. Very seldom is he
troubled with dyspepsia, or melancholy, or discontent
with his humble lot—evils which in most cases have
their origin in a disordered stomach. Just so rarely,
too, will you ever meet a Southern Yeoman who has

learned to fear mortal man, or who would under any circumstances humiliate himself to curry favor with the rich or those in authority. He always possesses a manly independence of character, and though not so impetuous as the gentry of the South usually are, still, in the midst of the dangers and carnage of the battle-field, and in the thickest of the fray, his eye never quails; but with steady tramp and unflinching nerve he marches right on to where duty and honor call, and with unblanched cheek meets death face to face. His wounds, like the scars of the old Roman, themselves bespeak his praise, for they are ever received from the front and never from behind.

The usual weapon of the Southern Yeoman is the deadly rifle—even in his sports—and this he handles with such skill as few possess, even in America. He likes the quick sharp report which announces in a clear tongue when the leaden messenger is *sent home;* and affects to despise the rattling fowling piece, the peculiar sporting gun of the Southern Gentleman. With his rifle the Yeoman shoots squirrels, ducks, turkeys, deer, bear, buffalo, and whatever else he pleases. The best riflemen are found in Georgia, Mississippi, Tennessee, and Kentucky—*the* best, perhaps, in the last-named brave and chivalrous Commonwealth. Herein turkey-shooting is practised by all classes, but chiefly by the yeomen. A live turkey is securely fastened to a stake at the distance of one hundred paces, and you pay five or ten cents for the privilege of each shot; if you hit the fowl in the head the carcass is yours, but any other *hit* is considered *foul,* and so passes for nothing. This is the kind of school in which were trained the hunt-

ing-shirt heroes of King's Mountain, and those unerr-
ing riflemen who, at the memorable battle of New-Orleans, made such havoc in the ranks of Packenham's
veterans. So also were trained those brave defenders
of Texan independence—Crockett, Travis, and their
compeers, who buried themselves beneath the countless
heaps of Mexicans slain at the heroic defense of the
Alamo. And it was because of a similar schooling
that Col. Jeff. Davis was enabled to say to the retreating Indianians at the battle of Buena Vista, pointing
proudly to the gallant yeomanry of Mississippi: "Stay,
and re-form behind that wall!" For well the brave
Colonel knew the rifles in the hands of his favorite
regiment would soon with their iron hail beat down
the advancing foe, and cause them to rush back in dis-
orderly rout to their tents and entrenchments. Indeed,
take them all in all, and we doubt if the world can
produce a more reliable citizen soldiery than the yeomanry of our Southern States. They only require the
right sort of leaders—officers under whom they are
willing to fight, and in whose mettle and abilities they
have perfect confidence. General Taylor was such a
man, and in this regard no American General of late
years has been his peer. Southern born himself, and
Southern bred, plain and unostentatious in his manners,
and at all times cool and determined in the hour of
danger; his soldiers loved the *man*, while they re-
spected and trusted the *general*. Noble old Soldier!
no true heart can fail to regret, that the exigencies of
politics forced you to lay aside the sword for our republican sceptre, and thus with the weighty cares and
perplexities of a station which you never were fitted to

adorn, too soon consigned you to the grave and deprived the Union of one of her most able and patriotic defenders. Green be the turf above you, honest Roman, and may your successors in office learn to emulate your virtues!

The Southern Yeoman much resembles in his speech, religious opinions, household arrangements, indoor sports, and family traditions, the middle class farmers of the Northern States. He is fully as intelligent as the latter, and is on the whole much better versed in the lore of politics and the provisions of our Federal and State Constitutions. This is chiefly owing to the public barbecues, court-house-day gatherings, and other holiday occasions, which are more numerous in the South than in the North, and in the former are nearly always devoted in part to political discussions of one kind or another. Heard from the lips of their neighbors and friends, and having the matter impressed upon their minds by the presentation of both sides of every disputed question at the same time, it is not strange that poor men in the South should possess a more comprehensive knowledge of the fundamental principles of our artificial and complex system of government, or should retain a clearer perception of the respective merits of every leading political issue, than if they derived their information solely from books or newspapers; which always furnish but one view of the matter in dispute, and which they must painfully peruse after a long day of toil, being more exercised meanwhile (aside from the drawback of physical weariness) in laboring to interpret the meaning of the "dictionary words," than in attempting to follow the facts

9*

or the argument of the writer, be he never so lucid and perspicuous.

We know a pretty general belief prevails throughout the entire North, and in Europe as well, (owing to the misrepresentations of our patriotic book-makers of the Free States,) that the great mass of the Southern people are more ignorant than the mass of Northern laborers; and, although this opinion is no sounder than the baseless fabric of a vision, there is yet a plausible excuse at least to be urged on behalf of those citizens of the North who entertain it. For the North, taken as a whole, is an inventive and manufacturing community, and her citizens, in consequence, love to agglomerate in towns, villages, etc. etc. Hence, they entertain a very foolish prejudice against the country, and every thing almost that pertains to country life; while such a personage as a country gentleman proper, is unknown from Maine to Oregon, and to speak of "our country cousins" as very annoying and troublesome, is a standing witticism in every Free State. But the South is almost evclusively agricultural, and, of course, the great mass of her citizens fall under the bann of the cockney prejudices of the trades-people of the North, equally with their own country cousins from Down East, or the sun-embrowned Hoosiers from the West. Now, we do not pretend to claim that the yeomen of the South are as intelligent or well-instructed about a great many things, as the mechanics, artisans, small shopkeepers, and others, who in a great measure constitute the population of the Northern towns; but we do insist, from a pretty extensive acquaintance with the peculiarities and characteristics of both, that the

Southern Yeoman is the peer in every respect of the small farmers in the Free States, as well as their superior in a great many. For, as has already been shown, he is certainly better informed than the latter about the political history of the country; is more accustomed to the use of fire-arms, particularly the rifle; and (which is no small recommendation) he has a better appreciation of good liquors, for, instead of' swallowing the vile stuff sent forth from Cincinnati and other places in the shape of mean whisky, the Southern yeoman usually confines himself to home-brewed ale, or native apple-jack, or home-distilled peach brandy, all of which drinks are said to be both wholesome and harmless, if taken in moderation.

From the yeomanry usually springs the overseer class—a very useful and important class of persons in the South; very much-abused and slandered though they always have been, owing to the drunken habits, libertinism, coarse brutalities, and general bad conduct of many of their number. But there are to be found among them men of sterling worth and incorruptible integrity—good citizens, intelligent managers, kind disciplinarians, and even sometimes they evince gentlemanly instincts, though but little polished in speech or manners.

We think the reading public, Southern as well as Northern, in forming its judgment of overseers, has never sufficiently considered the responsibilities and temptations of their peculiar position. They constitute the Southern police, or patrol, just as every Northern city has its squads of police to protect the property and lives of its citizens from the hands of thieves, burglars, incendiaries, garroters, midnight assassins, and street bullies. The "beat" of each Southern overseer, is the plantation on which he resides; and the collective body of overseers in every neighborhood, constitutes a regularly organized patrol—called by the negroes "Paterollers," and upon set times these "paterollers" form a troop and gallop from plantation to plantation during the whole night, arresting and punishing all slaves found off their proper premises without a permit from their master or mistress. But on the whole, the Southern overseer has a much more laborious duty to perform than his brother policeman of any Northern city. The latter has only to look after freemen—in most cases intelligent white men, who entertain some respect for the officers of the law; whereas the Southern overseer has confided to his care the kinky-headed descendants of those pagans who, only a century ago, made no bones of eating one another, and whose kindred yet remaining in Africa still look upon a white missionary stewed with onions and cayenne pepper, or even better perhaps eaten raw and without salt, as the greatest "delicacy of the season."

Did you never consider this fact, dear philanthropic Madam, who are so grateful to the policeman who breaks the pate of the drunken Irish bully, as kicks up "sich a divil of a row," right under your parlor window; but go into hysterics at the bare mention of a Southern overseer's knocking down a refractory Hottentot? And, besides, if you are so valiant in defense of the wholesale slaughter of Ghoorkas, Sepoys, and other colored Hindoos, by your beloved brethren, the English abolitionists, why, in the name of common-sense, do you scowl so because some bloody Southerner finds it necessary occasionally to give a rebellious slave a flogging? Is a tough New-England cowskin diligently applied to the back of a lazy, lying Congo, a more heineous offense in the sight of Heaven, than the breaking of a drunken loafer's skull by means of honest Charley's club, or the blowing of Sepoys from the mouths of British cannon, simply because, like our worthy revolutionary sires, they have dared to rebel against an usurped authority and a confessedly most inhuman tyranny? But bear in mind, our stout John Bull, we are casting no stones—save at the heads of those hypocrites, who sustain your virtuous queen in her recent bloody enactments in India, (all necessary, perhaps,) but at the same time rend the very heavens with their shrieks, because, in endeavoring to keep in subjection *our India*, we must needs resort to much milder and less sanguinary measures, though sometimes quite revolting to our humaner feelings. For he must be a very bold man who will deny that the overseers on many Southern plantations, are cruel and unmercifully severe, when permitted to be so by the carelessness or connivance of their employers. -Despite all which, however, we are yet prepared to contend, that, compared with the police of all other places, the world over, and taken *en masse*, there is not any where a more respectable and well-behaved patrol than the Southern overseers.

But that is not saying much after all! we hear you exclaim, thou worthy reader of books and not of men. To which we reply: Until you and we have been tempted as such men are always tempted, every where and at all times, and have proven ourselves to be better and holier than they, we have no right to condemn or pass judgment. God, who is Judge of both the quick and the dead, alone is competent to determine who is deserving of condemnation, and who of praise. At all events, let us not denounce the innocent with the guilty, as in all our short-sighted human judgments we are ever prone to do. Some men, for example, when they have read in the daily press the fulsome details of a *scan. mag.*—the minute particulars of how some second Judas has betrayed his master's cause, not *with* a kiss, but *for* the kisses and wickeder endearments of a straying lamb of his flock—are apt to congratulate themselves that they still remain bachelors, and that they have never been so foolish as to entertain any religious sentiments at all. Such men will solemnly and seriously vow and swear (and for one we believe they are honest in their declarations: who is not that measures the rest of mankind by himself?) that they doubt the existence of female virtue, and conscientiously believe there never was a clerical neck-tie yet which did not encircle the throat of a hypocrite and rogue. These very virtuous-minded individuals simply confound the innocent with the guilty, and are so affected by the prominence given to some glaring example of clerical hypocrisy, or breach of matrimonial and conjugal fidelity; they fail to note how many thousands of happy households all around them are patterns of virtue and good morals, or how many hundreds of ministers of the Gospel do not only point the road to Heaven, but also "lead the way." And just in the same spirit has it been the custom of

certain Northern busy - bodies, (whose mental equi-
librium is not well-poised,) because of the prominence
given to the cruelties practised now and then by some
Southern Overseers, to speak of the whole class as totally vile and sin-hardened, fit subjects for the wrath
of Heaven, and destined ere long to people the dismal
abodes of Hades — a place formerly regarded as the
final resting-bed of all sinners, but latterly devoted to
the exclusive accommodation of slaveholders, and those
engaged in the Slave Trade—barring the legitimate
traffickers in Coolie flesh, who (on account of favors
manifold) are to be landed after death in the Seventh
Heaven.   But, we would beg to remind all such astute
reasoners, of what they seem to be ignorant, namely, that
sometimes diamonds are picked up from the dirtiest
dung-hills, while the most beautiful of pearls are taken
often from the bodies of the ugliest of testacean bi-
valves.

So far as hospitality goes, the Yeomen of the South
are not a whit behind the Southern Gentleman, or any
other class of gentlemen the world over. And we
make this declaration boldly, despite the assertions to
the contrary of a certain literary Peripatetic of New-
York, who has been in the habit of taking a jaunt
through some portions of the South every few years,
and afterwards publishing in book-form an account of
what he saw and heard. Affecting the utmost candor
and impartiality, as well as the very essence and spirit
of Truth, this peripatetical maker of books scarcely
succeeds in spreading his poppies broad and thick
enough, to conceal even from simple eyes the malice which underlies his plausible style; and which, as

the venomous reptile concealed underneath the stone in the pathway takes every furtive opportunity to thrust its poisonous fangs into the flesh of the unwary pedestrian, so is ever showing its serpent head when occasion serves, hissing with spite and bitterness. This writer has spoken of the Southern Yeomen (not by name, 'tis true) as mean and stingy, selfish and rude, and as being besides devoid of even a semblance of hospitality. Now, making all due allowance for the temptation to misrepresent which such a writer would very naturally yield to, (since upon such a misrepresentation chiefly depends the sale of his book, while upon the said sale he himself depends for his daily bread;) we would yet mildly suggest, that, if ever again he should desire to share the humble crust of poverty, the proper way to attain his object is not to strive to be condescendingly kind and excruciatingly affable, as if one would say : " My poor country clown, I pity you ; for I am dressed in broadcloth and patent-leathers, and am much more intelligent than you, my poor country clown !" No, worthy Sir ! that is not the way to get at a poor man's heart, or his humble fireside either, as a welcome and honored guest. What is the right and proper way, let the following personal incident inform you, our over-dainty gentleman.

Perhaps you have not forgotten the Panic yet, fellow-citizens of the Free States? In the midst of your mad and headlong chase after sudden wealth ; in the midst of your wild and reckless speculations in stocks, bonds, railroads, lands, and every thing else, whereby money is to be made without any honest toil ; in the midst of your self-gratulations at the much faster me-

thod you had of getting riches, than your more conservative and plodding brethren to the South of you;
lo! there suddenly appeared a hand-writing on the
wall, and in one short hour all your visions of boundless prosperity came to naught. We need not remind
you of the scenes which ensued. They will not soon
be effaced from the memory of the present generation.
We need not remind you with what inward satisfaction you turned your doleful visages towards the hitherto despised South, and in view of her still undimin-
ished abundance, took heart again for the future of our
common Republic. You felt a pride, doubtless for the
first time, while beholding all the once firm-seated
thrones of Commerce and Finance toppling and tumbling down in irretrievable overthrow around you, that
one American Sovereign at least remained with head
erect—that, as ever before, COTTON STILL WAS KING.
Many of you, indeed, leaving your families in the Free
States, turned your steps Southward in search of employment. Never was there such an Exodus from the
Northern to the Southern States before. We happened likewise to hibernate in the Slave States during
that memorable era, and in passing from place to place
chanced to fall in with many of those unfortunates,
whom lack of employment and the Hard Times had
driven from their homes to seek shelter from the storm
in the sunny South. One of these was a Connecticut
man, a machinist by trade, and possessed of strong
anti-slavery prejudices, but prudent of speech and very
intelligent for a person of his calling and condition.
We met aboard a steamboat on one of the loveliest
rivers in the South; and although it was mid-winter,

still, sitting on the steamer's hurricane-deck, as it is called, and inhaling the soft and balmy air which already seemed laden with the odors of spring; he recounted to us the several adventures with which he had met in his various ups and downs, since he left the land of wooden nutmegs and steady habits.

We were much entertained. He told us with what hopes he had left his family in their New-England home, where he found it impossible longer to get employment at his trade, and how he had hastened Southwards with a joyful heart, confident of making enough to feed both himself and his little household during the winter months. But he was too late. Hundreds had rushed in before him, and every railroad shop was filled, (his business was to build engines,) as well as every other shop wherein he could hope to make himself useful. His money, what little he had, was soon exhausted; and then, to add to his misfortunes, at a lonesome village in Tennessee, he was taken sick of typhus fever, which kept him closely confined for some three weeks, and from which he recovered with difficulty, having not a beggarly dernier left; and so, weak and suffering, and without money or friends, he set out on his travels a-foot, being as yet barely able to walk. But he managed to walk thirty miles the first day for all that, and found himself late in the afternoon in the town of Columbia. Seeing two taverns in the place, he resolved not to impose upon the proprietors of either, but determined in the honesty of his heart that he would state the sad condition of his exchequer first to one, and, on refusal, then to the other, and afterwards throw himself on their charity for supper and a night's lodging. He was still well-dressed, which would make against him, he knew, but he flattered himself that his honest face would persuade even the most suspecting to believe his story. So he put a bold face on the matter, walked into the nearest of the two public houses, and going straight up to the landlord told him plainly how he was situated. For his pains and his honesty he was told to take himself off instanter. He then essayed to reason the matter with "mine host;" but the more the Yankee argued the more "mine host" swore and raved, until the former was glad to escape with a whole skin from the presence of the enraged Boniface, who must have been a genuine specimen of the native Southern Yankee, about whom we have already discoursed. But our Connecticut adventurer felt famished almost, having eaten nothing all day, and was determined not to die of starvation in the midst of plenty, so he forthwith sought out the other tavern. An old man was the proprietor of this—an old white-headed man, with a calm patriarchal demeanor. When he of Connecticut first looked on him, he thought to himself that if such a venerable old gentleman had no milk of human kindness in his composition, then surely charity must be a thing unknown in the State of Tennessee. Being taught by his recent experience, however, he was now a little more circumspect than in the first instance, and entering the public reception-room, proceeded to wash his face and then to comb his hair, which having finished, he walked deliberately up to the broad old-fashioned fireplace, in which blazed and crackled a rousing wood-fire, and leisurely took a seat in the midst of the numerous gentlemen who sat in a semi-circle about it.

There chanced (it being Court week) to be many law-yers, judges, and country gentlemen lodging with "mine host" at the time; and these, as they collected around the blazing hearth in the dusk of the gathering twilight, passed the time in story-telling, each spinning his yarn in turn, and vieing with all in the shouts of applause which were sure to follow any "decided hit." When every one had finished his story, seeing a stran-ger present, they courteously called on him to furnish them with his story, too. Our Connecticut friend was nothing loth, but proceeded immediately to do his best. His effort proved quite successful, and he was eagerly besought to tell another.

"I will tell you another in the morning," said the honest fellow. "I am too faint and hungry now. I am from Connecticut, gentlemen; I hope I am an hon-est man, too, but although you see me dressed so well, I have not a penny to save me from the gallows. I have walked thirty miles to-day, (turning to the land-lord,) and have eaten nothing since yesterday. I would like to lodge with you to-night. I can pay you nothing now—I only ask of you to trust me, however; for so sure as my name is ———, and I am an honest Yan-kee, you shall yet get every farthing."

"And you haven't eat any dinner this blessed day?" was the only reply of the gray-headed old gentleman, whose benign countenance from the first had so favora-bly impressed him of Connecticut.

"Not a mouthful!"

"Ned, come here. Show this gentleman to the din-ing-room, and see that he eats all he wants," said next the Good Samaritan, addressing his colored man; and then turning to his guest: "Of course, Sir, you can stay with us as long as you find it necessary."

"Yes," here interrupted the District Judge, "put him in my room, landlord, if the house is crowded; for I am invited to a friend's to-night, and shall not occupy it."

Well, here was a generous hospitality unlooked-for, and our Yankee's heart, as he expressed it, all of a sudden jumped up into his throat like a big bullfrog, and *stuck there*, and so impeded his utterance he had not a word to say by way of thanks, but simply bowed, and retreating to the dining-room proceeded to do ample justice to the generosity of his benevolent host.

But he could not afford to beg, and so sold his overcoat for twelve dollars, and started out once more a-foot with a little money: this, however, he soon spent, when, clad in only a thin, close-bodied coat, with ordinary pantaloons and vest, and a small bundle on his back, containing a clean shirt or two, he plodded wearily along, begging, like poor Oliver Goldsmith, as he went. And now came his experience of the hospitality of the Southern Yeomanry; for he purposely shunned the villages and the dwellings of the rich, and every night rested his tired limbs underneath humble roofs only. He was perfectly enthusiastic in his praises of the kind reception he every where met. We will tell you, our readers, just as he told us, how he was received in one house at which he stopped over night, and this will serve as an example of all the rest.

At this house there was a frolic of some kind or other, and the dancing and singing were kept up until a late hour. The guests assembled, like the host and

hostess, were all of the Yeoman class, plain, hard-working people, owning no slaves, and possessing a scanty
knowledge of either books or men ; hence their songs
were, as can be easily imagined, of the commonest and
most homely description. When, therefore, they called
upon the Yankee for his song, and he gave them the
pathetic ballad of Ben Bolt, sung feelingly and well,
all hearts were instantly captivated. Immediately they
passed him the bottle of old rye, pressing him to
wet his whistle and try again, and so kept him singing
and telling of the great world of which they knew so
little, until near upon the peep of day. And the next
morning, when he left, they would have him take along
a bottle of "sperrits" for his stomach's sake, as well as a
huge package of provisions, called in Southern parlance
a "snack." This certainly was enough of kindness for
one poor toiling family, and so our Yankee thought;
but when he was about a mile off, behold one of the
fair damsels of the house came clattering after him,
(riding her steed *bare-backed*, though with all delicate
and lady-like grace,) for the sole purpose of telling him
that there was a creek a little further on, which, owing
to the late rains, he could not cross without a horse and
a guide; and so, being as how all the men were gone
to work, mother had sent her to see the gentleman safe
over. And she did (O blushing daughter of fashion !)
absolutely take up before her on the bare-backed work-
horse this strolling and unknown fellow, and having
safely set him down on the other side of the swollen
stream, returned to her humble cot, never once dreaming that she had done a noble and generous action.

Ah ! wandering Peripatetic of New-York, you never

met with such hospitality, for you did not deserve it. Your cockney bearing and general stiffness of demeanor did not appeal to the humble tastes and simple habits of the yeomanry, and that is why you have declared them mean and selfish. What a wonderfully sapient fellow thou art, truly! Now, your brother Northerner, whose experience of the hospitality of the same class of people, we have already given, though he stopped for many nights in succession at their humble homes, bears witness that he was always entertained in the same hospitable spirit, and never but once was refused a night's lodging. On this occasion he had another Yank (as he called him) in company, a foot-passenger like himself, with whom he had been journeying for several days. When they called at the house alluded to, the mistress came to the door and told them that her good man was away; else, she would gladly take them in, but since he was absent she could not think of it. He of Connecticut thanked her, like a gentleman who could appreciate the delicacy of feeling which prompted the good wife to pursue the course she did : but his fellow Yank turned to him and whispered, " Let us go in, any how." " Sir," said noble Old Connecticut, (we called him Old Connecticut on board the steamer,) " you can do so if you like, but I shall not. But whether you go in or remain outside, I will have you to know that henceforth we travel separate roads. I shall no longer remain in company of a person who is a disgrace to his native land, and who in the country of strangers does not know how to conduct himself like a gentleman." Honest words these, worthy son of New-England! What a pity it is more of your countrymen do not feel as he must of necessity feel, who can honestly give them utterance. For, in that case, there would not be so many lying, sneaking, cowardly knaves, foot-padding it all through the Southern States, endeavoring by every devilish machination to kindle the fires of a servile insurrection, and writing calumnious letters to Northern newspapers, oftentimes defaming the characters of the unsuspecting patrons, at whose hospitable board their miserable carcasses are each day filled with abundance of every species of good cheer.

But to return once more to the subject of this chapter. Besides being given to hospitality, although in a very primitive way, as has been shown, the Yeomen of the South are also quite social and gregarious in their instincts, and delight much in having all kinds of frolics and family gatherings during the long winter evenings. On all such occasions, nearly, something serviceable is the ostensible cause of their assembling, though the time is devoted almost wholly to social pleasures: sometimes, 'tis true, there is a wedding, or a birth-day party, or a candy-pulling; but much more frequently it is a corn-husking, or the everlasting quilting—this last being the most frequent and most in favor of all the merrymakings which call the young people together. There is, indeed, nothing to compare to a country quilting for the simple and unaffected happiness which it affords all parties. The old women and old men sit demurely beside the blazing kitchen fire, and frighten one another with long-winded ghost stories; thus leaving the young folks all to themselves in the "big room," wherein is also the quilt-frame, which is either suspended at the corners by ropes attached to the ceiling, or else rests on the tops of four chairs.   Around this assemble the young men and the young maidens, robust with honest toil and honestly ruby-cheeked with genuine good health.   The former know nothing of your *dolce far niente* or dyspepsia, and the latter are not troubled with crinoline or consumption, but all are merry as larks and happy as it is possible for men and women to be in this lower world.   No debts, nor duns, nor panics, nor poverty, nor wealth disturbs their thoughts or mars the joyousness of the hour.   Serene as a summer's day, and cloudless as the skies in June, the moments hurry by, as they ply their nimble needles and sing their simple songs, or whisper their tales of love, heedless of the great world and all the thoughtless worldlings who live only to win the smiles of " our best society."   Meanwhile the children play hide and seek, in-doors and out, whooping, laughing, and chattering like so many magpies ; and, in the snug chimney-corner, Old Bose, the faithful watch-dog, stretches himself out to his full length and doses comfortably in the genial warmth of the fire, in his dreams chasing after imaginary hares, or baying the moon ; while, as the poet sings :

> " Around in sympathetic mirth
>   Its tricks the kitten tries ;
> The cricket chirrups in the hearth,
>   The crackling fagot flies."

In their religious convictions and practices, the Southern Yeomen very much resemble the Middle Classes ; are prone to shout at camp-meetings, and to see visions and dream dreams.   Although generally

10

moral in their conduct and punctilious in all religious observances, they do yet often entertain many very absurd ideas in regard to Christianity, ideas wholly at variance with any rational interpretation of the Sacred Scriptures; and hence they are led not infrequently, to mistake animal excitement for holy ecstasy, and seem to think, indeed, with the old-time priests of Baal, that God is not to be entreated save with *loud* prayers, and much beating of the breasts, and clapping of the hands, accompanied with audible groans and sighs. For all which, however, their officiating clergy are more to blame than themselves; for they are often ignorant men of the Whang Doodle description, illiterate and dogmatic, and blessed with a nasal twang which would do no discredit to New-England. They very seldom know any thing about their Bibles, but, like the star political priests of the North, seem to exert themselves to ignore all the facts and precepts of the Gospel of Jesus Christ as revealed in the Sacred Scriptures, preferring to teach " for doctrines the commandments of men ;" just as did the Levites and Pharisees with their talmudistic theologies in the days of our Saviour. And truly, it has always been to us a singular circumstance why religious people are so easily gulled. Although palpable to all the world else, they seem not to know—

> "A man may cry, Church ! Church ! at every word,
>   With no more piety than other people—
>   A daw's not reckoned a religious bird,
>   Because it keeps a-cawing from a steeple ;
>   The Temple is a good, a holy place,
>   But quacking only gives it an ill savor ;
>   While saintly mountebanks the porch disgrace,
>   And bring religion's self into disfavor !"

But to return.

As to the Vital Question of the Day, to make use of the cant phrase so greatly in vogue at the present writing, although not as a class pecuniarily interested in slave property, the Southern Yeomanry are almost unanimously pro-slavery in sentiment. Nor do we see how any honest, thoughtful person can reasonably find fault with them on this account. Only consider their circumstances, negrophilist of the North, and answer truthfully; were you so situated would you dare to advocate emancipation? Were you situated as the Southern Yeomen are—humble in worldly position, patient delvers in the soil, daily earning your bread by the toilsome sweat of your own brows—would you be pleased to. see four millions of inferior blacks suddenly raised from a position of vassalage, and placed upon an equality with yourselves? made the sharers of your toil, the equals and associates of your wives and children? You know you would not. Despite your maudlin affectation of sympathy in behalf of the Negro, you are yet inwardly conscious that you heartily despise the sooty African, and that you deny to even the few living in your own midst an equality of rights and. immunities with yourselves. You well know that you entertain a natural repugnance to coming in contact with Sambo—a repugnance so great that you slam your church doors in his face, shut him out of the theatres, refuse him a seat in your public conveyances, and, so fearful are you of the contamination of a black man's presence any where, in nine tenths of your States drive him away from the ballot-box, thus making your statute-books even belie your professions of philanthropy.   And yet you seek to turn loose upon your white brethren of the South *four millions of these same despised Africans*, congratulating yourselves meanwhile that you would be doing a most disinterested act of benevolence!   Shame on your consistency, gentlemen. Judged by your own acts, were you situated as the Southern people are to-day, stronger pro-slavery men than yourselves would not be found in the world. Hence we ask you again, did you occupy the position of the Southern Yeomanry in particular, is there a man in your midst who would favor emancipation?   You know there is not.   By the love you owe your race— by all the sacred ties of family and home—by every instinct of a superior nature—you would be restrained from perpetrating so iniquitous an act; an act which would sweep away in one overwhelming flood of an-archy and barbarism every trace of civilization, as well as every semblance of law and order.   And do you suppose the Yeomen of our Southern States are not rational and reflecting beings like yourselves?   Al-though not so learned as some others, they yet possess the hearts of men, of fathers and husbands, and they know as well as any political economist of you all, that their own class, in the event of emancipation, would suffer the most of all classes in the South, unless we ex-cept the negroes themselves.   For the Southern Gen-tleman would soon convert his property into cash, as did the wealthier planters of Jamaica, and immediately retire to some more congenial soil to enjoy his *otium cum dignitate.*   So, too, the thrifty Middle Classes would retire to the present Free States, and begin business in a different line ; but the Yeomen would be forced to remain and single-handed do battle with Cuffee, who, no longer forced to labor, and resorting again to toad-eating and cannibalism for the food necessary to sustain life, would in a few years reproduce on the shores of the New World a second Africa, all except the lions and elephants, the sandy deserts, and the anacondas.

And yet there are men in the North, claiming to be honorable, members of the Church, too, who are laboring to bring about such a catastrophe! Can any reasoning being doubt the motives which instigate such persons? We speak of the leaders of the abolition fanaticism, not of the rank and file who follow the former, to use an expression of Sam Weller's, "as a tame monkey does a horgan." But of the spirit which instigates the leaders in the blind crusade against Negro Slavery, the following facts speak with an eloquence more potent than words:

Near the close of the winter of 1857, the Rev. Wm. D. Chadick, of Huntsville, Ala., at the instance of S. D. Cabaniss, Esq., and S. C. Townsend, visited Ohio, for the purpose of selecting a home for a number of slaves belonging to the estate of Samuel Townsend, deceased, and who, according to his last will, were to be liberated and settled in some Free State. While in Ohio on this business, Mr. Chadick called on Gov. S. P. Chase, one of the lights of the Republican party.

" I was received by the Governor," says Mr. Chadick, "with apparent cordiality; and received from him much information in regard to the various negro schools and colonies, etc., in the State. But to my utter astonishment, Gov. Chase closed his conversation on the subject by remarking, with emphasis, that for his part, he would rather never see another free negro set his foot upon Ohio soil! I asked his reason. '*Because,*' said he, '*their moral influence is degrading.*' I then remarked that it appeared to me a glaring inconsistency in him and others in Ohio, to love our Southern slaves so much as to desire their freedom, and clamor for their emancipation, and yet hate them so much as to be unwilling to allow them a home in their own State; especially so, since, by the existing laws in the Slave States, the negro can not be liberated and remain where he is. He replied: ' I DO NOT WISH THE SLAVE EMAN-CIPATED BECAUSE I LOVE HIM, BUT BECAUSE I HATE HIS MASTER—I HATE SLAVERY—I HATE A MAN THAT WILL OWN A SLAVE.' "

Comment is unnecessary.

CHAPTER VI.

"From love of grace,
Lay not the flatt'ring unction to your soul,
That not your trespass, but my madness speaks;
It will but skin and film the ulc'rous place;
Whilst rank corruption, mining all within,
Infects unseen: confess yourself to heaven;
Repent what's past, avoid what is to come;
And do not spread the compost on the weeds
To make them ranker."

HAMLET.

NOT Plug Uglies and Rip Raps do we purpose to
discourse about at this time, gentle reader, for such
doughty shoulder-hitters and short-boys are not the
nceessary out-growth of Southern institutions, but only
vegetate in the purlieus of the cities of the South, just
as Dead Rabbits, *et id omne genus* of outcasts and vagabonds, grow up within the shadows of the marble palaces, gothic churches, and iron front five-storied ware-
houses of the cities of the North. But there is in most
of the Southern States a species of Bully entirely distinct from the above—a swearing, tobacco-chewing,
brandy drinking Bully, whose chief delight is to hang
about the doors of village groggeries and tavern tap-
rooms, to fight chicken cocks, to play Old Sledge, or

pitch-and-toss, chuck-a-luck, and the like, as well as to
encourage dog-fights, and occasionally to get up a little
raw-head-and-bloody-bones affair on his own account.
This is the Southern Bully *par excellence*, for in all the
world else his exact counterpart is no where to be found.
Ay, and a valiant Southerner is he too! No Giddings
of the North, no fiery Greeley ever felt one half so able
to thrash the trembling South into meek submission, (if
we are to credit their vaporing bravado while standing
out of harm's way,) as does the Southern Bully at all
times feel able and prepared—cocked and primed, in
his own vernacular—to flog the entire North; with his
tongue, that is, and very conveniently while the poor
North has her back turned. Thunder and bludgeons!
how he'd like to get at 'em, the crazy old milk-sops!
Split the Union? By all means, let her rip, the cussed
old concern! Yankees fight! Blamnation, man, we'd
lam 'em afore they could say Jack Robinson—we'd
put 'em through a course of sprouts in short order, so
we would! Ah! Messrs. abolitionists, you have your
lessons to learn yet, despite your eminent talent for
vaporing and vituperation. And truly we know of no
more competent instructor whom we could commend
to you than the Southern Bully: but in the kindness
of our heart now in advance, Messrs. abolitionists, we
warn you to beware of your instructor's ferule, beware
of his limber-jack; for he will cane you and cowskin
you, before even you, however nimble of tongue, will
be able to say, *Jack Robinson.*

However, since the Southern Bully is eminently the
production of the dram-shop or Southern groggery,
perhaps we can not do better than to describe, first, this

peculiar institution—a most devilish man-trap which daily ensnares its thousands—before proceeding to discuss the merits, or demerits, whichever you please, of the Southern Bully himself.

Now, as we all know, the temples devoted to the service of the Demon Alcohol in these United States, are Legion; and every where, all over the land, in cities and towns, in the most retired hamlets, and at every cross-roads, the independent Sovereigns of America exercise without let or hindrance the glorious privilege of getting beastly, senselessly, and riproariously drunk at their own royal will and pleasure. It is true, fair skeptic, and pity 'tis 'tis true. Have you read the report of the trustees of the Binghamton Inebriate Asylum? Even before the building is up, twenty-eight hundred applications, and among them three judges, twelve editors, *twenty-eight clergymen*, thirty-six physicians, forty-two lawyers, and, strangest and saddest of all, *four hundred and ten women in the upper circles of society!* But the most of these unfortunates would feel insulted did you accuse them of entering a rum-hole, a vulgar rum-hole! No, they keep a private shrine in their own homes, and they seek to bury their guilt and shame in fine houses and costly display of one kind and another. But the poor, alas! they must resort to the filthy, demoralizing rum-holes; for, laying aside all cant and all mere sermonizing, even the most casual observer can not fail to regret, deeply and sincerely regret, the wholesale destruction of morals, of honesty, of patriotism, of family affection, of domestic peace and domestic comforts, nay, of life itself, daily wrought in our midst by those terrible sinks of iniquity commonly called *dram-shops.*

10*

These are the bane of our great Republic, of the Free States as well as of the Slave. In all their protean shapes —whether as gilded saloon, or tempting bar, or polka-free-concert-and-free-cyprian Bier Keller, or reeking-groggery—they are but the visible "gates of hell," leading inevitably and surely into the jaws of a moral, if not always a physical, death. In the cities are to be found the worst specimens, for in such congregate indiscriminately wharf-rats, thieves, burglars, pimps, pickpockets, policemen, ward politicians, free negroes, and (alas! alas!) those Pariahs of our civilized society, those poor outcast wantons, whose miserable lives of crime and blasphemy, of lust and sottishness, are so harrowing to every honest man's soul to contemplate. However, in our Southern States (and of these alone do we now wish to speak) there is in the country and village groggeries enough of villainy and soul-murder, without the addition of pimps, thieves, pickpockets, degraded females, and the like abandoned characters, who mostly throng the liquor-dens of all cities, and support by the earnings of their infamy the sinful cause of murderous Alcohol.

A groggery-keeper in the South is usually a man of uncultivated mind, devoid of principle, habitually a blasphemer and Sabbath-breaker, a reviler of religion, and is sometimes also an abolitionist—owing to his secret traffic with the slaves, of which more anon. He is usually stout of person, being bloated from constant imbibing, and possesses a coarse beard, a blotched and otherwise spotted face, a red nose, hard, cold, watery and inflamed eyes, a dirty and badly fitting dress from crown to sole; and in speech is low, vulgar and obscene, a retailer of stale jests and disgusting stories of scandal and intrigue, and with every sentence belches forth from his accursed throat oaths and blasphemy.

The Southern groggery is usually a small wooden building, with two rooms; one intended for a sleeping room but used mostly for playing cards in, and the other devoted to the retailing of ardent spirits. His "sperrits" the groggery-keeper buys in Cincinnati chiefly, getting his rum however from New-England, though in both cases at second-hand of course; for the ordinary groggery-keeper rarely is able to go so far for the purchase of his wares. His usual custom is, to procure his whisky and rum from some wholesale liquor-dealer in the nearest large town to his domicil. Given the whisky, or neutral spirit preferred, he proceeds to manufacture his own wines and brandies from recipes furnished by dealers in New-York, who promise (we have seen their precious circulars) to forward the desired information on the reception of twenty dollars. The remainder of his liquors he mixes pretty thoroughly with wholesome water, and with unwholesome ingredients of some other description designed to give the requisite strength. Log-wood, juniper berries, dog-leg tobacco, and even strychnine, are all said to be used; and, owing to their different effects, have originated the expressive names of "bust-head," "rifle-whisky," "tangle-foot," "red-eye," and "blue-ruin." The water, however, luckily for the drinkers of the vile stuff, predominates not unfrequently, and we have heard of instances, even in the mild latitude of Mississippi, where genuine Old Rye has been known to *freeze* during a cold snap!

Of course the groggery-keeper's profits are enormous, provided he gets much custom. It requires very little figuring to prove this. Thus, B buys a barrel of A No. 1 whisky, takes out one half—which he converts, by an ingenious process known only to the initiated, into the most delightful old Cognac, genuine *eau de vie* —and supplies its place from the nearest well or spring, adding a modicum of pepper, dog-leg tobacco, strychnine, or what not, all of which, however, cost very little. He sells his brandy at so much the gallon or bottle, and his adulterated whisky for just double what it cost him. So you see he can afford to drink one half his liquors himself; if he can only dispose of the remaining half, he will still make money hand over fist, as he delights to express himself. The trouble is, there is no lack of competition in such a profitable business, and so our groggery-keeper has to keep a sharp look-out for customers. Luckily for him, he is surrounded by thieving blacks, who are always glad of an opportunity to exchange their master's meal, their mistress' poultry, or the neighbors' pigs, for a bottle of New-England rum, or a jug of Ohio whisky. Certainly the slave-owners object to such high-handed proceedings, flog the slaves whenever they detect them in any of their rogueries, or even when they find the poor fellows have gotten lawfully drunk on their honest savings, and crop the hair of the sinning liquor-sellers, feeding and housing them beside at the expense of the State, and robing them in the livery of convicted crime. But liquor is no respecter of persons or color, and the blackamoor who has once been under the dire influence of the Worm of the Still, like his infatuated white brother who is similarly situated, runs greedily into the very jaws of the reptile on every opportunity, and remaineth unsatisfied till he findeth himself swallowed entire, both body and breeches. Hence the Southern slaves always contrive, either by hook or by crook, to carry on their nefarious but secret traffic, often exchanging a whole porker, worth from five to ten dollars, for a single bottle of rum, worth intrinsically perhaps not more than fifty cents. But, if you consider how that the porker costs the darkey only the trouble of killing and cleaning it, and that the midnight purchaser runs the risk of the penitentiary every time he closes such a bargain, you will agree with us that, if any thing, the black man gets the best end of the trade. The good New-England rum will warm up the poor fellow's inner man and help to cheer him on his "journey frou' de wilderness," much more effectually than all that wordy sympathy so lavishly expended in his behalf by New-England orators in their heated harangues against his oppressors; while, if the worst comes to the worst, he will only have to undergo a flagellation at the hands of the overseer, by order of his master, or at the hands of the constable, by order of a Justice of the Peace—and there an end.

The extent to which this species of traffic is carried on would stagger credulity, even in the minds of the Southern people themselves. It is usually conducted in so secret a manner, that only occasionally are the miscreants detected in a way to furnish legal evidence of their guilt. Negro testimony is no where admissible against a white man in the South, and even if it were, the negroes would suffer almost any species of torture

before they would " peach ;" for those of them who engage in the traffic are generally the greatest devils on
the neighboring plantations, the greatest liars, the big-
gest rogues, as well as the most quarrelsome with their
fellow-slaves, and are so wedded to the love of liquor,
that it becomes to them a kind of necessity, a second
nature so to speak. Such fellows have the shrewdness
to know, if they were to inform on one groggery-keeper, they could never more obtain the confidence of another, and thus would have their grog cut off for all
time—a consummation by no means wished for, and to
which they would almost prefer death itself. Besides,
whenever two criminals have the same terrible secret to
keep, there is sure to spring up a sympathy betwixt
them ; hence, there is a real sympathy between the slaves
and the groggery-keepers, and this is why the latter are
sometimes abolitionists. These reason that, let the negroes only be emancipated, and their idleness will soon
force them more and more to the dram-shop, while
their facilities for robbing hen-roosts and pig-sties would
not be in the least diminished; and hence, like as Den-
nis, the public hangman, in Barnaby Rudge, aided in
the Lord Gordon riots simply because his own horrible
trade would thereby come into more request, so the
Southern groggery-keeper, that his own business might
thrive, would willingly aid in the overthrow of the
prosperity of the whole South, and would rejoice to see
her present teeming fields become one desolate wilderness.

And here will we pause a single moment, to address
a few words of friendly advice to the ultra abolitionists
of the North. Why, gentle Sirs, do you not more fre-

quently take the Southern groggery-keepers into your councils? Why do you not initiate them into your secret plots for fostering negro insurrections, for poisoning, maiming, and murdering the white families of the South, burning down their dwellings and laying waste their estates, in order that, as one of your leaders has declared, "you may laugh when their fear cometh?" It is known to a few, and suspected by a great number of American citizens, that you have your secret emissaries all through the Southern States, bound by secret obligations to carry out your nefarious and Catilinian conspiracies; and we ask you in all seriousness, why do you not enlist the Southern groggery-keepers under your black banner? They will prove the most efficient allies you can possibly hit upon. They know how to intrigue with the slaves, and to worm out family secrets, far better than those lank-jawed, thin-lipped, sharp-nosed, and bespectacled governesses whom you now use for that purpose; and they can tell you who are the most reckless, daring, villainous, and discontented of the negro men, with much greater precision than can those ostensible clock-menders, book-peddlers, and other Yankee foot-passengers generally, who are at the present time sneaking about from house to house in the Southern States, sharing the hospitality of the planters by day, and plotting with the slaves at night as to the best means by which a righteous and Christian insurrection may be inaugurated. Moreover, *whisky* is the most potent charm you could make use of to influence the negroes themselves; for we verily believe one good rousing dram would put more life and daring in their hearts than all the homilies ever preached by the political divines of the North, or all the bloody tracts ever published by the Secret Committee of the Massachusetts B. M. F. Society.

So much for the groggery-keepers and their groggeries—in which latter the Southern Bully so delights to lounge and drink, drink and lounge, and lounge and drink again, until he is fitly prepared for bets, brawls, oaths, blasphemies, quarrels, bruises, stabbings, shootings, manslaughters, murders; for in all these things he is more or less an adept. But the village groggery is not the only place loved and patronized by the Southern Bully. He haunts the village tavern equally as much—that is to say, when it is provided with a bar.

The village tavern is proverbially a dreary, dull, and ennui-begetting place, in all parts of the world, and is none the less so in the South, except on occasions. On occasions it becomes a sort of pandemonium, as the reader will presently learn. Most usually, when off the public highway and removed far from the routes of frequent travel, the establishment used as a tavern in all small Southern villages is nothing better than an old tumble-down shanty, the proprietor of which is a miserable old guzzler himself, coarse, ignorant, and vulgar, and quite indigent in circumstances—what little he makes being derived more from the sale of liquors at the bar than from any patronage of the travelling public. Indeed, a "solitary horseman" even, or other wayfaring man, hardly makes his appearance once in six months. Hence, the village Boniface makes no preparation for the entertainment of strangers, and in consequence keeps the vilest of vermin-habited beds, the mustiest of feathers, and the dirtiest of bed-linen;

while the floors of all the rooms are bare, the walls are bare, the chairs are rickety, the window-shutters are ragged in the extreme, and rattle and bang unceasingly at the sport of the wind; and the whole is looked after by a single slovenly wanton of a negro-wench, who is both chambermaid, cook, and scullion generally, and is besides a most brazen-faced, impudent hussy, (rendered so by the too frequent interchange of favors with the village bucks, and the overseers of adjoining plantations,) who will wink a modest man out of countenance any day.

The most profitable customer who ever patronizes the village Boniface of the South is the Horse or Hog Drover, wending his way from Virginia, Kentucky, Tennessee, Missouri, or North-Carolina, with his herds of wheezing swine, or droves of blooded horses and sleek mane-cropped, tail-cropped mules, to the more southerly latitudes, where such animals are always in demand at high prices. Since, however, the introduction of railways into most of the Southern States, hog-drovers do not so often patronize the village taverns as formerly, preferring to transport their herds to market by rail. Both the hog-drovers and the horse-drovers belong usually to the class of Yeomen, and are industrious but plain, plodding people—we mean when they raise their own animals, and merely drive them to the extreme South for a better market. For those of them who are not producers, but merely traders, afford some of the most illustrious examples of the native Southern Yankee to be found in the entire South. This is especially true of the horse-drovers; and it is on the occasion of a visit from these that the village tavern is for a while the scene of much bustle and activity, and becomes, as we expressed a few paragraphs back, a very pandemonium for noise and strife.

And here we may as well confess, we have no sympathy with horse-jockeys the world over. We have had our share of dealings with them, in both the North and the South, and we flatter ourself that we always succeeded in coming out of every such encounter, a "sadder but a wiser man." They are such a voluble, smooth-tongued, plausible race of miscreants, we do believe they could persuade an unsophisticated purchaser that black is white, or that any old broken-down, wind-galled, spavined, colicky, and otherwise generally used-up piece of horse-flesh, is a perfect paragon of equine cleverness—nimble as a cricket, gentle as a lamb, fleet as a reindeer, and possessing all the blood of all the best Arabians; and yet sold for never a fault in the world, and always at a sacrifice!

The Southern horse-jockey varies somewhat from the usual type, but chiefly in his outward man only; for inwardly he is ever the same sly, cunning fox, and thinks it a monstrous noble action to get the better of a credulous purchaser in a sale, and the very apotheosis of wit and shrewdness to swindle a poor countryman in a swap. He is usually unlettered, and in consequence despises your book-learning and all that such learning bestows upon its possessor; is rough in manners, and rude in speech, being much given to the use of slang expressions; never makes a wry face at a glass of any kind of grog; smokes an old rusty pipe incessantly; chews Virginia tobacco of the blackest and strongest brands; spits at random on every person and

every thing that comes within his reach; wears Kentucky "jeans;" swears roundly and all the time; tells
all manner of tough "yarns;" domineers over those of
his own class in worldly position; looks with a sort of
awe coupled with envy upon the Southern Gentleman,
but fairly bows his head to the ground in the presence
of the Cotton Snob. Do you demand why the fellow
does this last? Ask rather, why corrupt ward politicians are in such favor with our incorruptible Statesmen; or why the tradespeople on Broadway are so full
of genuflections at the appearance of gouty old Bullion,
the great millionaire; or why New-York saloon-keep-
ers are so loud in their praises of those youthful Fifth-
Avenoodles, who are wasting their patrimony in such
hot haste by means of their fast horses, fast women, and
riotous living, as well as every other species of folly
that a plethoric purse and an empty noddle conjoined
can devise—and you will have your answer: SELF-IN-
TEREST. It is the Cotton Snob who usually pays his
five hundred or his thousand dollars for his two-forty
nag. It is the Cotton Snob who suffers himself to be
flattered and cajoled by the cunning dealer in horse-
flesh, until he feels himself grown so large in his own
conceit as to imagine that his personal dignity, and the
dignity of his social position, both imperatively demand
that he should possess a *splendid rig* — none of your
ordinary concerns suited only to gratify the taste and
the financial credit of a Muggins. And do you suppose, generous operator on Wall-street, that the Southern horse-jockey, though clothed all in russet and wearing his pantaloons inside his boot-legs, is yet any less
shrewd than yourself to "watch the corners"—to look

after number One ? Note how eagerly the fellow pricks up his ears so as to catch every word the Cotton Snob may utter, ready always to make a flattering rejoinder, the obsequious slave ! Note how he affects to be amiably and confidingly drunk, plying all the while with the strongest of strong waters the poor pigeon he intends to pluck, until to save his soul the silly fool can not tell whether he carries his own shallow head on his shoulders or some body else's ; and how affectionately he locks arms with the drunken booby, and, as they two totter and stagger down the village street, endeavors to out-sing his thick-voiced companion, who only expresses himself distinctly at each return of the chorus. Yet there is all the time in the scheming horse-jockey's eye a cold, clear, snake-like gleam of cunning calculation, which proclaims to even the dullest observer how great is the sham he is perpetrating. So true—so true :

"The fox barks not, when he would steal the lamb !"

In view of the unusual flow of custom which his bar receives on such occasions, no wonder the village Boniface is all aglow with delight, (as well as mean whisky,) when the horse-drover makes his appearance, and demands entertainment for man and beast. Besides being enabled to get rid of his many times diluted and adulterated liquors, selling the same to the horse-jockeys, snobs, bullies, and the regular village topers and loungers, whom the occasion leads to assemble about the village bar-room ; he also succeeds in disposing of his musty corn and worthless fodder, to feed the

animals which the drovers have for sale. Wherefore,
in high spirits, our village Boniface blusters noisily
about, now here, now there, swearing all the time like
a trooper, looking withal very magisterial and self-im-
portant, and ready to turn up a glass with every new
comer; until he pretty soon feels " o'er a' the ills o'
life victorious," and is then about as jolly an old dog
of a landlord as ever wagged tongue against a " chaw"
of plug tobacco.

But, even in the midst of so much lying, drinking,
fighting, and cheating, there is much to be witnessed
that is both entertaining and diverting. It is nearly
always in the winter season that the horse-drovers take
their animals South ; when the evenings are long, and
even a village bar-room fire, built up of glowing hickory logs, despite the rough company and the big-bellied
black bottles frowning darkly in the shadowy background, sends a cheerful thrill through the frame, and
disposes even the most unsocial to merry-making and
fun. Hence, when the evening shades begin to appear,
having first supped and then attended to their horses,
the drovers consider that the day's labors are finished,
and feel prepared to devote the evening wholly to social pleasures. So " mine host" has a roaring big fire
built up in the broad fire-place of the bar-room, and
ensconcing himself snugly in the chimney corner, with
a well-filled pipe in his mouth, waits anxiously for the
story-telling to begin—for yarn-spinning is usually the
chief feature of the evening's entertainment. Pretty
soon assemble the village groggery-keepers, and all
the loose young bucks about town, two or three of the
drovers, a Cotton Snob or so about 'alf and 'alf, and

may be, some rattling, hare-brained son of a neighboring gentleman, whose untamed spirit is not sufficiently
under parental control, and whose mother is ignorant
of the fact that her darling " is out." These all arrange
themselves on cane-seated chairs about the blazing fire,
after the most democratic fashion, some with heels over
their heads, and others reclining in the laps of their
friends; while the body-servants of the wealthy young-
sters present, together with the traipsing tavern wench
before alluded to, stand grinning and giggling in the
door-way, (they rarely close doors during winter in the
far South,) occasionally emitting a loud guffaw, accompanied by a slap of the palm on the thigh, and a sway-
ing back of the entire body, just as some exquisitely
laughable yarn has been reeled off by any one of the
story-telling revellers within.   Nor is it long before all
ideas of caste are forgotten; and as the fire blazes
brighter and brighter, and the bottle begins to circle
more freely, and the jests and laughter become more
and more uproarious, whites and blacks guffawing and
huzzaing in chorus, no wonder the hours glide unper-
ceived away; and often it is long after midnight before
the merry wassailers retire to bed.

Such, then, are the usual resorts in which the Southern Bully delights to squander away the precious hours
of life: namely, the village groggery and the village
tavern.   And now, reader, having introduced you to his
haunts, we shall next proceed to show you what sort of
person the Southern Bully is himself.   And, *imprimis*,
he is not necessarily always poor.   Sometimes he boasts
of extensive estates, though not often, and then chiefly
when he is young; for as he grows old, his wealth seems

to take wings and fly away, so rapidly is it squandered. But as a general thing he is poor; and we shall therefore proceed first to speak of the seedy Southern Bully, and in conclusion will have a word to say about his wealthy *confrère* and fellow roysterer.

The poor Southern Bully, in nine cases out of ten, is a loafering ex-overseer, whose drunken dissolute habits have lost him his situation, as well as the character that would enable him to procure another. When not an ex-overseer, he is either a disgraced dry-goods clerk, a bankrupt groggery-keeper who has poured all his liquors down his own throat, or else the quondam rich Bully in the era of his decline. The poor Bully's dress is usually loose-fitting, dirty, tobacco-stained, liquor-stained, and grease-stained. His hat is woolen, with a limp flapping brim, battered crown, dirty and fuzzy, and on the whole might be called a shocking bad hat. His hair is habitually matted and unkempt, being in most instances of the Saxon peculiarity, that is, either red, or flaxen, or carroty-colored, or sandy. His beard is coarse and unkempt like his hair, and grows in great luxuriance all over his face, or else in ragged patches here and there, intended to represent imperials, mustaches, "literary dabs," and the like precious ornaments of the civilized man. His breath is foul with all diabolical scents—rum, filth, tobacco— just such a breath as you can inhale any day in any police-court the world over, and which once inhaled, you will ever more pray that it shall not come betwixt you and the wind again. But his speech is fouler than his breath. He can out-swear a special policeman; can out-lie a Toombs lawyer; can use more obscene language than the vilest pimp who ever laid snares to entrap lecherous countrymen; and can utter more blasphemy in a single hour than could the whole mess of Rutland Reformers in a week, assisted by all the black spirits and white, blue spirits and gray, who annually assemble in some one of the Free States, for the purpose of putting down the Bible and our Federal Constitution. It is wonderful, indeed, what a gift of gab the fellow possesses; what a multitude of strange and agglomerated oaths he can interlard his discourse with, and how he manages to survive'the constant damnings he is ever heaping upon every hair upon his head, and every bone in his body; verily, it surpasses belief! Oh! to see him at a chicken-fight—when there are game-cocks in the pit, and the bets range from one to five dollars! We tell you, Sir, it is sublime—the swearing and profanity he can give utterance to—perfectly sublime, so wholly is it beyond the conception of less depraved and more scrupulous minds! But if to see him at a cock-fight is glorious, to see him looking on at a dog-fight—bull-dogs, with cropped ears, stump tails, bow legs, and most villainous chops—is more glorious still, while most glorious of all, grandest of all, most inspiring of all, is, to witness the conduct of the Southern Bully, as he stands outside the imaginary ring in which is being waged a bloody *man-fight!* O thou soul-stirring spectacle! Hip, hip, hurrah! See, with what a gentlemanly grace Jones bungs up Smith's peepers! See, with what a sweet smile Smith plucks away half of Jones' yellow beard! How comfortable must have been that "left" which Jones let fly into Smith's bread-basket! How refreshing to the sight the claret fountain

so unceremoniously started from Jones' mug by the noble Smith! Hurrah for Jones! Hurrah for Smith!
Go in, boys! Let 'er rip! Never say die! Hit 'im
agin! Dam—! Y-a-a-a-a-ou! Ugh-h-h! O-o-o-o-oh!
And the glorious work is done!

And yet you still advocate human bondage? Pray,
thou good motherly soul, what has human bondage to
do with such scenes? You miserable old woman, why
do you always discover an African in the fence, let one
turn whithersoever he may? Only go, worthy madam,
into your own tenant houses, poor-houses, work-houses,
groggeries, brothels, and the like nurseries of vice and
infamy, and you will soon discover that the real cause
of such human debasement, is not the kind of bondage
to which you allude, but is that wickeder bondage of
the soul which leads man a willing captive, bound and
manacled, into the very camps and courts of the devil.
To say nothing of other Northern cities, how many
murders were committed in New-York alone during
the year of grace 1858? *Sixty-six;* or at least we find
that set down as the number in the public journals.
But we hang the murderers in the Free North. You do?
How many were hanged during the year of grace 1858,
in the above-mentioned city of New-York? ONE;
and he, poor fellow, for a little more would have been
pardoned by the kind, and amiable, and soft-hearted
Governor. Query, are not all such Governors a little
soft in the head as well as in the heart?

We tell you, thou venerable grandam, it's all bosh.
The South is no more a heathen country than the
North. You, O mother of Israel, have bullies all
around you, thieves all around you, murderers all

11

around you, *et id*, etc. etc. ; and when you lift up your hands in such holy horror at the shortcomings of your neighbors, you only make yourself an object of pity in the sight of the truly wise, and in the sight of God a hypocrite and Pharisee.   Indeed, we think we may safely assert, that the South, in some particulars, even has an advantage over the North ; for, however coarse, vulgar, brutal, and besotted the Southern Bully may be, still he is rarely ever a downright thief, and seldom murders in cold blood, and never attempts to make a dishonest livelihood by swindling the innocent and helpless—widows, and fatherless girls, and the like. But, according to the statistics and estimates of the New-York *Tribune*, in the one city of New-York alone, about fourteen thousand persons make annually nearly sixteen millions of dollars in the various walks of crime and vice, for which our leading metropolis is so infamous.   Moreover, although we do not pretend to gainsay that the Southern Bully is a miserable nuisance in every sense, as well as a disgrace to civilization, and all that, we yet stoutly maintain that he is a greater enemy to himself than to any other person, and for wickedness does not begin to compare with those swindlers in high places—the Schuylers, Huntingtons, and other *gentlemen* of the like kidney, presidents of banks, coal companies, railroad corporations, et cetera, et cetera ; who are every day growing rich on the hard earnings of the poor, pilfering from the day laborers, and absolutely stealing the little savings intrusted to them by toiling servant-girls ; and yet who continue to be smiled upon by " our best society," and are allowed the ineffable privilege of snoring in our most orthodox and fashionable churches. Neither is the poor Southern Bully to be compared for meanness to the rich Southern Bully, of whom we come now to say a few words; for the poor Southern Bully can plead in extenuation of his shortcomings the temptations of poverty and ignorance, as well as the lack of any refining associations or surroundings; which is not the case with his rich fellow-drunkard, fellow-gambler, fellow-blackguard, fellow-libertine, and fellow-brawler, since the latter *could* be a gentleman if he *would*.

This style of Southern Bully is found more often in the Cotton States, than elsewhere; which is owing to the fact, that fortunes are more frequently made in those States than in any others, by ignorant men— overseers, negro traders, and others of a similar class. For it is the son of the vilest of the Southern Yankees, who usually, no matter how great his wealth may be, does not even approach the comparative respectability of a Cotton Snob, but is nothing more nor less than a bully—an ignorant, purse-proud, self-conceited, guzzling, fox-hunting, blaspheming, slave-whipping, uproarious, vulgar fellow! who is at all times as willing and ready to pink a fellow-being as to wing a pheasant, or to shoot a hare. Even if sent to college, (which sometimes does happen, since his father, however ignorant, is yet anxious that his son shall know more than himself,) he seldom learns any thing from books, and cares for nothing but his daily drams, his cocktails, and brandy-straights, his pistols and his cards, his dogs and his sooty mistress, and, greatest knave of all, himself! While at college, however, he lives extravagantly, though but meanly supplied with funds by his miserly parent; and, as a matter of course, is always over head and ears in debt. But wo to the poor tradesman who menaces him with a bill! The Honorable Algernon Percy Deuceace, worthy scion of the noble house of Crabbs, knew not better how to brain a dunning tailor or starving cobbler, than does the warm-hearted noble-souled Southern Bully, of *good* family and *respectable* standing. And as for presenting one of the son's bills to his miserly father, were we an honest storekeeper, we should much prefer to bear in patience with the wrath of the hot-headed juvenile, than to run the risk of encountering the supercilious frowns of his honorable sire.

When the rich Southern Bully comes into the possession of his estates, his first care is to fill his cellars (in case he has any, otherwise his store-room) with barrels of Old Rye, as well as brandy, gin, rum, and other kinds of strong waters, but rarely with any thing in the shape of wine. Wine may do for babes, but not for such a puissant gentleman as he fancies himself to be. Having laid in his stock of liquors, he proceeds immediately to gather about him a set of boon companions like himself—idle loafers, drunken overseers, and may be one or two other fellows of like kidney; and now he devotes his nights to gaming, drinking, and coarse libertinism, and his days to fox-hunting, horse-racing, and the like. Ah! thou blot on the fair escutcheon of the South, what a rabble is it indeed dangles ever at your heels! How they yell, and whoop, and halloo, louder than the deep-baying hounds, while they pursue the manly old English sport! One would almost fancy the whole of Bedlam had broke loose, so great is the confusion they create. And as they ride crashing and dashing through the thick underbush in the wide-reaching stretches of Southern woodlands, or through the tangled mosses which hang in festoons from the cypresses of the swamps, you will observe not infrequently two bottles of different kinds of liquors, dangling, one on either side, from the pommel of the Southern Bully's saddle— from each of which he drinks by turns, between every swallow shouting furiously, tally ho! tantivy! to his hounds, and waves to his liegemen to follow on, so that they may all be "in at the death."

Like the Cotton Snob, the rich Southern Bully is great on horse-flesh. His conversation runs chiefly on dogs and horses, horse-trappings and the like; and he himself much affects jockey caps, and other sporting articles of costume, and fills his house with wood-cuts of all the celebrated racers, as well as with whips, saddles, bridles, spurs, etc. etc. Besides, from associating so constantly with jockeys and grooms, he soon learns all the slang phrases peculiar to jockeydom, and rattles them off most volubly on all occasions; for his groveling conception of what constitutes a well-bred gentleman, never allows of his looking to any thing beyond a shrewd dealer in horse-flesh. Hence, he will tell you that he wants no scallywags about him—no *short stock*, as he delights to characterize all horses of unrecognized or uncertain pedigree. He must have the full blood or none; and in consequence his stables are filled with racers, trotters, natural pacers, and saddle and harness horses without number, all of undoubted descent from some imported stallion, and any one of which he will back against the world for almost any stake you shall name. Hence, he is all the time running his crack nags against the crack nags of the sponging worthies who dangle always at his heels; nor does he allow any of the public races near him to come off without his being in attendance, together with his horses, grooms, and motley crowd of retainers. Of course he loses money in the end; as who does not that follows the turf any length of time? But, in addition to his losses from bets, he loses also from the negligent carelessness with which his plantation and negroes are looked after; for how can these be expected to thrive, when he keeps his overseer all the time with himself, and more than half the time drunk? Moreover, to cap the whole, he is ever losing money at cards: for, if he plays in his own old tumble-down dwelling, he loses there; and if he plays in the little back-room to the village groggery, he loses there; and if he plays in the tap-room of the village tavern, with the horse-jockeys and other equally honest, hearty blades, he loses there too, since, poor ignorant simpleton! he is always fuddled with rum or brandy, and falls therefore an easy prey to every sharper who crosses his path. When, however, he has played out his last card; when he suddenly wakes up out of his sottish stupor, to find himself a thriftless beggar; when he sees the auctioneer crying off his paternal acres and the lazy blacks, (for whom he never entertained one half as much sympathy as he still cherishes for his blooded horses, that are also now snatched from him by the officers of the law,) his wits seem to return to him in a measure, and pretty soon he becomes a peripatetical blackleg, gambling for a livelihood. He travels on the river steamboats mostly, and lives by plucking all such poor pigeons as remind him of his former self; else, acts as a decoy to entice such verdants to play, so that keener sharpers may do the plucking, dividing with him the spoil. Any man who has travelled much on the Mississippi, or the Alabama, or the Red, or the Arkansas, or any other of our Southern rivers, can not fail to have noted the rich Southern Bully in this particular stage of his decline and fall. He must not be confounded, however, with the keenest and most adroit of such peripatetic *chevaliers d'industrie ;* for these are nearly always foreigners, or else have served their apprenticeship to crime in some one of our large cities. The Southern Bully is not so polished or self-possessed as all such precious scamps usually are ; and is besides so constantly addicted to ardent spirits, that his face is full of blotches, and has not that genteel pallor and thoughtfulness of expression so characteristic of the regularly-bred gambler.

But in a very few years we miss the Southern Bully on the river steamers, and must either search for him in an untimely grave, or else far out on the South-western frontier. Here he chases after buffaloes and Indians, and shoots wild cats and Comanches with equal nonchalance; and astonishes with the boastful narratives of his former exploits, the simple-minded backwoodsmen — those rude American vi-kings who wear leather breeches and buckskin shirts, and live by following the chase ; but who are honest and rudely chivalrous, though unschooled in the arts of civilized life, all of which they as heartily contemn and despise, as did those ancient barbaric heroes of the Niebelungen Lied. Wearying after a while, however, of this no-madic life, the Southern Bully makes yet another change, and as a last resort turns fillibuster. Like Cortez in Mexico, or Pizarro in Peru, or the English in India, or the French in Algeria; he seeks by plun-dering and pillaging a helpless people, to make up for his past losses, as well as to bury in the excitement of adventure and the changeful fortunes of the tented field, all remembrances of a past life, misspent, squan-dered, and most wickedly wasted in riot and dissipa-tion.

And here let us remark, in conclusion, for all such emprises the Southern Bully is eminently the right man in the right place; and it is much to be regretted that so many far better men and truer gentlemen, have been misled to consort with him in his hazardous and unlawful enterprises. For, although we feel persuaded the United States will, purely in self-defense, be com-pelled at no distant day to seize on Cuba, Mexico, and all Central America, we yet think when that time does arrive, it will then be plenty soon to rid the Republic of these pestilent, quarrelsome fellows, who now infest both the North and the South, and whose room is much more desirable than their company. Ah! when the hour for action comes, how admirably will it serve us to pit such dawdling, lazy drones, against the still more worthless raggamuffins who possess, only to abuse, those fertile and highly-productive lands lying along our Southern boundary. What a poetical justice will that be—the allowing the miserable riff-raff and rabble of both communities to kill one another off, and thereby make room for the honest workers.

> " So, neighbor confines, purge you of your scum ;
>   Have you a ruffian that will swear, drink, dance,
>   Revel the night; rob, murder, and commit
>   The oldest sins the newest kinds of ways ?
>   Be happy, he will trouble you no more !"

Let us not disguise the fact, however, that it is painful to every virtuous or Christian mind to reflect, that such happy results are only to be consummated by such unhappy adventures. So, also, it is painful exceedingly to look upon a gallows ; or to gaze into the iron-barred windows of a Sing Sing or a Newgate ? Yet these all have their necessary uses ; and so too have those. For, in man's present transitory and changeful state, wars, pestilences, and famines, though usually regarded as scourges, are in reality only blessings in disguise.

11*

CHAPTER VII.

POOR WHITE TRASH.

" The ways of Heaven are dark and intricate,
  Puzzled in mazes, and perplexed with errors ;
  Our understanding traces them in vain,
  Lost and bewildered in the fruitless search ;
  Nor sees with how much art the windings run,
  Nor where the regular confusion ends."

ADDISON.

THE intelligent student of history needs not to be
informed that the peasants of Western Europe and the
British Isles, the descendants of the vassals and serfs of
the Middle Ages, are not by any means so bountifully
blessed with all creature comforts—food, clothing, and
the like—as they should be; and are in fact but little
better off than were their old-time progenitors, who
wore the badge of servitude, and passed by inheritance
from the Baron to his heir, equally with his manor-
house and other landed estates, his sheep and his swine,
his horses and dogs, or the gloomy pictures on his cas-
tle-walls, or the ancestral coat-of-arms. Why their condition at this time is so sorry, we leave to the political
economist to inquire. It may be that the old order of
things, the old relationship between landlord and vil
lein, protected the latter from many hardships to which
the nominal freemen of the nineteenth century are sub-

jected, by the blessed influences of free competition, and the practical workings of the good old charitable and praiseworthy English maxim: "Every man for himself, and devil take the hindmost." Again, it may result from the over-crowding of the Old World with shiftless *prolétaires* and starving *sans culottes*, in order to pamper and fatten a dissolute family of princes and kings, who revel in every luxury that art can devise or heart desire. And yet again, it may be that the laboring classes of Europe, having been used many hundreds of years (in the persons of their ancestors, that is) to the control and guidance of others, have proved inadequate to the task of providing for and taking care of themselves. But, no matter what the cause may be, the fact is indisputable, that the peasants of all the European States are in a very sorry condition, and are but little if any better off than were their forefathers who lived before the ancient feudal tenures were abolished. Else, why the social upheavals which have periodically convulsed Europe for the past half-century and more? Why the strikes, trades-unions, socialist and communist tendencies of the times?

Now, without presuming to solve this great social problem, still, and with all due deference to those of our readers who may be of a contrary mind, we contend there is a great deal in *blood*. Who ever yet knew a Godolphin that was sired by a miserable scrub? or who ever yet saw an athletic, healthy human being, standing six feet in his stockings, who was the offspring of runtish forefathers, or of wheezy, asthmatic, and consumptive parents? And do you suppose, Sir, or Madam, the heroes of our Revolutionary history

ever would or could have sprung from the loins of a
dissolute aristocracy on the one hand, or a down-trodden and servile race of villeins on the other? Never,
we warrant you. Their and our forefathers had to undergo a schooling of near upon ten centuries to prepare
them and us, their latest offspring, to snatch the golden
fruits of Independence from the Cerberean guardian-
ship of Tyranny, and thereby prove to all mankind
what dignity and worthiness the human race is capable
of, under proper training and a proper system of education. 'Tis true, however, we are already beginning
to forget the philosophy of this great marvel of the
present age, and are foolishly clamoring that every nation and every people under heaven are just as fit and
capable to control and govern themselves as we; while
some of us, in our Quixotic madness, are ever running
a tilt against windmills, until many a poor gentleman,
of amiable and kindly heart but weak head, has run
stark mad—his little modicum of brains proving insuf-
ficient to sustain the weight of all the Inalienable
Rights of Man, to say never a word of Woman's
Rights, about which so great a clatter is made in certain quarters.

Alas! the disease which has deprived such unfortunates of their wits, is not to be reached by any reme-
dial agency known to science, whether the science of
medicine or of political economy. The instructive lessons of history convey no intelligence to such minds;
the experience of the past serves not to guide their
footsteps by its clear radiance, while, in their blind in-
fatuation, they even dare to disregard the immutable
decrees of the All-wise Father. Fancying they them-

selves have discovered the long sought-for Philosopher's
Stone, they feel assured the world must certainly go to
eternal smash, unless they can prevail upon mankind
to practise and to reverence their own crude teachings
—those Utopian absurdities they so love to cherish in
their heart of hearts, as something wiser than the wisdom of Solomon, more sacred than the Ten Commandments, more perfect than the Constitution framed by
the Fathers of our Republic, as well as the source of
greater blessings to the sons of men than the Gospel of
our Lord Jesus Christ. Alas! poor imbeciles! how
fortunate would it be for yourselves, your country, and
the rest of mankind, could you all be securely caged
and placed in a *Maison de Santé*, and there be confined
to a strict regimen of cold water and asses' milk—the
water to be applied outwardly to your empty noddles,
to relieve the swelling thereof, and the milk to be taken
inwardly, as the kind of nourishment most suitable for
babes!

We apprehend there is no need to inform the intelligent reader why we have bored him with these pre-
liminary remarks. He must be aware that certain persons in the Free States are always denouncing the
South because of her "peculiar institution," and that
they leave no stone unturned but they will have their
spiteful fling at the "oligarchs." Time was, when
such worthies swore roundly (and at that time not
without reason, as confessed by Southerners themselves) that the institution of African slavery was un-
profitable, and should therefore be abolished. But
suddenly came the great demand for cotton; negroes
advanced in value from five to fifteen hundred dollars

a piece; the South furnished about three fourths of all
our exports, and the peculiar institution became deci-
dedly the most profitable and safe investment in the
whole country. In consequence of this unlooked-for
checkmate, the denouncers of the slaveholders were
forced to change their tactics, and so began a new species of agitation. They now acknowledge that to the
owners of negroes the system of labor peculiar to the
South is beneficial, but is, they contend, a terrible
curse to the non-slaveholding whites, and ought to be
abolished on account of the latter. Look at the Poor
Whites of the South, cry these wiseacres, and behold
the fruits of slavery. And in the same breath they
exclaim, Down with the Oligarchs! Down with the
Chivalry! They do not trouble themselves to inquire
what are the natural causes of the existence in the
South of a class of lazy vagabonds known as Poor
Whites, or how great the number of these may be, but
rush madly and recklessly to the conclusion, that they
form the bulk of the Southern masses, and are rendered
the pitiable wretches they are by reason of the peculiar
institution. Behold now, attentive and reflecting reader, how soon a plain unvarnished statement will render
this whole subject intelligible.

As we took occasion to state in the first chapter, the
early settlers of the South were not of equal fortune, or
blessed alike with the same refinement and culture.
We have already spoken of the Cavalier class, and
their present descendants and representatives; of the
past and present standing of the thrifty Middle Classes;
of the Yeomanry and the useful position their offspring
yet occupy; and we would now like to know, what

has become of those paupers and convicts whom Great
Britain sent over to her faithful Colony of Virginia—
of those indentured servants who were transported in
great numbers from the mother country, or who followed their masters, the Cavaliers and Huguenots,
when these bade adieu to the white cliffs of merry England and the purple-clad hills of La Belle France, to
seek their fortunes in the New World? Sir William
Berkley, in 1770, in answer to interrogatories submitted to him by the Lords' Commissioners of Foreign
Affairs, in which they inquire, "What number of English, Scotch, and Irish have for these seven years last
past come yearly to plant and inhabit within your government; and also what *blacks* or *slaves* have been
brought in within the same time?" answered: "Yearly
there comes in of servants *about fifteen hundred;* most
are English, few Scotch, and fewer Irish, and not above
two or three ships of negroes in seven years." The
servants here spoken of were indentured servants or
paupers, who were sold pretty much like the Coolies
are sold to the Cubans at the present time. They were
considered as mere "goods, wares, and merchandise,"
to be sold publicly at places appointed by law, as the
reader will learn from the following clause from an act
passed in 1680 by the Virginia House of Burgesses:
"And all goods, wares, English servants, negroes and
other slaves, and merchandises whatsoever, that shall be
imported into this colony from after the 29th day of
September, which shall be in the year 1681, shall be
landed and layd on shore, bought and solde at such
appointed places aforesaid, and at noe other place whatsoever, under like penalty and forfeiture thereof."

Now, does the reader fancy there is any thing in the nature of our soil and climate which would soon transmogrify such untutored, uncultivated, and servile creatures into freemen and gentlemen? Does he imagine that the glorious Declaration of Independence would alone suffice to put bread and meat into the mouths of paupers, or clothes upon their ragged backs? Is he so foolish as to believe that the over-throw of the Law of Primogeniture, the bestowal of the elective franchise, and the other levelling doctrines of Mr. Jefferson, would of themselves elevate to a position of thrift and intelligence, necessary to success in an honest competition with their more self-reliant fellows, those outcasts and paupers, picked up in the back slums and cellars of London, and transported at the public charge to Virginia, and there sold in the market-house to the highest bidder? If yea; then we must say, O candid reader, that you are a greater ninny than we supposed you were, be you sir or madam, miss or master.

For observe, if you please, the actual result has been far different. Just as the abolishment of the old feudal base tenures has been as yet productive of no percep-tible advantages to the Old World peasants, so likewise the removal of the English paupers to the New World, to the enjoyment of all the immunities of freemen, and to a land of such cornucopian abundance that it may be said almost to flow with milk and honey, has as yet been productive of no material improvement in their condition as a class. An individual here and there may have become imbued with a more manly feeling than what he otherwise would have attained unto; but

as a class, as a community, they remain in *statu quo.*
Every where they are just alike, possess pretty much
the same characteristics, the same vernacular, the same
boorishness, and the same habits ; although in different localities, they are known by different names.
Thus, in the extreme South and South-west, they are
usually called Squatters ; in the Carolinas and Georgia
Crackers or Sandhillers ; in the Old Dominion, Rag
Tag and Bob-tail ; in Tennessee and some other
States, People in the Barrens—but every where, Poor
White Trash, a name said to have originated with the
slaves, who look upon themselves as much better off
than all " po' white folks" whatever.

To form any proper conception of the condition of
the Poor White Trash, one should see them as they
are. We do not remember ever to have seen in the
New-England States a similar class ; though, if what
a citizen of Maine has told us be true, in portions of
that State the Poor Whites are to be found in large
numbers. In the State of New-York, however, in the
rural districts, we will venture to assert that more of
this class of paupers are to be met with than you will
find in any single Southern State. For in examining
the statistics of pauperism, as prepared by the Secretary of State for New-York, we learn that the number
of her public paupers, permanent and temporary, is
set down as 468,302—to support whom requires an annual outlay of one million and a half of dollars, which
has to be raised by tax for the purpose. They are
also found in Ohio, Pennsylvania, Indiana, and all the
States of the North-west, though in most of these last
they came originally from the South. But every

where, North and South, in Maine or Texas, in Virginia or New-York, they are one and the same; and have undoubtedly had one and the same origin, namely, the poor-houses and prison-cells of Great Britain. Hence we again affirm, what we asserted only a moment ago, that there is a great deal more in *blood* than people in the United States are generally inclined to believe.

Now, the Poor White Trash are about the only paupers in our Southern States, and they are very rarely supported by either the State or parish in which they reside; nor have we ever known or heard of a single instance in the South, in which a pauper was farmed out by the year to the lowest or highest bidder, (whichever it be,) as is the custom in the enlightened States of New-England. Moreover, the Poor White Trash are wholly rural; hence, the South will ever remain secure against any species of agrarianism, since such mob violence always originates in towns and cities, wherein are herded together an unthinking rabble, whom Dryden fitly describes as,

> " The scum
> That rises up most, when the nation boils."

The Poor Whites of the South live altogether in the country, in hilly and mountainous regions generally, in communities by themselves, and far removed from the wealthy and refined settlements. Why it is they always select the hilly, and consequently unproductive districts for their homes, we know not. It can not be, however, as urged by the abolitionists, because the slaveholders have seized on all the fertile lands; for it is well known, that some of the most inexhaustible soils in the South have never yet felt the touch of the ploughshare in their virgin bosoms, and are still to be had at government prices. Neither can it be pleaded in behalf of the Poor White Trash, that they object to labor by the side of slaves; for, as we have already shown, the Southern Yeomanry, who, as a class, are poor, work habitually in company with negroes, and usually prefer to own a homestead in the neighborhood of wealthy planters. We apprehend, therefore, that it is a natural feeling with Messrs. Rag Tag and Bobtail—an idiocyncrasy for which they themselves can assign no good reason—why they delight to build their pine-pole cabins among the sterile sand hills, or in the very heart of the dismal solitude of the burr-oak or pine barrens. We remember to have heard an overseer who had spent some time among the Sandhillers, relate something like the following anecdote of a youthful Bobtail whom he persuaded to accompany him out of the hill-country into the nearest alluvial bottoms, where there was any number of extensive plantations in a high state of cultivation, which will aptly illustrate this peculiarity of the class. So soon as the juvenile Bobtail reached the open country, his eyes began to dilate, and his whole manner and expression indicated bewilderment and uneasiness. "Bedadseized!" exclaimed he at last, " ef this yere ked'ntry haint got nary sign ov er tree! How in thunder duz folks live down yere? By G-o-r-j! this beats all that Uncle Snipes tells about Carlina. Tell yer what, I'm goin' ter make tracks fur dad's—yer heer my horn toot!" And he did make tracks for dad's, sure enough.

In the settlements wherein they chiefly reside, the Poor Whites rarely live more than a mile or two apart. Each householder, or head of a family, builds him a little hut of round logs; chinks the spaces between these with clay mixed with wheaten straw; builds at one end of the cabin a big wooden chimney with a tapering top, all the interstices being "dobbed" as above; puts down a puncheon floor, and a loft of ordinary boards overhead; fills up the inside of the rude dwelling with a few rickety chairs, a long bench, a dirty bed or two, a spinning-wheel (the loom, if any, is outside under a shed,) a skillet, an oven, a frying-pan, a triangular cupboard in one corner, and a rack over the door on which to hang old Silver Heels, the family rifle; and both the cabin and its furniture are considered as complete. The happy owner then "clears" some five acres or so of land immediately surrounding his domicil, and these he pretends to cultivate, planting only corn, pumpkins, and a little garden truck of some kind or other. He next builds a rude kennel for his dog or dogs, a primitive-looking stall for his "nag," ditto for old Beck his cow, and a pole hen-house for his poultry. This last he covers over with dirt and weeds, and erects on one side of it a long slim pole, from the upper branches whereof dangle gourds for the martins to build their nests in—martins being generally regarded as useful to drive off all bloody-minded hawks, that look with too hungry an eye upon the rising generation of dunghills.

Being thus prepared for house-keeping, now comes the tug of war.

But, whatever may be said of the poverty of Rag

Tag and Bobtail, of their ignorance and general spiritual degradation, it is yet a rare thing that any of them
suffer from hunger or cold. As a class, indeed, they
are much better off than the peasantry of Europe, and
many a poor mechanic in New-York City even—to say
nothing of the thousands of day-laborers annually
thrown out of employment on the approach of winter
—would be most happy at any time from December to
March, to share the cheerful warmth of the blazing pine
fagots which glow upon every poor man's hearth in the
South; as well as to help devour the fat haunches of the
noble old buck, whose carcass hangs in one corner
suspended from one of the beams of the loft overhead,
ready at all times to have a slice cut from its sinewy
hams and broiled to delicious juiciness upon the glowing coals.

Indeed, the only source of trouble to the Sandhillers
is the preservation of their yearly "craps" of corn.
Owing to the sterileness of their lands, and deficient
cultivation, that sometimes fails them, running all to
weeds and grass. But they have no lack of meats.
Wild hogs, deer, wild turkeys, squirrels, raccoons,
opossums—these and many more are at their very
doors; and they have only to pick up "old Silver
Heels," walk a few miles out into the forest, and return
home laden with meat enough to last them a week.
And should they desire to purchase a little wool for
spinning, or cotton ditto, or a little "swat'ning" to put
in their coffee and their "sassefack" tea, or a few cups
and saucers, or powder and shot, salt, meal, or other
household necessaries—a week's successful hunting
invariably supplies them with enough venison to pro-

cure the wished-for luxuries, which they soon possess themselves of accordingly, from the nearest village or country store. Having obtained what they want, they hasten back again to their barren solitudes; their wives and daughters spin and weave the wool or cotton into such description of cloth as is in most vogue for the time being; while the husbands, fathers, sons, and brothers, betake themselves to their former idle habits —hunting, beef-shooting, gander-pulling, marble-playing, card-playing, and getting drunk. Panics, financial pressures, and the like, are unknown amongst them, and about the only crisis of which they know any thing, is when a poor fellow is called upon to "shuffle off this mortal coil." Money, in truth, is almost a perfectly unknown commodity in their midst, and nearly all of their trafficking is carried on by means of barter alone. In their currency a cow is considered worth so much, a horse so much, a dog so much, a fat buck so much, a wild-turkey so much, a coon-skin so much, et cetera, et cetera; and by these values almost every thing else is rated. Dollars and dimes, or pounds, shillings and pence, they never bother their brains any great deal about.

The chief characteristic of Rag Tag and Bobtail, however, is laziness. They are about the laziest two-legged animals that walk erect on the face of the Earth. Even their motions are slow, and their speech is a sickening drawl, worse a deal sight than the most down-eastern of all the Down-Easters; while their thoughts and ideas seem likewise to creep along at a snail's pace. All they seem to care for, is, to live from hand to mouth; to get drunk, provided they can do so without having to trudge too far after their liquor; to shoot for beef; to hunt; to attend gander pullings; to vote at elections; to eat and to sleep; to lounge in the sunshine of a bright summer's day, and to bask in the warmth of a roaring wood fire, when summer days are over, and the calm autumn stillness has given place to the blustering turbulence of hyemal storms. We do not believe the worthless ragamuffins would put themselves to much extra locomotion to get out of a shower of rain; and we know they would shiver all day with cold, with wood all around them, before they would trouble themselves to pick it up and build a fire: for we recollect to have heard an anecdote of a gentleman who was once travelling through a section of country peopled by Sandhillers, on a cold and raw winter's day, when he chanced to come up with a squad of great strapping lazy bumpkins on the side of the road in a woods, sitting all huddled up and shivering around the smouldering remains of what had once been a fire. The traveller was himself quite chilled, and thought it prudent to stop and warm before proceeding any further on his journey. But imagine his astonishment, on asking the miserable scamps why they had suffered their fire to burn so low, to hear them answer, that they " were afeared they mout git too cold pickin' up sticks!" Very humanely he gathered together a pile of dry brushwood lying close at hand, built up in a little while a roaring fire, warmed himself, and again mounting his horse, rode on his way; leaving the great loutish clowns quarrelling among themselves, as to which one of them was entitled to the *warmest side* of the fire!

In physical appearance, the Sandhillers are far from

prepossessing. Lank, lean, angular, and bony, with flaming red, or flaxen, or sandy, or carroty-colored hair, sallow complexion, awkward manners, and a natural stupidity or dullness of intellect that almost surpasses belief; they present in the main a very pitiable sight to the truly benevolent, as well as a ludicrous one to those who are mirthfully disposed. If any thing, after the first freshness of their youth is lost, the women are even more intolerable than the men—owing chiefly to their disgusting habit of snuff-dipping, and even sometimes pipe-smoking. The vile practice of snuff-dipping prevails sometimes also among the wives and daughters of the Yeomanry, and even occasionally among otherwise intelligent members of the Southern Middle Classes, particularly in North-Carolina. The usual mode is, to procure a straight wooden tooth-brush— one made of the bark of the hickory-nut tree preferred —chew one end of the brush until it becomes soft and pliant, then dab the same while still wet with saliva into the snuff-bottle, and immediately stick it back into the mouth again with the fine particles of snuff adhering; then proceed to mop the gums and teeth adroitly, to suck, and chew, and spit to your heart's content. Ah! it is almost as decent as smoking cigars, and is fully as *distingué* as chewing tobacco!

Being usually addicted to this filthy and disgusting vice, or whatever else one may choose to call it, it is not at all strange that the female Sand-hillers should so soon lose all trace of beauty, and at thirty are about the color of yellow parchment, if not thin and pale from constant attacks of fever. Besides, they are quite prolific, and every house is filled with its half-dozen of dirty, squalling, white - headed little brats, who are familiarly known as Tow-Heads—on account of the color of their hair, as well as its texture and generally unkempt and matted condition. In the main the entire family, both male and female, occupy the same apartment at all hours of the day and night, just as do the small farmers of the North-west, or the very poor in all large cities. But it is a rare circumstance to find several families huddled into one poor shanty, as is more often the case than otherwise with those unfortunates in cities, who are constrained to herd together promiscuously in tenant - houses and in underground cellars. On the contrary, each Sandhiller has his own lowly cabin, and whilst it is sad to contemplate the hard necessity which forces father and mother, sons and daughters, all to live in the same narrow room ; still it is pleasant to believe, that the sacred nature of the relationship between the parties, casts a vail of modesty over the scene, which is wanting where two or more stranger families are thus promiscuously thrown together in such close contact.

Of course, intelligence of all kinds is at a low ebb with Messrs. Rag Tag and Bobtail. Few of them can read, fewer still can write, while the great mass are native, genuine Know-Nothings, though always democratic in their political faith and practice. Indeed, puzzled to comprehend for what other purpose the miserable wretches were ever allowed to obtain a footing in this country, we have come to the honest conclusion, that it was providentially intended, in order that, by their votes, however blindly and ignorantly cast, they should help to support the only political party which

12

has been enabled thus far to maintain a National organization. Nor can they be blamed for voting the democratic ticket, live they in the North or the South; for to the democratic party do they owe the only political privilege which is of any real use to them—the privilege of the elective franchise. This fact, indeed, is nearly the sum total of their knowledge of our Government, or its history. They remember Washington because he was the Founder, if we may so speak, of the Republic: they remember Thomas Jefferson because he effected the change in the policy of the country, whereby they became *sovereign freemen*, the voice of each one of them counting *one*, while that of an Astor or a Girard could count no more: and they remember General Jackson because he whipped the British so bad at New-Orleans, and afterwards, while he was President, dared to "remove the Deposits" in the teeth of opposition from all the moneyed men in the nation; and it is said that, in certain very benighted districts of Central New-York and the mountains of East-Tennessee, General Jackson is voted for still at every presidential election.

In religion the Poor Whites are mostly of the Hard-Shell persuasion, and their parsons are in the main of the Order of the Whang Doodle. They are also very superstitious, being firm believers in witches and hobgoblins; likewise old-time spiritualists, or, to render our meaning plainer, believers in fortune-telling after the ancient modes—such as palm-reading, card-cutting, or the revelations of coffee-grounds left in the bottom of the cup after the fluid has been drained off. Poor simple souls! they have not yet risen to the supernal glories of table-tipping, horn-blowing, and the other modern improvements in the mode of consulting such as have familiar spirits : for, although these boast that they number a million or so of adherents in the more enlightened Free States, we suspect they could hardly drum up in the entire South one thousand fools credulous enough to embrace their miserable dogmas. Yet in scarcely a settlement of Poor Whites will you fail to find some gray-headed old crone, who professes to be able to tell you all about your past life, as well as to predict what is to be your future career : but she does not charge very exorbitant prices for her disclosures, being well satisfied to receive the small sum of twenty-five cents for each consultation. Whereas, in the enlightened city of New-York, in which are hundreds of professed star-readers, (the united annual incomes of nineteen of these Professors of the Black Art being one hundred thousand dollars,) and where, it is said, sixteen hundred persons are foolish enough every week to consult such damnable impostors ; the regular fee varies from one to five dollars. Besides, this can also be said in behalf of the old women among the Sandhillers who tell fortunes ; they never use their pretended gifts for the purpose of entrapping poor but silly girls, into such peculiar institutions as are kept by our virtuous and refined Dawsons : which is more than can be said of one half those dirty dens of superstition which flourish in the very centres of our refinement and civilization, and the proprietors of which dare, with unblushing audacity, to advertise in the daily press the location of their horrid penetralia.

Another evil which prevails greatly among the

Sandhillers — a royal evil too, in the present as all
past ages, if poor King Clicquot of Prussia washing
his face in the vermicelli soup at Milan the other day,
and afterwards grinning with a drunken leer upon his
guests through the strings of worm-like paste that hung
from his royal beard, is to be considered a specimen of
modern potentates—is the iniquitous practice of drinking alcoholic beverages to excess.   And then, too, such
vile stuff as the poor fellows are wont to imbibe!   Too
lazy to distill honest peach or apple brandy, like the
industrious yeomanry, they prefer to tramp to the nearest groggery with a gallon-jug on their shoulders,
which they get filled with "bust-head," "rot-gut," or
some other equally poisonous abomination ; and then
tramp home again, reeling as they trudge along, and
laughing idiotically, or shouting like mad in a glorious
state of beastly intoxication.   Hence, as is the case
elsewhere in all parts of our glorious Union, many of
the poor fellows annually die of *delirium tremens* or
mania a potu ; to the memory of all whom some doggerel poetaster has indited the following epitaph :

> " Here is laid a luckless Bobtail,
>   Died, poor fellow, of mean whisky,
>   Strychnine whisky, sharp as lightning,
>   Ruin-blue and Minié rifle—
>   Knock-'em-stiff and flaming red-eye—
>   Such as kill 'em at the counter,
>   Forty rods or any distance.
>   Perished thus the wretched Bobtail,
>   By imbibing strychnine whisky,
>   Sold by some confounded bummer,
>   At a bit a glass, or cheaper—
>   Strychnine whisky—whisky strychnine."

To so great an extent are Rag Tag and Bobtail addicted to this shameful vice, that, in those Congressional districts in which they mostly abound, as we were once told by a Southern member of Congress, no person who is temperate and lives cleanlily and like a gentleman, and who will not therefore condescend to drink and hurrah with Tom, Dick and Harry, need ever hope for political preferment. And the character of our informant bore ample testimony to the truthfulness of his assertion; for a more drunken and besotted wretch we should hardly wish to see. He said, that, in certain parts of his district, the "red-eye" was passed around in an old tin coffee-pot, and every man helped himself by "word of mouth"—whatever this slang expression may mean. And we may here observe, this accounts for the great dissimilarity in the character of our Southern Congressmen. While these all are more or less innocent of any participation in the corrupt practices of those Forty Congressional Thieves, who have brought such deserved opprobrium upon our National Legislature; and while as a general thing, there is more of good-breeding, of gentlemanly bearing, of chivalric tone and statesmanlike deportment about the Southern Representatives than most others—still, it can not be safely denied, that some of them are nothing better than tippling, gambling, and debauched libertines, not a whit more intelligent or honest than the corrupt ward politicians of our large cities; men who never make a speech in our Legislative Halls for any other purpose than Buncombe. Which is true likewise of many Northern Congressmen—especially of those who live in the North-west, where lager-beer and corn-juice have in a measure usurped the place of wholesome water.

Neither have we, Honorable Sirs, Northern or Southern, any apology to offer for these animadversions; and for two very good reasons. In the first place, we shall have offended *no gentleman,* for all such who are members of our Federal Congress, acknowledge and lament, equally as sincerely as we do, the truth of what we have charged. And in the second place, although it is not the fashion for the delicate wits and kid-gloved moralists of this decent age to speak the truth plainly and bluntly, we will yet plainly and bluntly declare, we do not consider it a mortal offense to excite the ire of those political demagogues who *are not gentlemen;* but whose coarse and vulgar habits and tastes, whose wicked and open blasphemies, and whose vaporing Buncombe speeches, serve only to disgrace the Republic at home and abroad, and to demoralize their own immediate constituents, as well as the masses of the people at large. O you miserable agitators and radicals, North and South, what a pity it is you can not see yourselves as others see you! For truly, while you are so furiously ventilating your windy fanaticism and overhot zeal in the Halls of Congress, wholly regardless of the honor and the vital interests of the Republic, you only serve, be you Fire Eater or Black Republican, to give point and significance to these lines from a translation of a satire in Monsieur Boileau :

> " Thus one fool lolls his tongue out at another,
> And shakes his empty noddle at his brother!"

But to return.

The Poor White Trash rarely possess energy and self-reliance enough to emigrate singly from the older Southern States to the South-west, but usually migrate by whole neighborhoods; and are thus to be seen nearly every summer or fall plodding along together, each family having its whole stock of worldly goods packed into a little one-horse cart of rudest workmanship, into which likewise are often crowded the women and children, the men walking alongside looking worn and weary. Slowly thus they creep along day by day, camping out at night, and usually carrying their own provisions with them—bacon, beans, corn-meal, dried fruits, and the like simple and unassuming fare. When they reach a large river whose course leads in the proper direction, they build them a rude kind of flat-bottomed boat, into which, huddling with all their traps, they suffer themselves to drift along with the current down to their place of destination. Having reached which, they proceed immediately to disembark, and to build their inevitable log-cabins, squatting at their free will and pleasure on Uncle Sam's domain; for they seldom care to purchase land, unless they can get it at about a "bit" an acre. Owing to this custom of occupying the public lands without making entry of the same according to law, in most of the new Southern States the Poor Whites are almost invariably known as Squatters. When the lands temporarily occupied by them, finally come into market, the Squatters once more hitch up their little one-horse carts, pile in all their worldly store, together with their wives and little ones, and again facing to the westward, go in

search of their New Atlantis—which the poor creatures find so soon as they get beyond the limits of civilization; when they "squat" as before, raise their little "craps" of corn and garden truck, shoot bears,
deer, and Indians, and vegetate generally like all other
nomadic races. And thus will Rag Tag and Bobtail
continue to pass further and further westward and
southward, until they will eventually become absorbed
and lost among the half-civilized mongrels who inhabit
the plains of Mexico; unless it should chance that
some new life and energy shall be instilled into them
during their sojourn on our Western frontier, both by
contact with the hardy race of backwoodsmen and
hunters who there abound, and the stern necessity of
learning to defend themselves against the predatory
bands of Camanches and Arapahoes, who are always
prowling around, seeking whom they may scalp and
plunder. If such a life fail to work a change for the
better in the miserable wretches, we are inclined to
think their ultimate absorption by Mexico will prove
a happy riddance to us; for they are of so little account at present, that, could every one of them be
blotted out of existence to-morrow, neither the South
nor the North, nor the commercial world would be any
the poorer for their loss. Let us cherish a hope, however, that the experiences of a rough border-life will
in time regenerate Rag Tag and Bobtail, and render
them at some future period both useful and ornamental
citizens of our great Republic. *Homo sum, et humani
a me nil alienum puto*, said Terence, and so say we:
and we confess, moreover, that we feel for the humblest
descendant of our common father Adam, a brotherly

sympathy. Not, however, of the patent sort, of the popular double-self-acting-backward sort, kind Sir, which leads your worship into the gross errors of socialism, communism, and the like stuff and nonsense, but a rational sympathy which would lead us to give ten talents to the man endowed with sufficient capacity to use ten talents; to give five talents to him who could only manage five; and three talents to another whom five would make a fool of; but not even one talent to the poor imbecile, who, not knowing the value of the gift, would surely wrap it up in a napkin and bury it in the ground, or else throw it away entirely as something worthless and unprized.

The Poor Whites of the South seldom come in contact with the slaves at all, and thousands of them never saw a negro; still, almost to a man, they are pro-slavery in sentiment. Unlike the Southern Yeomen, who are pro-slavery because these dread the consequences to the humbler whites of the emancipation of the negroes, and because also they are intelligent enough to understand what would be the nature of these consequences; the Poor White Trash are pro-slavery from downright envy and hatred of the black man. We presume this feeling must have originated many years agone when the pauper ancestors of the Sandhillers were first "layd on shore," as our worthy ancestors expressed it, like all other "goods, wares, and merchandise," and very possibly met with a somewhat supercilious reception at the hands of the bepowdered and bejewelled body-servants of the grand old cavaliers of those times. The blacks on their part, too,

12*

reciprocate the feeling of hatred at least, and look with ineffable scorn on a " po' white man."

Nevertheless, although as a class the Poor White Trash are intensely pro-slavery, now and then one will find amongst them fierce abolitionists. These, however, are not usually of the pure, unadulterated pauper blood. Their origin is somewhat mixed. Thus it happens not infrequently that a poor Sandhiller is blessed with a more than commonly pretty daughter, whose rosy cheeks, blue eyes, pearly teeth, and wealth of golden hair (despite a few freckles, and tan, from constant exposure) win the affections of some robust, honest, hard-working young Yeoman, or better still, the son of a well-to-do farmer of the Middle Class; and soon the loving twain are made one flesh, and begin life on their own hook, as the bridegroom's father expresses it. Now, love-matches of this nature, as all of us may have observed, generally result in a pretty large family of children, all of whom are more or less blessed with good constitutions and a fair share of intelligence. Very seldom is it, indeed, but at least one of the humble household is possessed of more than ordinary abilities: this one, let us suppose, is a boy. Before he is ten summers old, he is put to hoeing tobacco, or corn, or cotton, and is enabled to get from two to three months only of schooling during the whole year. But his mind is quick, his perceptions and desires run ahead of his years, and an inborn spirit of gentlemanship prompts him to strive to occupy a position in society more honorable than what his parents do. He feels, yea knows, that he is the equal of the sons of the neighboring gentlemen, with whom he comes often in con-

tact at the district school, but who habitually treat him
as an inferior—just as your own darling Charlie, philanthropic Madam, is accustomed daily to snub that
poor Irish lad who occupies the same seat with him at
the Free School. Of course our young Yeoman feels
keenly the gibes and slights put upon him; for he is a
lad of spirit, and we do not blame him. Neither do we
blame him that he firmly resolves to toil night and day
but he will yet occupy an equal position with those
who now look down upon him with such ill-disguised
contempt. We do not blame the worthy lad for laying
by his hard-earned "fo'pences" and "bits," hoarding
them closer than miser ever hoarded his gold, in order
that he may buy such books as he may need, as well
as to enable him by and by to work his way through
some second or third-rate college, assisted it may be by
some benevolent gentleman who takes an interest in
the plucky spirit of the struggling boy. In all this he
is to be honored and applauded by every generous mind.

But if, after he has gained the knowledge and social
position to which he so ardently aspires, and has thereby become the pride of his doting old mother and the
boast of his hard-working father; he still continues to
harbor in his bosom resentment against those whom
fortune favored more than himself in the outset of life,
and secretly entertains proposals from the deadliest enemies of his native land merely because of such personal spite, to gratify which he also lends himself to
aid the schemes of Northern abolitionists; where is
there an honest man who would not utterly loathe and
despise his meanness of soul? We know he may delude himself into the belief, that the social position of

his father as well as that of his mother's family connection is due mainly to the institution of slavery; but is this an excuse for treason? Is it any excuse for his wishing to deprive other men of their property, or for his aiding to stir up a servile insurrection, hoping to see the roofs of his supposed enemies blazing at midnight and tumbling in upon the devoted inmates, while the emancipated blacks are dancing savagely around the ruins in the delirium of a brutal joy? And yet, if these things be inexcusable, how much more damning and black becomes his record when, driven by force out of the State he seeks to rend with intestine feuds and all the horrors of a servile war, he takes refuge in the Free States and still, in bitterness of soul, continues his unnatural war upon his native land! Before, there was a shadow of palliation for his treason, since he honestly felt that the peculiar institution was the sole cause of his humble origin and the poverty of his race; now, however, he knows better. He finds the poor just as plenty in the Free States as in the Slave States, and that social distinctions are just as nicely drawn in the one as in the other. He sees that the sons of gentlemen as habitually scorn to associate with the sons of laborers, either in Massachusetts or New-York, as in Virginia or the Carolinas; and this should teach him that the real cause of all such social distinctions is not to be sought for in any institutions whatever, no matter how peculiar, but in the lamentably narrow and crooked nature of man himself. For, we care not how vociferously the demagogues of New-England, or any other section of the North, may rant about social equality, they all know in their hearts that such a thing is simply an impossible abstraction.

Why then do they prate so constantly about it? O unsophisticated questioner, we much fear you have not yet cut your eye-teeth! Why? Because *it pays*, dear Sir; and will therefore be kept up, until the people shall learn to appreciate at their real value the professions of those political mountebanks and charlatans, who imagine the surest way to office and preferment is, to flatter and cajole the thoughtless and variable rabble. At present, however, the windy demagogues have every thing their own way, and do indeed play such fantastic tricks in the sight of high Heaven as are enough almost to make the angels weep. It is chiefly owing to the influence of such worthies that Massachusetts, rightly boastful of the culture and scholarly refinement of her citizens, has been led to discard her Everetts, Winthrops, Cushings, and Choates, for—whom? Well, let the history of the old Bay State, since the voice of the great Webster was hushed in death—the absolute nothingness of her political influence in the Republic—the utter incompetency of her later representatives, dealing in slash-buckler rhodomontade and pedantic imitations of the old classic masters, instead of the dignified statesmanship and chaste oratory of her earlier political giants—let the many hurtful isms which are rapidly being embraced by her citizens at large, isms hurtful alike to good morals, to good manners, to political integrity and a pure Christianity—let these all furnish the answer. In the words of the deep-voiced and heavy-browed sage of Marshfield, but with a far different significance: "There she stands; let her answer for herself!"

We know, Rev. and Hon. Sir, what your ready reply is. We have heard it again and again, until the sound thereof vexes our ears like a twice-told tale. You contend that the present uninfluential position of Massachusetts, is owing solely to the temporary ascendency of what you are pleased to call the Oligarchs: and you seek to console yourself and your friends, with the pleasing anticipation of what wonders the old Bay State will perform when her time comes to wield the sceptre of empire and destiny. But, Sir, allow us to suggest, that possibly that "good time coming" may be tardy in its approaches, and that, when it does come, (if ever?) the event will prove even to Massachusetts herself far other than propitious. For (and mark well our words!) you, Sir, half priest and the other half demagogue, wearing the surplice and wielding also the secular arm of power, have been for a long time preaching a crusade against the rights of property—have taught men every where, that to deprive their neighbors of property valued at millions and millions of dollars, instead of being an infraction of the Divine Law and therefore criminal in the sight of God, on the contrary would entitle them to receive praise and honor in the present life, and insure to them in the life to come rewards imperishable. And upon what pretense, forsooth? Because your neighbors, as you claim, can possess no rights of property in men and women—in human flesh, and brawn, and blood, and brains, to use your own vernacular of cant. And so in truth they ought not *in foro conscientiæ*, without making an equivalent return, either in the nature of protection, food, shelter, attention in sickness and the like; the most of which the Southern slaveholders are constrained by law to grant in return for the service exacted of their bondmen. But, you clamor, they do not return an exact and equal account—they charge too much for their kind superintendence and benevolent regard! Ah! Sir, it is just here that you have trodden upon an adder, which will in time turn and sting your Reverence. For, truly, the poisoned darts you have so resolutely hurled against the South will, rebounding, yet find a mark the archer little meant, and one close to your own hearthstone.

Unconsciously to yourself, you have been advocating all this time only a new species of agrarianism. Unconsciously you have been sowing the wind, and sooner or later will surely reap the whirlwind for your pains. Already your laborers, your operatives, your journeymen mechanics and others, secretly moot the question: How it happens they remain so poor, while their employers are constantly growing richer and richer; build their marble palaces, educate their children in idleness and dissipation, and besides spend half their own days tuft-hunting and toad-eating upon the continent of Europe. Already, we repeat, this terrible question is being mooted in secret conclave; and should the time ever come when it shall be mooted openly—when loud-mouthed and earnest men, *fresh from the people*, shall bestride Faneuil Hall, bawling for an equal and exact distribution to every mechanic of whatever craft, to every operative of whatever mills, to every laborer of whatever grade—bawling, we say, for an equal and exact distribution to the workmen of the net proceeds of their combined labor; and denouncing in the same breath pampered capitalists, as so many lordlings growing rich on the earnings of the moiling and toiling poor, reaping where they have not sown, and gathering where they have not scattered; upon what plausible pretext will you, Sir, then seek to gainsay them? You will have none. Dumb and quaking with fear you would be constrained to acquiesce in their logic; for they would only use in their own behalf the identical arguments you have assiduously tried to impress upon their minds for ten years and more, in order to persuade them to interfere in the affairs of their neighbors.

But you think we are begging the question? You think such a terrible chimera never has troubled the thoughts of the sober citizens of New-England? You feel assured that men and women, little boys and girls, can stand to work from ten to thirteen hours every day, winter and summer, in heat and in cold, making at that only a beggarly pittance which barely suffices to keep body and soul together; and yet never once inquire, honest souls! how it chances that their employers, who neither toil nor yet do spin, are still reckoned among the merchant-princes of the land, dress in fine broadcloth and spotless linen, and in every other respect fare sumptuously every day? Oh! dear, no; you couldn't begin to think of such a thing. Why should you? Your Reverence is paid from three to five thousand dollars per annum for talking billingsgate religion, maudlin sentimentality, and a cheap philanthropy, and of course it never occurs to you that what is so profitable to your individual self, is yet sowing broadcast the seeds of many future disasters to the Constitution and the Union. It never occurs to you, O astute politician, that those whom you so earnestly teach how to remedy the sad lot of others, are all the time, although unread in classical lore, revolving over in their minds the sentiment so often quoted from Horace: *Mutato nomine, de te Fabula narratur.* But, we have written that this question is even now agitating the breasts of thousands of the sons of toil in New-England; and what we have written that do we know to be true. For we have heard it discussed in whispers, and under one's breath as it were, within the very shadows of Faneuil Hall and Bunker Hill Monument. Nay, within the classic precincts of old Harvard, under the venerable elm trees which there spread so far-reaching their umbrageous boughs, as well as in the shadowy alcoves of her magnificent Library; we have heard agrarian utterances from learned schoolmen and collegians — utterances alike antagonistic to the spirit of our Federal Constitution, and the generally accepted ideas in regard to the laws of *meum* and *tuum.* We have there heard ultra anti-slavery men, when driven to the wall by force of irresistible argument, confess that they equally abhorred capitalists as slaveholders; and that the only reason why they did not not wage as relentless war upon the rich men of the Free States, as upon the Southern Oligarchs, was owing entirely to the dictates of policy. *The time has not come yet,* was the plea they invariably set up; but after disposing of the Chivalry, then would come the turn of their own rich men. So-ho, ye stout gentlemen of *backbone!*

> " When the Devil is sick,
> The Devil a monk would be;

> But when the Devil is well,
> The Devil a monk is he!"

The Chivalry are not disposed of yet, however, and the prospect is, that they will not be disposed of for many a day to come. In the mean time, the leaven of unsound political doctrine has been doing its perfect work in the Old Bay State. Her great lights have all been hid under a bushel, and farthing candles only now serve to guide with flickering uncertain beams the feet of her groping citizens; who, as was to have been looked for under the circumstances, have stumbled into all sorts of social and political quagmires — in their blind flounderings even stultifying themselves so much as openly to put at defiance the laws of Congress, and shamefully to despoil of his ermine a noble Judge, whose sole crime was that he dared to respect his oath of office. But the end is not yet, we much fear. What with ovations to Brown, the hanged horse-thief and murderer—with lawlessness and bigotry—with pampered capitalists on the one hand, and starving operatives on the other—with drinkers of five-dollar whisky-skins in her pulpits, and infidel ranters in her lyceums —with every where a form of godliness, and no where any evidence of its power to make men charitable to the opinions of other people; we must confess, we should be astonished at no calamity which might befall such a community. But, *procul, O! procul* be the day of its trouble and the hour of its disaster; and soon arise once more with healing in your beams, thou Sun of Prosperity, and light up with golden splendors the granite hills of New-England, which have blackened so long under the lowering clouds of financial panic and commercial depression. For know, O land of the Pilgrims—land of grassy meadows, mountain streams, and bonnie lassies—with all your faults (and these are not few) we love you still! Yes; there is a charm in your frosty but kindly atmosphere—there is a breath of poesy in your lovely landscapes—there is a wealth of intellect in your teeming cities, a wealth of invention in your crowded workshops, and a wealth of energy in your hardy sons, which we shall never fail to admire and esteem. While, highly prized above all the rest, we revere the very stones of your flinty hillsides, which mark the spots where fought and fell the noble patriots of 'Seventy-Six; and ever swells our bosom with pride and emotion, when we recall those memorable events which preceded and followed the Declaration of Independence, and in which brave, true-hearted New-England played such an honorable and conspicuous part. For truly, fellow-countrymen, though we smite you hip and thigh when our blood is up, we feel all the time that you are our countrymen still: and although with no sparing hand we probe you in your sore places, like the good physician, we seek to wound only that we may heal.

CHAPTER VIII.

THE NEGRO SLAVES.

" In fact, in his perennial speech,
  The Chairman owned the niggers did not bleach,
        As he had hoped,
        From being washed and soaped,
  A circumstance he named with grief and pity;
  But still he had the happiness to say,
        For self and the Committee,
  By persevering in the present way,
  And scrubbing at the Blacks from day to day,
        Although he could not promise perfect white,
        From certain symptoms that had come to light,
  He hoped in time to get them gray!"

THOMAS HOOD.

A GREAT many philanthropic men, possessing too exalted an opinion of human kind, are ever seeking to find fault with God (either directly or indirectly) for the misery and sin which are in the world. They will not consent to acknowledge that man is, when unregenerate, essentially a bestial sort of animal, grovelling in ignorance and vice, and influenced at all times by such sentiments only as are inspired either through fear or self-interest. Filled with their own idea of what a man ought to be, they delude themselves into the belief that he would be the beau ideal of their imagination, had God never allowed the devil to leave Hell;

for they do not consider that there is in every man a private devil of his own, which can turn his bosom into a hell or heaven as the man himself of his own free will shall choose to act.

All such short-sighted and one-ideaed philosophers are in the main miserable—full of impracticable theories, and ever disposed to be skeptical as regards any kind of religious belief. Though boastful of their charity and humanity, however, their hearts are filled instead with all bitterness, being perfect strangers to that heavenly Love, which "suffereth long and is kind;" for they seem to delight in looking at the darker aspects only of every subject, and refuse to perceive that their Creator is always

"From seeming evil still educing good."

Hence, they are the genuine representatives of Procrustes in this present nineteenth century : whoever does not agree with them in sentiment, they damn incontinently, pronouncing anathema maranatha upon the heads of all such. Hence also, they may be fitly styled the latter-day Popes, from whose decrees there is no appeal. Yea, verily, as was predicted of Anti-Christ, they do not scruple to set themselves up as superior to the authority of the Holy Scriptures, and boldly and impiously teach for doctrines the whims and caprices of men. Thus they denounce what Abraham, the chosen friend of God, and what the Jews, his chosen people, all practised, as the "sum of all villanies." And they likewise pronounce Jesus Christ an impostor, because (as they blasphemously assert) he was influenced to let slavery alone from political considerations, although he did not allow these to prevent him from overturning the old Jewish laws allowing of concubinage and fornication. And in precisely a similar spirit do they denounce St. Paul, because he, acting as the inspired Apostle of Christ, sent Onesimus, a runaway slave, back to his master, and enjoined upon all other slaves to count their masters worthy of all honor, especially those masters who were fellow-believers of the glorious Gospel which Paul preached.

Now, on the minds of such men we do not expect to produce the slightest impression, by any thing we may have to say touching the condition of the negro slaves in our Southern States. Their understandings are as impervious to logical sequences, as the hide of the two-horned rhinoceros is to rifle-balls. They may be called, indeed, not inaptly the pachydermatous race of bipeds. Like the tree mobwana of Central Africa, no matter how much you may clip, and pollard, bark, or even cut them down, they still flourish and seem to draw their nourishment from thin air alone. But, from an intimate acquaintance with many Northerners who have been seduced by the ceaseless clamor of such senseless babblers, to entertain strong anti-slavery convictions; we feel assured that we shall not labor in vain while endeavoring to present a fair and truthful statement of the result to themselves, as well as to the rest of mankind, of the forced labor of the Negroes in our Southern States.

We are well persuaded that many good men, pious men—men of earnest natures and delicate sensibilities, not in the North alone but even in the South—do honestly look upon slavery as both a great moral evil and an equally great social curse. And when we consider their early prejudices and peculiar cast of mind, we can not greatly blame them because they sincerely are of opinion, that, had the peculiar institution never been introduced into this country, we should all have been much better off as a people and as individuals. For, well we know, they do not consider, while entertaining the honest convictions they do, that they thus assail the wisdom and goodness of the Great Ruler of Nations; that they are carping at the overruling providence of the Omniscient Being, in whose sight the wisest of men barely rise to the rank of fools. Alas! so short-sighted are we all. " I could write down twenty cases," says Cecil, "wherein I wished that God had done otherwise than he did; but which I now see, had I had my own will, would have led to extensive mischief."

And the experience of Cecil is the experience of all mankind. We are all miserably short-sighted, and hardly a day passes but we are disposed to find fault with *what is;* but the morrow invariably proves to us, that we could not possibly have benefited matters had we had the power. So, at the present time, many of us are hourly expecting and hoping that God will signally rebuke the sin of slavery, and by a special interposition of Divine Providence bring what we conceive to be the greatest of evils to an instant and final end. In our folly, we do not consider that Jehovah never would have permitted the first human-freighted ship to leave the shores of Africa for the New World, had he not designed a beneficial result should flow from the introduction of the sable children of the tropics into the fruitful fields of our own temperate latitude. Yes, Madam, with our conception of the nature of Deity, we can not believe that the All-wise Ruler would purposely allow a great evil to grow and increase to such magnitude, as to become indeed the very centre and pivot of the world's commerce; merely to signalize his disapprobation of it by the overthrow of the world's prosperity, when he might have crushed it in the beginning without harm to a single individual. We honestly believe, therefore, God had a design in permitting the old Slave-trade—a design to bless and benefit the human race.

What! God have a hand in the horrors of the Middle Passage? Consider, Madam, the horrors of war, of pestilences, and famines. God surely has a hand in all these. Consider the horrors of our Revolutionary struggle, and, above all, the sad fate of the poor Indian, whom your own Puritan ancestors helped to drive off, at the point of the bayonet, from the hunting-grounds of his fathers, to the unknown wildernesses of the West. Will you deny that God had a hand in all this? And yet the Red-men have faded from before the presence of the Pale-faces, as the morning mists melt away before the rising sun. We have slain in battle many more of them, than ever perished of blacks in the Middle Passage, and at the same time we have utterly corrupted the living with our damnable fire-water, thus rendering them useless to themselves and to the world; neither have we converted any numbers of them to Christianity, as is the case with millions of the Africans held in bondage on the American Continent. Still, in the face of these facts, your anti-slavery minister will tell

you in all soberness, that God had a hand in removing
the savages in order to make room for the saints. And
he will tell you the simple truth. We have no fault
to find with him for entertaining such a belief. But
we do find fault with him for turning upon the men
of the South in the same breath, and saying to them in
regard to their negroes, what the lawyer said to his
client when told *whose* bull it was did the goring:
"Ah! that alters the case." Yes, thou Reverend Pharisee, we do blame you for your inconsistency, while
acknowledging the hand of God in the merciless
slaughter of whole tribes of artless children of the forest, in order to make room for the children of civilization; in refusing to perceive the benign Providence
that snatched the idolatrous children of the desert from
their cannibalism and their bloody human sacrifices, to
place them under the control and tutorage of enlightened men and women of a superior race.

For, although we might compare the present condition of the Southern slaves with the condition of other
laborers elsewhere, we yet fancy such would hardly be
the proper method by which to arrive at any just
knowledge of the benefits or evils resulting from African servitude. Certainly we believe the comparison,
if made, would show that the negroes of the South are
happier as a class than the peasants of other countries.
We know from actual observation that they fare better
than the poor of any of our cities—are more warmly
clad, work less, and are a thousand-fold more cheerful
and contented. We know, too, that they are infinitely
better off than the peons of Mexico, who are bought by
the year for any nominal sum which they are presumed

13

to owe the purchaser, and are liable in their old age to be turned adrift without a home, and with not a living soul to take an interest in their welfare. We also believe, and so must every thoughtful honest man, that their lot is even enviable compared to that of the poor Coolies and other *free apprentices*, those new-fangled slaves whom Cant and Hypocrisy are engaged in selling for *a term of years* to our tropical neighbors. But we repeat, there is no necessity to make the comparison. To arrive at any rational conclusion as to what has been the result of African slavery in the United States, we must consider what was the character of the negroes when first landed on our shores, and what is their character now. Have they improved in speech, in morals, in personal appearance, and in usefulness; or have the "degrading effects" of a century of slavery rendered them more savage than they were when they wandered about in the jungles of Congo and Guinea, feasting on human flesh, and worshipping dogs and monkeys, stocks and stones? or have they cursed the soil by their presence, rendering it as barren and unfruitful as their original desert wastes, whereon their kindred still roam, rejoicing in the rude comforts of an untutored barbarism, and in all the wealth and simplicity of Adam's fig-leaf? This is the question, and the only question.

However much sophists and demagogues may seek to mislead and confuse the public mind in regard to the subject of Negro Slavery, the above is the only view to be taken of its merits or demerits. How this master or that master may maltreat or abuse his slaves, has nothing whatever to do with the question. No more than, to judge of the influence and results of Christianity, would it be just to cite the examples of a Borgia or a Hildebrand. No more than, to weigh the blessings of the sacred institution of marriage, would it be proper or reasonable to dwell only on the frequency of divorces, or to direct attention to the many mismated couples, whose union is a lasting torment to each. Would you not call that man a fool, who should pretend to denounce the Bible on account of Judas Iscariot and the bloody old Popes of the Middle Ages, or the thousands of modern Christians who are only wolves in sheeps' clothing? Unquestionably. We give our readers credit for common sense and common honesty. We take it for granted that we are addressing no Hottentot, no Fourierite, no free-lover, no latter-day-saint, no carping philosopher, superlatively wise in his own conceit. We beg the question therefore. Our readers will all acknowledge that the merits of Christianity are greater than its abuses, and that its abuses even may be considered blessings, when compared with the greater evils which would undoubtedly afflict mankind if shrouded wholly in heathenish darkness, and deprived of even the most glimmering ray of Gospel light. Thus Dr. Livingstone, the Protestant anti-slavery missionary, coming from the jungles of Ethiopia into the Catholic Portugese colony of Algona, honestly confesses that he would rejoice to see the poor degraded negroes of the interior even no better Christians than the saint-worshipping half-castes of the coast-country, rather than they should remain in the forlorn and hopeless state of barbarism and savage idolatry in which he found them universally steeped. To his enlightened vision, even

the most priest-ridden of untutored Catholics appeared
as saints, compared with the incomparably vicious and
degraded pagans whom he had left behind him, and
whose whole religion consisted in the worship of Barimo, or Evil Spirits.

As for the benefits flowing from the institution of
Christian marriage, we presume there are only a few
radicals in this enlightened country who will question
them.   Not because there are no abuses, but because
without marriage there would be greater abuses.   And
why shall we not apply the same just and humane reasoning to the existence of African slavery in our Southern States?   Can any honest man tell why Negro
slavery should be condemned, if it can be shown that,
with all its abuses, it has still been the source of incal-
culable good to millions? that, had it not been introduced into America, greater abuses would have been
the consequence?   If there be such a man in these
States, an honest anti-slavery man who loves God and
hates the devil, who honors Truth but despises Cant,
who pins his faith to the lively oracles of the Living
Jehovah, and not to the trash and stale fustian of the
Bunkum orators of the tabernacles, we beseech from
him a candid hearing.   Lay aside all your early prejudices, Brother after our own heart, and read the following pages thoughtfully, calmly, and dispassionately,
and afterwards decide the matter for yourself as be-
seemeth a.man, and do not crouch down like a trembling slave for fear of public opinion, and in consequence adopt some one else's sentiments as your own.

Imprimis, then, do you know how it came about that
African slavery was first introduced into the New

World? We warrant you not one in ten of the negro-
philists of Europe or this country can properly answer
this question. We warrant you, also, that fully one
half the enemies of the peculiar institution do not know
that negroes have always in all lands been held as
slaves, from times so remote that the memory of man
runneth not to the contrary; but firmly believe, that
the whole blame of the great oppression rests upon the
heads of the slaveholders of the present generation. To
all such allow us to say, the introduction of African
slavery into America originated in the humane breast
of Las Casas. At that period the aborigines of this
country, the poor untutored "salvages," were sorely
oppressed by the discoverers and conquerors of the
land, who used the poor creatures like so many beasts
of burden, not even sparing their lives on occasions.
Having been accustomed, before the coming of the pale
faces, to the utmost personal freedom, devoting their
time to idleness and hunting, they very soon proved
unequal to the misfortunate change, being incapable of
performing the tasks imposed upon them by their new
masters, and so perished miserably by hundreds of
thousands.

To remedy so great an evil, Las Casas bethought
him of the experiment of removing the negroes from
Africa to the New World, that they might take the
place of the poor "salvages." The negroes were already slaves in their own country—slaves to masters
whose authority was absolute—and had been such from
time immemorial. Not only were they slaves to men;
they were doubly the slaves of every species of degradation as well. Sunk in the most deplorable barba-

rism, and guilty of all the wickednesses of the cities of the plain, they also waged incessantly cruel wars amongst themselves, tribe against tribe, and village against village. Chiefs built their huts of human bones, and drank the blood of their enemies out of human skulls, and yearly offered up whole hecatombs of human sacrifices; and on the death of every headman of a tribe, hundreds of his slaves were butchered over his grave, that they might accompany and serve their dead master in the other world.

Surely, thought the humane Las Casas, there can be no harm in removing such wretches from the thraldom of their heathen masters to the milder sway of civilized men. And at that time, all humane men every where were of the same opinion. Catholics, churchmen, non-conformists of every persuasion, and infidel philosophers also, all regarded the move as both philanthropic and evangelical. Certainly good men reprobated the horrors of the Middle Passage then, as earnestly as they do at the present time; but when they reflected on the horrors left behind—the man-eaters and the bloody human sacrifices—the constant wars between the different tribes—their spiritual degradation and mental darkness—they felt constrained to look upon even the horrors of the Middle Passage as an advance from the blacker horrors of the accursed country, whence the poor creatures were being removed. And so our own New-England Puritans became the leading traffickers in slaves, and Boston one of the best slave-marts in the country. The clergy of Massachusetts then did not scruple to buy human flesh at the market price, and felt that they were conferring a favor upon the poor pagan purchased, which they were.

Wisely, however, the Slave-Trade did at last come to an end; at least so far as the United States are concerned. We say *wisely*, and what we say we mean; for had the traffic continued, the Southern people would have soon found themselves in a similar predicament with the man who purchased the elephant. They would have come into possession of such a multitudinous horde of savages, that they never would have succeeded in controlling them, much less in civilizing or christianizing them; but would have been doubtless themselves swept away by the black inundation, leaving the whole land covered with a darker barbarism than what marred its face when first discovered by the great Genoese.

Altogether, we only received from Africa about three hundred and eighty thousand blacks. At the time of their importation, they were valued at and sold in the market for about an average of fifty dollars a piece. They were worth no more, and in Africa not so much; indeed, a hundred-fold less. Even at the present time slaves can be bought in Africa at one dollar a head. Dr. Livingstone saw a slave boy sold in Algona for only five shillings. Now, say what you please about selling God's image, we think it looks encouraging to see the said image bring a thousand dollars instead of the paltry sum of five shillings: it indicates improvement, to say no more. Had the Slave-Trade continued, however, we doubt much if the negroes would by this time have been worth a baubee. And had not England turned anti-slavery, and emancipated all the

blacks in her colonies, thus giving the South the mo-
nopoly of most slave-grown products, the negroes
would, in all probability, have been worth not more
than half what they are valued at now ; and in consequence would not have been one half so humanely
cared for as they are at present, since self-interest
prompts every man to bestow the greatest care upon
what is of the greatest pecuniary value. The reader
will perceive, therefore, that, while acknowledging the
hand of Providence in the introduction of African
slavery into the New World, we also consider the abolition of the Slave-Trade at the proper time as equally
providential.

But let us come back to our " sheeps."

When the honest reader reflects what was the character of the negroes when first brought to America ;
when he reflects, also, that the merchantable value of
" God's image cut in ebony," has been enhanced just
about one thousand per cent, by one hundred years of
servitude ; he will certainly agree with us, that whips,
and chains, gyves, buckings, burnings, and flagella-
tions, have not been so much in fashion at the South,
as certain light-headed gentlemen would have one believe.

But the best test of the improvement of the African
race in this country, is not the increased value of the
negroes as chattels. It has grown to be almost a political axiom, that nations as well as individuals propa-
gate the species according to the abundance or lack of
proper nurture, protection from the inclemencies of the
weather, attention in sickness, and the removal of dis-
quiet from the mind. If we apply this test to the con-

dition of the slaves on our Southern plantations, we will find that they have fared better than the laboring classes of almost any nation on the globe. From the original three hundred and eighty thousand, by natural increase, aside from their descendants now free, in 1850 according to the census there were in the South 3,204,000 slaves of the African race. These, allowing the same percentage of increase for ten years, as the census returns show during the last decennial period, would now number nearly five millions. And as an evidence of their moral improvement, the number of these connected with the churches is 468,000, or about one seventh part of the entire number. Probably in no State in this nation is one seventh part of the whites professors of religion. These Christian slaves are distributed as follows :

Connected with the Methodist Church South, are.......200,000
Methodist Church North, in Virginia and Maryland......15,000
Missionary and Hard Shell Baptists...................175,000
Old School Presbyterians.............................15,000
New   "   "..................................20,000
Protestant Episcopalians.............................7,000
Disciples of Christ..................................10,000
All other sects combined.............................20,000

These figures appear the more remarkable, when we consider that, as a result of all foreign missionary efforts, the native heathen church membership in 1855 was only 180,000. Add to which, that none of our Southern slaves are addicted to the paganism of their ancestors ; none of them are liable to lose their lives except for offenses against the country's written laws ;

13*

none of them are cannibals; all of them are more or less warmly clad in garments which cover the whole body, and all of them are kept under wholesome restraint to prevent their lapsing again into. barbarism ; and we are at a loss to perceive, how any reflective person can refuse to acknowledge, that it is manifestly a Divine Providence which has wrought so great a change for the better, in so short a time.

But, aside from this great improvement in their own physical and moral condition, are these enslaved Africans of no benefit to the rest of mankind ? What is the value of the annual product of their labor ? It is estimated at ten hundred millions of dollars ! almost enough to buy up the whole continent of Africa. The surplus annual produce alone brings in over two hundred millions of dollars ; we mean that surplus which the South exports to foreign countries. And this is no fictitious wealth—it is solid and substantial. The Panic which has so recently collapsed the speculative bubbles of the North; which destroyed the financial credit of the whole country, and shook the entire continent of Europe with a great monetary crash ; scarcely affected in the least the wonderful prosperity of our Slave States. This fact is now conceded by all. It is proven by the continued high prices paid for negroes and land in the South, but more especially by the little decrease in the value of her exports for the fiscal year of 1857–8, and their undoubted increase in value for the fiscal year of 1858–9. According to the official report of the Secretary of State, our exports of domestic products for the last fiscal year show the following figures :

Free States exclusively............... $5,281,091
Free and Slave States in common...... 84,417,493
Slave States exclusively.............188,693,498

the balance of our exports being made up of specie and foreign productions re-exported. Indeed, had it not been for the products of slave labor during the two years last past, not only would our own country have become bankrupt, but the leading nations of Europe would have shared a like fate, and fully ten millions of white freemen would have been thrown out of employment, and thereby reduced to absolute starvation.

And yet in the face of all these wonderful but undeniable facts, there are men in the world who have so befogged their minds with the senseless vaporings of our mouthing anti-slavery orators, they fail to note the finger of God in so marvellous a development! They refuse to confess the goodness of the Almighty in snatching the poor naked heathen from the burning plains of Africa — clothing them in the habiliments worn by civilized men—enlightening gradually their benighted minds, and rendering their labor (before expended in wars and a constant struggle with torrid wastes of sand for the commonest necessaries of life) so productive as to fill all the ports of commerce with activity, and to crowd the navies of the world with cargoes more rich and rare than those brought from ancient Ind : giving thereby bread and life to the toiling millions of God's poor, who would else be left to perish succorless and friendless. On the contrary, full of fanatical zeal and blind prejudice, they seek to undermine the institutions of the South by every foul

means known to conspiracy, and, failing in their trea-
sonable designs, out of sheer madness exalt to the dignity of a martyr a hanged horse-thief and murderer!
And this too, while one of their most cunning and oily-
tongued leaders confesses in the words following, that
they are remiss in their own conduct towards the free
blacks in the Northern States. Hear him :

"How are the free colored people treated at the
North? They are almost without education ; with but
little sympathy for ignorance. They are refused the
common rights of citizenship which the whites enjoy.
They can not even ride in the cars of our city railroads.
They are snuffed at in the house of God, or tolerated
with ill-disguised disgust. Can the black man be a
mason in New-York? Let him be employed as a
journeyman, and every Irish lover of liberty that carries the hod or trowel would leave at once or compel
him to leave. Can the black man be a carpenter?
There is scarcely a carpenter-shop in New-York in
which a journeyman would continue to work if a black
man was employed in it. Can the black man engage
in the common industries of life? There is scarcely
one in which he can engage. He is crowded down,
down, down, through the most menial callings, to the
bottom of society. We tax them, and then refuse to
allow their children to go to our public schools. We
tax them, and then refuse to sit by them in God's
house. *We heap upon them moral obloquy more atrocious
than that which the master heaps upon the slave.* And,
notwithstanding all this, we lift ourselves up to talk to
the Southern people about the rights and liberties of
the human soul, and especially the African soul !"

These are the words of H. W. Beecher, who called John Brown a "servant of Christ," and declared from his pulpit, that it only wanted a cord and gibbet to make of that old felon's life a complete success! Consistency, thou art a jewel!

This is what the abolitionists in the North have done for the negro: let us see now what their English cousins have done for him. Many facts of importance in regard to the Underground Railroad have been brought to light by the *fiasco* of Old Brown and his companions at Harper's Ferry, but none of greater importance than the disclosures in regard to the actual condition of the negroes of Canada. By the proceedings of the Court of Assizes of Essex county, (Canada,) it appears that the grand-jury have made a presentment to the court, based upon a representation emanating from the authorities of the township of Anderdon, in regard to the negro population of the county. The grand-jury submit the document that was presented to them to the court, and urge that some action be taken in the matter. The Anderdon authorities say: "We are aware that nine tenths of the crimes committed in the county of Essex, according to population, are committed by the colored people." And they further urge, that 'some measures may be taken by the government to protect us and our property, or persons of capital will be driven from the country." The court, in alluding to this presentment, remarked that "he was not surprised at finding a prejudice existing against them (the negroes) among the respectable portion of the people, for they were indolent, shiftless, and dishonest, and unworthy of the sympathy that some mistaken parties extended to them; they would not work when opportunity was presented, but preferred subsisting by thiev·ing from respectable farmers, and begging from those benevolently inclined."

We may now return to our subject. And it may be that some reader will object, How do you know, had the negroes been left unmolested in their native land, they would not of themselves have attained to even greater civilization than they have achieved in this country? This objection is easily answered by considering the present status of Cuffee in his native Africa: and let us pause a moment to regard him, as described by the latest and most reliable travellers.

Richardson and Barth have furnished us with the most reliable information in regard to the negroes of North-Africa. Although both these travellers were sent out by the British Government, and were themselves strongly anti-slavery in sentiment, they yet bear testimony to the utter degradation of the natives of Negroland, and prove conclusively that these are to-day just where they were one hundred—yes, five hundred years ago, and that now as always slavery is their normal condition. Dr. Barth even is of opinion, (in opposition to the popular sentiment,) that the foreign slave-trade has very little to do comparatively with the horrors of slave-hunting and the like inhumanities; but that the domestic slave-trade of Africa alone is the chief support of such barbarous acts. Hear him:

" Now, it should always be borne in mind that there is a broad distinction between the slave-trade and domestic slavery. The foreign slave-trade may, comparatively speaking, be easily abolished, though the difficulties of watching over contraband attempts have been shown sufficiently by many years' experience. With the abolition of the slave-trade all along the northern and south-western coast of Africa, slaves will cease to be brought down to the coast; and in this way a great deal of mischief and misery necessarily resulting from this inhuman traffic will be cut off. *But this, unfortunately, forms only a small part of the evil.* There can be no doubt that the most horrible topic connected with slavery is slave-hunting; and this is carried on not only for the purpose of supplying the foreign market, but, *in a far more extensive degree, for supplying the wants of domestic slavery.*"

In this assertion, Dr. Barth is sustained by the facts, and by the unanimous testimony of all explorers worthy of the name. It has not been six months, in fact, since the death of Guezo I., King of Dahomey, has been announced; and his son and heir caused *eight hundred slaves to be slain on his grave*, in order that these might accompany their dead sovereign into the land of spirits : while of the two hundred thousand population of this kingdom, one hundred and eighty thousand are slaves.

Passing down into South-Central and South-Africa, on the testimony of Dr. David Livingstone, a devout missionary, a practical Christian, a learned Englishman, the most wonderful of modern travellers and explorers, and withal both by constitutional and national prejudices anti-slavery in sentiment; we learn what is the present condition of those native Negro tribes, from whom our own Southern slaves have doubtless in the main derived their origin. Dr. Livingstone has evidently done his best to present us the most pleasing aspect of the condition of those tribes : being therefore a witness for the prosecution, his testimony must of necessity be regarded as at least impartial when used by a pro-slavery advocate.   Now, Dr. Livingstone describes nearly all the black tribes with whom he came in contact as more or less enslaved, except the Bechuanas and Makalolos.   But what is the character of these black freemen of Africa, according to the testimony of Livingstone himself?   We shall see.

First, as to the Bechuanas.

The different tribes comprehended under this general name, live in Southern Africa, near the English possessions of Cape Colony, and have b en under missionary influence for about fifty years.   Dr. Livingstone lived among these people a long time as a missionary himself, and married the daughter of Mr. Moffat, who has labored in the same field forty years or more, and who has also translated the Bible into the Bechuana language.   In his zeal for establishing that the Bechuanas are free, the worthy missionary even goes so far as to contend that their very name means *free men.*   Now, to show what is considered freedom in benighted Africa, read the following account of the conversion of Sechele, the chief of one of the Bechuana tribes.   We quote the author's own words :

"Seeing me anxious that his people should believe the words of Christ, he once said: ' Do you imagine these people will ever believe by your merely talking to them ? I can make them do nothing except by thrashing them ; and if you like, I shall call my headmen, and with our litupa (whips of rhinoceros hide) we will soon make them all believe together.'"

This may look like freedom to an Englishman, especially when in Africa, where the chiefs of most tribes are wont to run a muck, (when they have nothing more serious to occupy their thoughts,) killing every person they meet; but we presume most Americans will be puzzled to perceive wherein is any difference between such a free use of litupa by the headmen of Sechele and the same use of cowskins by the overseers on our Southern plantations.

But again, speaking of these same Bechuanas:

"No one refuses to acquiesce in the decision of the chief, *as he has the power of life and death in his hands, and can enforce the law to that extent if he chooses.* . . . This system was found as well developed among the Makalolos as among the Bakwains, or even better, and is no foreign importation."

The Bakwains here spoken of are a tribe of Bechuanas—the same of whom Sechele was chief.

As for the intellectual advancement of the Bechuanas, despite fifty years' intercourse with the English, Livingstone gives the following not very flattering report:

"The acme of respectability among the Bechuanas is the possession of cattle and a wagon. It is remarkable that, though these latter require frequent repairs, none of the Bechuanas have ever learned to mend them. Forges and tools have been at their service, and teachers willing to aid them, but, beyond putting together a camp-stool, no effort has ever been made to acquire a knowledge of the trades. They observe most carefully a missionary at work until they understand whether a tire is well welded or not, and then pronounce upon its merits with great emphasis, but there their ambition rests satisfied."

So much for the Bechuanas.

As we have before observed, the Makalolos were another tribe of freemen with whom Livingstone became acquainted. They reside to the north of the lake Ngami, in the heart of what has heretofore been considered a *terra incognita*, namely, Ethiopia. They never saw a white man before the coming of Livingstone; never had any intercourse with the Portuguese or other slave-traders, and pretended indeed to know nothing of the slave-trade whatever. According to their oral traditions, they came originally from further north, and conquered by their superior prowess all the tribes then inhabiting their present country; *and these tribes they continue to hold in bondage, calling them Makalaka, their word for slaves.* What the nature of this slavery is, as well as the character of the enslaved tribes, can be conjectured after perusing the following extracts:

" On land the Makalaka fear the Makalolo; on water the Makalolo fear them, and can not prevent them from racing with each other, dashing along at the top of their speed, and placing their masters' lives in danger. In the event of a capsize, many of the Makalolo would sink like stones. A case of this kind happened on the first day of our voyage up. The wind, blowing generally from the east, raises very large waves on the Leeambye. An old doctor of the Makalolo had his canoe filled by one of these waves, and, being unable to swim, was lost. The Makalaka who were in the canoe with him saved themselves by swimming, and were afraid of being punished with death in the evening, for not saving the doctor as well. Had he been a man of more influence, they certainly would have suffered death."

Another example:

"An interesting-looking girl came to my wagon one day in a state of nudity, and almost a skeleton. She was a captive from another tribe, and had been neglected by the man who claimed her. Having supplied her wants, I made inquiries for him, and found that he had been unsuccessful in raising a crop of corn, and had no food to give her. I volunteered to take her, but he said he would allow me to feed her and make her fat, and then take her away. I protested against his heartlessness, and, as he said he could not part with her, I was precluded from attending to her wants. In a day or two she was lost sight of. She had gone out a little way from the town, and, being too weak to return, had been cruelly left to perish. Another day I saw a poor boy going to the water to drink, apparently in a starving condition. This case I brought before the chief in council, and found that his emaciation was ascribed to disease and want combined. The chief decided that the owner of this boy should give up his alleged right rather than destroy the child. When I took him he was so far gone as to be in the cold stage of starvation, but was soon brought round by a little milk given three or four times a day."

The reader will now know why these Makalolo are not slaves—they are a precious lot of slaveholders! Besides, they are not negroes proper, but rather copper-colored, being evidently in part of Arab descent. The Makalaka, on the contrary, are darker-hued, and pretty fair specimens of the negroes of dry latitudes.

The Makalolo and their slaves usually dress alike, the fashion being to appear in *puris naturalibus*, or at best with a very shabby apology for Adam's fig-leaf. The slaves delve in the ground for food to feed their masters, while the latter are nearly always at war with some tribe or other, or engaged in the old Highland sport of *lifting* their neighbors' cattle, etc. etc. When they attack a village, their custom is to slay without remorse or any distinction of age or sex, and to reduce all the captives, whose lives are spared, to bondage. And this is the sum of all that can be said of Dr. Livingstone's enlightened free tribe of blacks in the interior of Ethiopia, about whom some respectable journals, in both Great Britain and the United States, have circulated many exaggerated not to say apocryphal stories.

As for the other negro tribes with whom Livingstone was made acquainted in South Central Africa, he has himself been forced to make the following confession :

" The statement of Pereira that twenty negroes were slaughtered in a day, was not confirmed by any one else, though numbers may have been killed on some particular occasion during his visit ; *for we find throughout all the country north of* 20°, WHICH I CONSIDER REAL NEGRO, *the custom of slaughtering victims to accompany the departed soul of a chief ; and human sacrifices are occasionally offered, and certain parts of the bodies are used as charms.*"

You here behold, O negrophilist of the North, what

the negro slaves on our Southern plantations would have been, had not their ancestors been providentially removed to a land of Christian enlightenment, and placed under the severe but necessary pupilage of life-bondage to white men. And this very necessity Livingstone has unwittingly confessed, while giving the reasons which led him to refuse a slave-girl presented to him by Shinte, a chief of the Balonda—a tribe remarkable for the toilet of its females, who literally have " nothing to wear."

" If I could have taken her into my family for the purpose of instruction," says the Doctor, " and then returned her as a free woman, according to a promise I should have made the parents, I should have done so; but to take her away, and probably never be able to secure her return, would have produced no good effect on the minds of the Balonda; they would not then have seen evidence of our hatred of slavery, and the kind attentions of my friends, *as it almost always does in similar cases*, would have turned the poor thing's head. The difference in position between them and us is as great as between the lowest and highest in England, and we know the effects of sudden elevation on wiser heads than hers, whose owners had not been born to it."

Immediately following this confession is a very singular paragraph, which we must quote, if merely to show how a good and wise man can be blinded by either national, or sectarian, or constitutional, or whatever other kind of prejudice you may please to call it. For, directly after having refused the gift of a slave from conscientious scruples, this really Christian gentleman,

in every sense of the word, proceeded to show the natives the pictures in the magic lantern—and the very
first picture represented Father Abraham, a *slaveholder !*
But let the Doctor tell it in his own words :

" The first picture exhibited was Abraham about to
slaughter his son Isaac ; it was shown as large as life,
and the uplifted knife was in the act of striking the
lad ; the Balonda men remarked that the picture was
much more like a god than the things of wood or clay
they worshipped.   I explained that this man was the
first of a race to whom God had given the Bible we
now hold, and that among his children our Saviour appeared. The ladies listened with silent awe ; but when
I moved the slide, the uplifted dagger moving towards
them, they thought it was to be sheathed in their own
bodies instead of Isaac's. ' Mother ! mother !' all shout-
ed at once, and off they rushed helter-skelter, tumbling
pell-mell over each other, and over the little idol huts
and tobacco bushes."

After the learned missionary had gotten through
with the illustration of this subject, having previously
delivered them a good orthodox anti-slavery sermon,
we should have liked much to witness the effect on
himself and his auditory of the public announcement
that the same "friend of God," even Abraham, was a
slaveholder, and bought and sold human chattels at
their market value !   We apprehend there would have
been seen then and there *real pictures*, which, for effect,
would have greatly surpassed the cunningest devices
of the camera-obscura.

And now, will the reader pardon yet another digres-
sion ? For just here we wish briefly to allude to a

very singular fallacy, which has begun to mislead the minds of men of late years—and that is a belief in the absolute non-superiority of races; in other words, the absolute equality of all men, of every creed and every color. A new sect of philosophers is springing up in this country and in Europe, who, shutting their eyes to the experience of thousands of years, and refusing to acknowledge the notorious superiority in all climates and all lands of the pure white races, have the impudence and temerity to declare that this superiority is only apparent, and does not indicate any inherent superiority of blood. We have often been amused to note what poor shifts these learned wiseacres are forced to resort to in defense of their cherished hobby. The weakest and most shallow of them all, is the latest which has come to our knowledge. It originated in this country, we believe, and is urged by the abolitionists in support of their designs for compassing the emancipation of our Southern slaves, or at least in the hope of putting the institution "in course of ultimate extinction."

It is this very sapient proposition: The whites in these United States are superior to the negroes, because the latter are exotics in our latitude; but are inferior to the same blacks in Africa, because there the blacks are the indigenous race, while the whites are the exotics, and in consequence must succumb to the climate.

Now, can the reader tell wherein lies the wit of the above sage proposition? Why, in this: It is like the celebrated question of a certain learned philosopher, asking the reason why a pail full to the brim of water can yet be made to contain a fish weighing two pounds, without spilling a single drop of the fluid. *Both pro-positions are false in fact.* When you put the fish weighing two pounds into the pail, you find that the water does run over; and so, too, when you come to study the map of Africa, you find the white race, there as here, invariably superior to the black, and this from time immemorial. Bayard Taylor assures us, that, on the walls of the Egyptian monuments and palaces, the thick lips, woolly head, black skin, and other peculiarities of the negro, are often to be seen, but in every instance the blackamoor is represented as serving in the capacity of a slave.

Confining ourselves, however, to modern times, we find the Boers in South-Africa holding the blacks in a state of bondage, in spite of the English, the negroes, *and the climate, all combined.* So, too, on both the East and West Coast we find the Portugese doing the same thing. And as for Northern Africa, the testimony of Dr. Barth and almost every other traveller, proves beyond cavil that the mass of slaves used there for domestic purposes are brought from Negroland, and are sold to the Arabs, Berbers, etc. etc.; all of these latter being not in the least tainted with negro blood, if not pure white. At a late meeting of the Boston Society of Natural History, however, Dr. Bodichon, a resident of Algeria, presented a paper on the races of the north half of Africa, in which he contended that the Numidians or Berbers, and the Arabs, are white. The former live in the mountains, are small in stature, warlike, independent, democratic, and polygamous. They dwell in villages, and plant vineyards. They are fine soldiers, able to compete with Europeans. They are an indigenous race also; at least Bodiehon so declares. The Arabs live in the plains, are a tall race, of dark complexion, equestrian, nomadic, warlike, religious, poetical, and polygamous. Dr. Bodiehon also found in the interior a Germanic race, with blue eyes and light hair, and who are probably the descendants of the ancient Carthaginians. " *These all*," concludes Bodiehon, "*possess the characteristic superiority of white races—the enslaving of the neighboring blacks.*"

Wherefore, our philanthropic friends, whenever again you feel inclined to swallow unquestioning, like so many young crows, whatever your gowned clergy and much-be-flattered paragons of the Lyceum may choose to thrust down your gaping throats; we beseech you, in Truth's name, to keep your mouths shut until you have learned the nature at least of the nutriment you are invited in such honeyed phrase to receive into your capacious stomachs. What if you do possess all the wonderful digestive capabilities of the ostrich, is that any reason why you should stultify yourselves by evincing as little discretion as that silly bird, fowl, or whatever you may please to call it, which never can distinguish between a fat healthy worm and a tenpenny nail? Even if you have "a taste for being diddled," have sufficient self-respect not to make yourselves the laughing-stock of the wise, by giving point to the keen satire of Hood:

> " Only propose to blow a bubble,
> And lord! what hundreds will subscribe for soap!"

But to return to our subject once again.

Having demonstrated to a certainty that the four

14

millions of enslaved blacks in the United States are superior in every respect to the blacks remaining in Africa, whether free or slave; and having demonstrated, also, that the negroes every where are an inferior race; therefore, exclaims the reader, believing slavery to be the natural and normal condition of the negro, and that his removal from Congo or Mozambique is to benefit both him and his posterity, of course you advocate the revival of the slave-trade? Not of necessity, dear Sir! Not of necessity, permit us to assure you, thou venerable and respected grandam! Draw a little nearer, if you please, Madam, seeing that age has rendered your hearing a little defective. Well. Now, there is your paragon of grandsons, the hopeful Augustus—(he is twisting the cat's tail, we observe!) who is ever tearing his dear granny's dress, and plucking at the scanty beard which grows from a mole directly under your venerable chin: Augustus dearly loves sugar-plums, doesn't he? And a few of them, well melted in the mouth before being swallowed, rarely give him the colic or the gripes, eh? Oh! they only sweeten the dear child's temper, we hear you mumble, admiringly. But when he bolts down his sugar-plums whole without any previous lubrifaction, (which he always does, if allowed,) and crams and crams until, however much like poor Oliver he may cry for more, he finds it impossible to coax or force another plum into his distended stomach, what are the sad consequences? Ah! how often has your grandmotherly soul been grieved within you, while you watched by his sleepless pillow after every such feat of gormandizing, administering to the saintly infant tinctures and powders, from ten of the clock at night until the crowing of the old family rooster at day-break! Truly we will not harrow your warm old heart by dwelling on such painful reminiscences. Observe, however, that there may be a surfeit of slaves as well as of sugar-plums.

But these things are not left to man to decide. A Higher Power disposes—man is like the dog in the treadmill, he goes his little round, but can never get beyond the length of his tether. Under the guidance of the Divine Hand, at the proper time, a missionary exactly fitted for his mission has penetrated to the most secret recesses of Ethiopia, and, returning safely thence, has made known to the Christian world such facts as lead us to predict: That, fifty years from to-day, the slave-trade on the high seas will be entirely unknown. The only thing which encourages the traffic at present is the difference in value between a slave in Algona and the same chattel in Cuba, Brazil, or the United States. Whenever the day comes that a man's labor shall be worth as much in Central Africa as in Alabama or Louisiana, it will then no longer be profitable to engage in the slave-trade; and, we don't care how much the preachers pray, or the politicians twaddle, or the old women whimper, or the young misses snivel, or the British cruisers cruise, or the laws denounce the traffic; nothing under heavens will ever stop the slave-trade, but *the certainty of no profits.*

Now, as we have declared above, we believe the time will come when there will be no gains for those who would like to engage in the slave-trade, or the Coolie trade either, which is altogether the worse of the two. Were the writer a member of the English

Cabinet, and did his voice possess sufficient weight, he flatters himself that he could put a stop to the slave-trade at least, in the short space of twenty years. Dr. Livingstone has shown that all Central Africa, once considered a waste of sand, is reticulated with many noble streams, of a size sufficient to carry large steam-boats, and watering millions of acres of cultivable land, all lying idle at present, owing to the ignorance, lazi-ness, and vice of the indigenous races. Nine tenths of these are already slaves, degraded below the level of the brute creation around them, and holding their lives at the absolute disposal of their masters, who are in all respects as sunken and degraded as themselves. These slaves could be purchased on the spot by Englishmen for one dollar a piece on an average; and the whole territory could likewise be bought up from the different black tribes for a mere song. By judicious leveeing the present fluvial wastes of the Leeambye region could all be reclaimed, and very soon cotton estates, sugar estates, coffee estates, and others could be opened and successfully cultivated, the masters living in the high and healthy districts, leaving the blacks to till the river lands under white tutorage and control. Ere long, wealth would spring up on every hand; towns, vil-lages, gentlemen's parks and preserves, schools, church-es, railroads, steamboats, and telegraphs would follow; and in another generation the negroes themselves would forget their paganism, and would be placed on a par with our own negro slaves, speaking the English lan-guage, freed from their former degradation, clothed in decent apparel, church-goers, Christians many of them, and, compared to what they now are, civilized all. Men might bawl out, slavery! despotism struck in! and all that; yet such is the only method by which Africa can ever be speedily civilized, or rendered of much commercial importance to the rest of the world.

"To this complexion will it come at last."

And, honestly; would not such a system be eminently humane compared with the policy England has pursued in India, and which she will doubtless pursue in Central Africa also, when she once gets a foothold on any of the waters of the Leeambye? In India, although acting in the name of Freedom, the English have oppressed the natives much more despotically than our slaves are oppressed in the South. Perhaps our British cousins have been as lenient as possible under the circumstances; we are not prepared to deny it; but there is, as we all know, a material difference between a clean shirt to a laboring man's back and bacon and greens and johnny cake for his digestion, and a simple strip of calico about the loins with only rice to eat from the cradle to the grave. That the latter condition appertains to the shudras and all the lower castes in India, all must acknowledge. Besides, the Hindoos still remain wedded to their gross superstitions; they despise the religion of their English conquerors; and, as is well known, the recent terrible rebellion was caused solely on account of their abhorrence of cartridges greased with the fat of their sacred animal, the cow. Indeed it has been asserted (how truly we know not) that the English have not cared to Christianize the natives, preferring to make money out of their superstitions, selling them idols of wood and brass fabricated in England, and levying a government tax on the offerings placed in the temples of Brahma, Vishnu, and Juggernaut. Verily this may be called Freedom which produces such results, and that Slavery which in two or three generations converts a horde of lazy savages into useful and partly civilized beings; and because one is called Freedom and the other Slavery, men may be swift to applaud the former and denounce the latter; but, for all that, in the eyes of God, there is nothing in a name!

Now, we have stated above that Great Britain will probably pursue the same line of policy in Africa that she has pursued in India; but that she will continue to do so any length of time, we are inclined to doubt. There is a great difference between the two countries, particularly as regards population. In India there are millions upon millions of laborers, and the killing off of a few hundred thousand is a downright advantage to the survivors. But in Africa the population has always been kept thin and scanty, owing to the constant wars between the petty chiefs, and cannibalism, and human sacrifices, and the slave-trade; in consequence whereof John Bull will soon discover that, if he wishes to develop the resources of the latter country, he will have to put a stop to every practice which causes the destruction of human life. Hence, although the English in the outset may begin in Ethiopia as they began in Calcutta, we opine still that it will not take a great while to convince so practical a people that such a policy *will never pay;* particularly when unemployed Saxons, clamoring for "work or bread," shall throng the streets of Liverpool and Manchester, London and Leeds; and when the price of slave-grown cotton shall have advanced to from twenty to thirty cents per pound.

But let their policy be what it may, we firmly believe that South Central Africa will in time come under English domination. We think this thing has been fore-ordained — predestinated from the foundation of the world. It is a subject of prophecy indeed, and ages ago the decree went forth, that the heathen should become the possession of the followers of the Cross before the second advent of Christ. " I shall give the heathen for thine inheritance, and the uttermost parts of the earth for thy possession; thou shalt break them with a rod of iron; thou shalt dash them in pieces like a potter's vessel." This may be done in the name of Freedom, as the English now rule the Indies, and in time are destined, consociate with the French, to rule Africa; or it may be done under the name of Slavery and superiority of race, as we of America will ever continue to rule our negroes, and those shiftless vagabonds—Indians, half-breeds, and no breeds at all—who wander about from place to place over our vast territorial domain, both present and prospective; or it may be done under the auspices of a supreme autocracy, like that of Russia, which will eventually absorb at least half of Asia, and nearly, if not the whole, of the empire of the Ottomans. But, however accomplished, the event is as certain as fate. No opposition on the part of one-ideaed philanthropists, nor incredulous sneers on the part of infidel philosophers, nor intrigues of selfish cabinets, nor the rant and cant of the tabernacles and Exeter Hall, will avail ought to prevent the fulfillment of the irrevocable fiat of Jehovah-God. In the heavens, sitting on his everlasting throne, the Ancient of Days will laugh at their abortive attempts to retard the progress of true knowledge, of pure religion, and of the only feasible enterprise whereby the millions of Adam's posterity, now so sunk in every beastly degradation, can ever, by any possibility, become regenerated.

Certainly, (and we make the confession with sorrow unfeigned,) before the glorious consummation can be achieved, there must of necessity be innumerable and bloody wars, as well as great oppression of the weak by the strong, and most pitiful crushings of the bruised human heart in all nations. But let us not forget the only, the sad alternative: without such wars, and the subduing of the savage nations by the civilized, there would still greater calamities befall the former through their own ceaseless fightings and discords, while their savage natures would remain world without end the same. Certainly, also, many a Warren Hastings, many a Koompanee Jehan, will grow hugely rich out of the spoil of the poor, while many a heartless Legree will continue to oppress the enslaved African; but even the wickedness and grasping cupidity of such spoilers will result in blessing many a laboring man's hearthstone and humble mechanic's fireside, cheapening the necessaries of life, which they would otherwise be unable to purchase, and enabling them to clothe their families in garments of such warmth and comfort as they otherwise could never provide.

We pray our readers not to misunderstand us, however. We do not seek to defend the outrages perpetrated by Messrs. Koompanee Jehan, Legree, and their compeers in crime and oppression; so neither do we admire the spots on the surface of the sun, but shall we be so foolish as to wish the light of Phœbus extinguished because of such blemishes? No: let Koompanee Jehan answer for himself—let all the rascals the world over answer for themselves; and do you, our readers, take care to stand upright on your own bottoms, and our word for it you will find but precious little time to discuss, or even rail at, the lack of perpendicularity on the part of your neighbors. Christ chose twelve Apostles, yet Judas was one of them. Do you, Reverend Sir, pretend to say that you would object to being an Apostle, because the Apostle's office can be and has been most shamefully abused? Do you believe that by standing in the shoes of Paul you would have to stand in the shoes of Iscariot as well? And yet you are teaching just such nonsense every day of your life. Every day you are teaching your spiritual flock to concern themselves more about the shortcomings of others than their own, until the doctrine taught by Christ, of individual responsibility and individual righteousness, is almost wholly unknown in the land.

O Paul, thou man of Tarsus, how would your eyes have been opened had you lived in this blessed nineteenth century! A little wine for thy stomach's sake, and thine often infirmities, says Paul. Nay, answers the Rev. Water Bunkum; touch not, taste not, handle not the unclean thing, for it is shamefully abused by many, and by using it at all you become a participant in their guilt and debasement. Marriage is honorable in all, says Paul, and the marriage-bed undefiled. Nay, respond the New Lights; marriage is often the source of numberless wrongs, therefore marry not at all, but

14*

let your loves and affinities enjoy the "largest liberty."
If you are called being a slave, seek not to be free, says
Paul. Nay, answer the Priests of Higher Law; administer poison in your master's meat, or march with
pikes and Sharpe's rifles into his mansion, bent on murder, and let your watchword be, God and Liberty! Be
obedient to rulers, says Paul, and to all those who are
in authority, knowing that all governors are appointed
of God. Nay, bawl out the political parsons of these
enlightened times; not so fast, Brother Saul! We
find that it pays to mingle politics and religion, and we
speak advisedly when we say that all governments are
the work of the devil, and hence we advise men every
where to pray for anarchy—for we believe in the largest liberty in all things, and are of those who would
cry,

> "Havoc! and let slip the dogs of war!"

Alas! alas! where shall we find the humble, pray-
erful, and consistent disciple of the Christ who declared,
"My kingdom is not of this world?" Æsop tells us,
in one of his fables, that he took a candle with him on
a certain day to help him in his search for a *man;* but
in the present age of the world, something other than
a candle would be needed to help the most diligent in-
quirer find a *Christian.* We are of opinion, however,
that we are on the eve of a great change for the better;
though we feel sure, notwithstanding, from the predictions of Holy Writ, that the world will continue in a
very deplorable condition even until the sounding of
Gabriel's trumpet. Hence we are astonished at the
simplicity of those soi-disant philosophers, who per-

suade themselves and their disciples that this or that form of oppression, this or that wickedness shall cease before the ushering in of the Millennium. A favorite idea with them is, that in a very few more years there will exist no where on the globe either a slave or slaveholder, king or subject, prince or vassal. Now, to convince such windy babblers of the impiety of their predictions, we would beg to remind them that St. John, foretelling the final destruction of the human race preparatory to the creation of a new heaven and a new earth, uses the following language:

"And I saw an angel standing in the sun; and he cried with a loud voice, saying to all the fowls that fly in the midst of heaven, Come, and gather yourselves together unto the supper of the great God; that you may eat the flesh of KINGS, and the flesh of captains, and the flesh of mighty men, and the flesh of horses, and of them that sit on them, and the flesh of all men, BOTH FREE AND BOND, BOTH SMALL AND GREAT."

Thus it will be seen that kings, captains, *free men* and *slaves*, great men and small, will continue on the earth the same as now, up to its final destruction; or, as was declared by Christ himself, that great day will come as a thief in the night, just as the flood came in the days of Noah—finding men marrying, and trafficking, and lying, and swindling, and corrupting, and degrading, and oppressing their fellow-men as always before. Wherefore let us hope that those visionary gentlemen who are idly dreaming of the fraternization and equality of all races of men will soon lay aside their Utopian schemes, and learn to look upon man as he is, and labor to help him in the condition in which they find him.

For assuredly, Messieurs, the mountain will never come to Mohammed, but Mohammed can go to the mountain if he will. With all your dreaming and theorizing, your cant and your tabernacle trash, you will change man's nature not a whit; but a little practical charity and godliness will effect much. It is just as difficult a matter to whitewash a white man as a blackamoor; and you may remember Thomas Hood's account of the great Philanthropical Society which undertook to wash the latter, and whose members, honest souls! are rubbing and scrubbing poor Cuffee yet:

" Great were the sums collected!
    And great results in consequence expected.
    But somehow, in the teeth of all endeavor,
            According to reports
            At yearly courts,
    The Blacks, confound them! were as black as ever!

" Yes! spite of all the water soused aloft,
    Soap, plain and mottled, hard and soft,
    Soda and pearlash, huckaback and sand,
    Brooms, brushes, palm of hand,
    And scourers in the office strong and clever,
        In spite of all the tubbing, rubbing, scrubbing,
        The routing and the grubbing,
    The Blacks, confound them! were as black as ever!"

And this brings us once more to the consideration of our main subject.

Although the negroes in our Southern States have been improved almost beyond computation, by the necessary pupilage of one hundred years of bondage, they are still totally unprepared for emancipation. This fact is demonstrated clearly by the result in Liberia,

Algona, Jamaica, South and Central America, and every where else in fact that the blacks have been liberated in any numbers. They very soon relapse again into the heathenish practices of their ancestors, superadding to the same the vices of civilization. We once knew an intelligent German gentleman, a graduate of a leading German university, who had afterwards lived three years in London, in which city he was employed by English capitalists to visit Jamaica, for the purpose of superintending some important chemical experiments with sugar-cane. He remained in Jamaica five years. When he first went there, like nearly all the Germans, he was strongly anti-slavery in sentiment; but at the time we made his acquaintance, although then an assistant Professor in one of the leading colleges of New-England, he vowed that no negro was fit for any thing else than slavery. The London *Times*, indeed, after a review of the actual condition of the British West-Indian Islands, closes with the following emphatic paragraph against the policy of black emancipation :

" We wish to heaven that some people in England —neither government people nor persons, nor clergymen—but some just-minded, honest-hearted and clear-sighted men would go out to some of the Islands—say Jamaica, Dominica, or Antigua, not for a month, or three months, but for a year—would watch the precious protege of English philanthropy, the free negro, in his daily habits : would watch him as he lazily plants his little squatting : would see him as he proudly rejects agricultural or domestic service, or accepts it at wages ludicrously disproportionate to the value of his work. We wish too, they would watch him while, with a hide thicker than that of a hippopotamus, and a body to which fervid heat is a comfort rather than an annoyance, he droningly lounges over the prescribed task, on which the intrepid Englishman, unaccustomed and uninured to the burning sun, consumes his impatient energy, and too often sacrifices his life. We wish they would go out and view the negro in all the blazonry of his address, his pride, his ingratitude, contemptuously sneering at the industry of that race which made him free, and then come and teach the memorable lesson of their experience to the fanatics who have perverted him into what he is."

Now, Freedom is a good thing in its place, but there is not in any language a word which is more often misapplied. Nothing is more common than to mistake *license* for *liberty*, nowadays. People seem to have forgotten that a man has to be educated to appreciate Freedom, as much if not more than to appreciate music, or literature, or to be a connoisseur in Art. Properly speaking, there is not a *free man* on the globe: we are all more or less restrained from doing what we like, and such restraint is in nearly every instance not only wholesome but absolutely essential to our well-being. Man needs indeed to stand in greater awe of himself, than of what a fellow-man can do to him. Wherefore, because a man desires the largest liberty, is no reason why he should have it: so, too, do we all desire wealth and the honors of the world, but do not these often render their possessors miserable, changing wise men into fools, and fools into knaves? Why, there is not a beggar in our streets but would like to be put on horseback, and yet he would no sooner find himself in the saddle than he would ride post-haste to the devil, as the old adage hath it. So neither is there a convict in any of our penitentiaries but damns in his heart the whole penal code ; yet the well-being of himself as well as society, demands that he should be restrained of his liberty for all that. The same rule applies to minors also, persons *non compos*, idiots, and others. Wherefore shall it not be held equally applicable to negroes, Indians, Chinese, and all other inferior races, who are incapacitated to take care of themselves ?

Confining ourselves to negroes for the present, we must say, that such works as Uncle Tom's Cabin have created an entirely erroneous sentiment, touching the present mental, moral, and social status of the Negro, to say nothing of their tendency to deceive the public as to the physical condition of the great mass of our negro slaves. Mrs. Stowe wished, doubtless, by writing her book, to reform abuses; but, like the young physician who advised the cutting off of a man's head to cure a tumor on its side, she made a great mistake touching the proper method of reform. Although she must feel flattered by the great success of her book among those who have nothing whatever to do with the abuses of slavery, she can hardly fail to blush when she remembers that no practical good has resulted from her labors; for slavery, according to the often-repeated assurances of her greatest friends and admirers, is daily growing in strength and power.

Now, to arrive at any proper conception of the actual average condition of the slaves on our Southern plantations, the reader must not lose sight of the fact that they are, about three fourths of them, only two or three generations removed from those naked gibbering savages and cannibals, who, fifty or a hundred years agone, offered up human sacrifices on the Continent of Africa. After living some twenty years in the midst of such pagans, Dr. Livingstone, the stout anti-slavery Englishman, is forced to write :

"The Israelitish slaves brought out of Egypt by Moses were not converted and elevated in one generation, though under the direct teaching of God himself. Notwithstanding the number of miracles he wrought, a generation had to be cut off because of unbelief. Our own elevation, also, has been the work of centuries, and, remembering this, we should not indulge in over wrought expectations as to the elevation which those who have inherited the degradation of ages may attain in our day."

This is the whole argument in a nut-shell. With this thought in our minds, the great marvel is, that our negro slaves are not more degraded than we really find them. While it is possible that some of them may continue to this day to worship their fathers' gods, the Barimo, we have yet never met with or heard of any instance of the kind. The nearest approach to any species of paganism amongst the most degraded of them, of which we have any knowledge, is an absurd belief in charms, medicine-bags, witches, conjurers, and the like. Nearly all of the negroes, indeed, except those who have been reared up in direct contact with intelligent whites, and those who are practical believers in Christianity, are more or less wedded to superstition, and firmly believe in the potential agency of conjura-

tion, and in the efficacious influence of "medicine."
What they mean by this expression, is perfectly synon-
ymous with what the Balonda, the blackest and most
woolly - headed of all the inhabitants of Negroland,
mean by the same term, as interpreted by Dr. Livingstone : and we have noticed in the South, too, that the
blackest of the blacks are in the main most generally
addicted to this miserable superstition. What their
"medicine" is composed of, we do not know. They
usually tie it up in little dirty rags, and either suspend
it from a bush over some path often frequented by the
enemy they wish to "kunger," or else try to get a
small bit of the latter's beard which they tie up in the
same rag with their other " charms, " and then "kunger"
him at their leisure. Their bag of " medicine" they call
a "waiter." They believe it to possess wonderful
powers, and that it will protect them against every species of misfortune. Whenever they have done any
thing amiss, they immediately begin to manipulate
their " waiter" in order to " kunger" off whippings, or
any other mode of punishment: and if they can only
procure a bit of their master's beard or of the overseer's,
they are rendered perfectly invulnerable, in their own
eyes, against hurt from either. Of course only the
most degraded of them are such fools, but it is impossible to drive this gross superstition out of the thick
skulls of those who are wedded to it.

We know a Southern gentleman who owns one of
the most inveterate conjurers alive. He is one of your
in-grain lazy devils, and in consequence finds himself
in hot water very frequently ; but so great is his faith
in his medicine-bag, he is accustomed to tell his fellow-

slaves, that he can always "kunger off" a whipping if apprized of its coming soon enough. His master, to cure him of his laziness and his superstition at the same time, used to tell him to prepare his "waiter" several days before he purposed to chastise him, in order that he might make a fair trial of his art of conjuration. The negro's name is Wesley—called Wes' for short— and though he has tried time and again to charm away the remorseless hickory, still, poor fellow ! he has most signally failed in every instance. Notwithstanding, Wes' still clings to his medicine-bag as tenaciously as ever. Like our modern Spiritualists who fail some-times to raise the spirits, Wes' considers that the fault is in himself and not in his "art." Like our modern abolitionists whose hopes are yearly growing "smaller by degrees and beautifully less," he feels assured of a better day a-coming. Like our disappointed politicians who long for the Presidential Chair, he thinks while there is life there is hope : at least Wes' is determined to stick to his "medicine" through thick and through thin.

Connected with this superstition of the medicine-bag and conjuration, is the diabolical practice of poisoning : for the negro poisoner is nearly always a great conjurer, or witch, in the estimation of the other blacks. No person who has not lived in the South, can form any adequate conception of the effects of African poison, or of the frequency of its use. Had the amiable Mrs. Stowe ever heard of the wicked practice, she could have introduced into her book one of the most original as well as useful of characters. How pleasantly, in truth, could she have killed off poor Legree with the slow

African poison, and all for the sake of Humanity! How well she could have painted for our delectation his remorse, and the terrible visions seen during those paroxysms of pain and madness, which the same devilish poison so often produces! Believe us, our readers, it would have been better than a play. It would have proven dreadfully edifying and instructive. Besides, there can certainly be no more charming character to grace a blood-and-thunder novel, than the genuine African poisoner; for usually she is an old toothless hag, who either came direct from Africa herself, or is but one generation removed from those who did—is black as midnight, and, being superannuated, sits all day long in her cabin-door like a great black spider, the while with busy brain and a leer that would shame the devil himself, either laying new schemes for murder or gloating over the murders with which her skinny hands are already stained. The secret (for it is a secret) of her diabolical skill undoubtedly originated in the very heart of Negroland, and is even now known to the fewest number of blacks, and we presume to no living white person whatever.

Some of our readers may possibly remember that Fred. Douglass, the chief negro lecturer of the North, publicly prayed in the presence of several thousand of the *élite* of the city of Chicago, during the Fremont excitement, and on a solemn Sabbath day, too, (the better the day the better the deed, you know!) that the Southern slaves might dare to administer poison to their masters in the food cooked for their tables. Now, we would suggest to honest Fred, that any information as to the nature of the genuine African poison would prove of great service to his quondam fellow-slaves, provided it enabled science to discover an antidote; for, singularly enough, the negroes nearly always poison one another, and rarely even attempt the life of a white person. And it is utterly confounding for what trivial causes they will take the life of a fellow-slave. Sometimes it is simply a dispute about a game at cards or marbles; sometimes the being supplanted by a rival in the confidence of the master or overseer is the exciting cause; but much more frequently jealousy leads to the fatal deed, or a strong desire to get rid of a troublesome wife or husband, in order to solace themselves with some new "affinity."

When a negro has determined to take the life of another negro, he or she, as the case may be, proceeds under cover of night to the cabin of the most famous witch or conjurer in the neighborhood, and in a roundabout, circumlocutory manner states his or her business. They do not use the word poison on such occasions; they call it "medicating." They hint to the old hag of a sorceress, therefore, that they want so and so "medicated." Having communicated their wants and paid the customary fee, the bloody-minded wretches skulk back to their own quarters, feeling a devilish satisfaction. It is but fair to say, however, that many of them have no more correct idea of how such "medication" is effected than our readers; and we are charitable enough to believe, that they sometimes become accessories to murder by poisoning, when their firm conviction is that the little dirty medicine-bag does all the mischief. Occasionally, 'tis true, the negroes attempt to destroy their victims without consulting a witch or conjurer; but in nearly all such instances their attempts prove abortive, for these tyros in villainy seldom advance beyond "jimson weed," ground glass, snakes' heads, lizards stewed in oil, and such like simple poisons. The effects produced on the human system by these are not necessarily fatal, and are altogether different from what is produced by the genuine African poison; the direful effects of this are *sui generis*, and can not be mistaken. This is eminently a slow poison, and rarely kills under six months, and sometimes the victims linger for several years. If it be not in reality what the medical faculty have named African consumption, then it is so nearly allied thereto as to be altogether its cousin-german. We incline to the opinion that they are one and the same thing.

The effects produced by African poison are different in different individuals, but still possess a general similarity in all cases. We never saw its effects upon but one *living* victim, that we are aware of; but we have heard them described so often, we think our description will be true to the facts. And here we may remark, that the same cowardly mode of assassination prevails in Hayti also, which affords additional evidence that the secret is of African origin.

We know an aged gentleman who, when a young man, knew in lower Virginia a certain old Doctor Flournoy, an illiterate root or Indian doctor, as he was called, who was famous for curing cases of negro poisoning, and whom the gentleman in question once employed to attend two of his own negroes, who were dying of (supposed) African consumption—a case of which, the whole faculty assert, has never been cured.

When Flournoy visited the negroes they were in the last stages, and he immediately pronounced them incurable, stating at the same time that they had been poisoned, (which the patients had all the while stoutly maintained,) and, also, that had he been called upon for advice before the *pains ceased,* he certainly could have effected a cure. For one thing remarkable in both African consumption (so called) and African poison, is the fact that the patient or victim suffers horrible pains at the outset, but gradually becomes perfectly free from all pain whatever, and then slowly dwindles away to a mere skeleton, and so dies. Very frequently too, in the first stages of the complaint, the victim is troubled with terrible dreams, both sleeping and waking. The visions which haunt him upon his couch at night are usually horrible and ghastly—visions of blood and murder, of grinning skeletons and shapeless monsters, which cause him to start up in his sleep and cry aloud for very fright; but the waking fancies of the wretched man are far more terrible. He imagines that his body is full of creeping things—snakes, lizards, and the like reptiles; and he solemnly assures the physician that he can feel them crawl and twist and wriggle under his flesh, along the thighs, up the spinal column, and over the whole body in fact; and will in a frenzy sometimes clap his hand over the particular spot indicated, and exclaim excitedly: "Ah! here he is—here he is!" At other times the wretched victims of this terrible poison will declare that invisible arrows have been shot clean through them, and will point to the spot where each entered, as well as to the spot whence it issued again from the body. And it sometimes happens that they fall down suddenly, declaring they are bewitched, precisely like the old Puritans used to do in the days of Cotton Mather. The venerable and sage Flournoy, indeed, who flourished some thirty or forty years ago, when such murders by poison were much more common than now, and who was besides both ignorant and superstitious, did stoutly maintain that witchcraft had about as much to do with such strange procedures as any thing else; and whenever the poor blacks began to tumble over around him, either because of fainting fits or fright, the old gentleman was accustomed to lift up his hands in superstitious awe, and exclaim: "Well, boys, what darts is flyin' in the a'r now!"

As we have said, however, the acute pains, the frenzy, the crawling motions under the skin, all soon pass away; the victim loses his appetite; his skin becomes dry; the secretions irregular; the pulse somewhat excited and feverish—until, in the final stages, a slight hacking cough ensues. But the great source of the whole physical derangement is in the bowels. These are filled with tuberculous ulcers, very similar to those to be found in the lungs in an ordinary case of consumption. We were once led by curiosity to witness the dissection of a young negro man, who had been for eighteen months dying inch by inch of this terrible malady. The physicians endeavored to persuade the poor fellow that he had African consumption, but he maintained to the last that he had been poisoned. So when he died, the learned doctors, to prove they were in the right and the negro in the wrong, determined to open his body to see if they could discover what had caused his death. In company of an elderly friend we were permitted to enter the room in which the dissection took place; nor shall we soon forget the scene then and there presented to our gaze. The room was dark and dirty, shrouded in gloom and silence, except directly under the light of a solitary window, beneath which lay the outstretched corpse on a table or something of the kind, while gathered about in little squads the learned disciples of Esculapius discussed in low tones the merits of the case. The wisest of the M.D.s, a pursy old gentleman of about sixty-five, sat coolly smoking a pipe of strong tobacco, to prevent his inhaling the noisome effluvia emitted from the dead body, while with steady hand he proceeded unconcernedly to lay open the stomach of the deceased, exposing to view a most revolting spectacle. The whole body of the intestines presented one mass of fetid tubercules, and the sole wonder was how any human being could have lived an hour, much less a whole year, with his bowels in such a condition.

After a very brief consultation, the doctors present sagely concluded, that the negro had not been poisoned as he ever contended, but must have died of the incurable African consumption—a name used to designate a disease about which, as a general thing, the Faculty know nothing positively, save that in some respects it is similar to the old orthodox consumption of the lungs. From the fact of its being seated in the bowels and seeming to attack negroes exclusively, they dubbed it in the outset *African* consumption, and have ever since shaken their profoundly sagacious wigs at all those who dare to dissent from their dictum. But

for all that, we contend it is simply African poison ·
and they would do well to study its nature more closely, for possibly an antidote can be found somewhere
in the vegetable kingdom.

As we have already mentioned, the name of this
dreadful life-destroying agency is a secret, (known only
to a few old negro women and men,) which must have
come originally from Africa; for cases of this kind of
poisoning were much more frequent fifty years ago—
when fully one half our slaves were natives of Negroland—than at present, when it is seldom you meet an
aged "culled pusson" who was born a subject of the
King of Dahomey, or of any other African prince.
After reading Livingstone's work, we are led to entertain this conviction stronger than ever before. Indeed,
one of his own sable attendants evidently died of the
same complaint, in the very heart of the African continent. Here is his account of the matter :

" We were detained here so long that my tent became again quite rotten. *One of my men, after long
sickness, which I did not understand, died here.* He was
one of the Batoka, and when unable to walk I had
some difficulty in making his companions carry him.
They wished to leave him to die when his case became
hopeless."

When it is remembered that Livingstone is a regular M.D., the presumption is pretty strong, that a disease which he confesses not to understand must have
been very different from such diseases as are produced
by natural causes.

So much for " medicine," " waiters," " medication,"
and the like. Nearly all the other negro superstitions

15

are of a harmless character, which, in the main, the poor creatures have learned from their white masters— the good Puritans, Baptists, Methodists, and other religious sects, who first obtained possession of their ancestors. Thus they believe in fortune - telling, in witches, ghosts, hobgoblins, etc. etc. ; and many of them still nail (or did a few years back) the all-powerful horse-shoe over their cabin-doors, in order to prevent the ingress of all incorporeal beings whatever. One of their most orthodox convictions is, that witches ride the horses at night, and they will very seriously point out to you the saddles in the mane of the colts, asseverating the same to have been used by the imps of the Foul Fiend. They likewise entertain a great horror of hearing a hen crow like the cock, for they. assert it is an evil omen prognosticating a death in the family before a great while. So, too, would they fear to carry a hoe on the shoulder into the house, or to step over another person's leg, as well as to do many other things in themselves simple and harmless.

As for their mode of life on the plantations, their habits of work, conversation, religion, etc. etc., we think the following descriptive passages from a Northern writer in the main very just and truthful.

"On most plantations a certain amount only of work is daily required of each competent person, men, women, and children or youths; the 'task' prescribed being graduated in accordance with age and condition, from the 'quarter-hand' of the youngest to the 'half hand' and the 'three-quarter hand' of older years, up to the 'full-hand' of mature and healthful adult strength; thence retrograding, in like degrees, toward declining force and years. Industriously performed, these tasks are generally finished early in the afternoon, and often by two o'clock; when the laborer leaves his field and saunters homeward or whither he listeth. Perhaps it is to gossip in the sunshine over his pipe, or, perhaps, if he be thrifty or short of funds, to raise vegetables in his own private garden-patch, or to look after his eggs and poultry and pigs, for all of which his master will pay him the market-price as to any other trader. The tasks are begun at sunrise, and toward eight o'clock the darkeys have a good time for half an hour or so over the breakfast which has been brought for them to the field. At noon those who please dine, riding home for it if they are using horses, or having it brought to them, or waiting until the completion of their tasks.

"Men and women all smoke habitually, whether at work or at rest. Near any squad or gang a fire may always be seen, made for the double use of lighting pipes and as a rendezvous in gossip hours, for your genuine African is never quite warm enough. The appearance of the negroes at work in their plantation rig is not very elegant, and not so picturesque as it might be with a little change from the inflexible regulation hue of hueless gray; though, to be sure, the hankerchiefs worn on the head by the women (they never don bonnets, not even on Sunday or on gala days, [our Northerner is at fault here]) afford some slight relief. In the cut of coat and skirt there is always variety enough, and so in the fashion of the ever-changing hat. The conversation, though it seldom gets beyond the little current aches and experiences of their own lives, the doings of their family and friends, and pigs, with sometimes a little talk about their master's household, is often gay and jolly enough, judging by the loud and hearty ' yah ! yahs !' sounding all about, *heah* and *dar*.

" We once heard a jovial young scamp—the pet and gallant, the merry-maker and the mischief-maker of his set—a sort of ' Dandy Jim of Caroline,' relating to a wondering circle a certain alligator adventure he once had. How he killed an indefinite number, too numerous to mention, of the reptiles, and then tied one obstreperous juvenile by the tail to a branch of a tree ; how he left him there and thus suspended some three feet from the ground, and straightway forgot all about him, until returning by that way a matter of a year afterward he found the young prisoner doing well, and grown so much that his head now fairly rested upon the ground !

" ' Lor' a massey !' cried an astonished demoiselle, ' what you do to him den, Jim ?'

" ' What I do to him den, Miss Clarissa ? Why, I tie up his tail a little higher an' gib him chance to grow down some more. Yah, yah !'

" The authority of the plantation is vested in the overseer, by whom it is re-delegated in parcels to the more enterprising, intelligent, and reliable of the blacks.   The subordinate officers are called ' drivers,' and their office is to apportion the tasks and direct the labor of the gang placed under their care; to administer reproof and correction when needed ; and to be responsible for conduct and work to the superior officer.

" Each family of negroes has a house or cabin of its

own, generally with sufficient garden-ground, piggery, hennery, and so forth. These cabins are often made of logs, but sometimes are neat and cozy frame dwellings. They are usually placed, at suitable intervals, in rows, or double rows, with a wide street between. When it pleases the occupants to keep their homes so, they are pleasant enough, surrounded with neat palings and well protected by the beautiful shade trees of the country. Here, as in old Albion, their house is their castle, and rarely does even the master know any thing of their domestic affairs except when bad conduct or sickness makes it necessary for them to be looked after. They are constitutionally joyous and *insouciant;* and it is often pleasant to witness their glad, thoughtless recreations as the twilight and the evening hours set in.

"They are supplied, even under the requirements of the law, with a reasonable amount of clothing, and ample rations of food are served out every week. These consist chiefly of meal, rice, vegetables, molasses, bacon, fish, and coffee, according to their wants and occupations. Most of them have a surplus of these staple articles of diet, which they exchange at the nearest store for nick-nacks more to their liking. The law forbids the sale of liquor; but they manage, in some way, when so disposed, to get quite enough of it.

" Sunday is the great gala-day of the negroes, always excepting the annual festival at Christmas. At this time they interchange visits with relatives and friends on the neighboring plantations, generally bearing with them some present or other; most often of an edible character, as a turkey, a chicken, a goose, a cake, or a confection. Whether at home or abroad, however, on

Sunday they are pretty sure to repair to the church, when an accessible one is open. The whites occupy the front seats, while the blacks fill up the rear, the two classes entering by different doors.

"As a people, they seem to have a genius for piety, and in a pretty close ratio to their need of it, the greatest scamps being usually the most devout worshippers. Strange to add, there is no hypocrisy in this contradiction. The same unreflecting impulsiveness which prompts them to steal any desirable thing within reach, also leading them to mourn, briefly, over their sinfulness in sackcloth and ashes. They are fond of preaching, and the ministerial office among them is seldom wanting in candidates. Every plantation is, more or less, well supplied in this wise. To be sure they make strange work in their confident ignorance, often weighing anchor with but half an idea on board."

But we will speak of their religious tendencies more at length on a future page.

In nearly all the Southern States the negroes, as a general thing, are much attached to coon and opossum hunting, and on most of the large plantations one will find from six to a dozen coon-dogs, which belong exclusively to the slaves. They also are fond of hunting hares, whenever they can prevail upon their young masters to suffer them to use the fox-hounds for that purpose. They chase the hares until these are forced to betake themselves to a hollow tree, when the negroes either twist them out with a slim stick, or else smoke them out by means of fire. But above all things else, Cuffee dotes on fishing, and is a most enthusiastic disciple of the quaint old Izaak Walton. Angling requires little exertion, and your genuine Cuffee most cordially hates exertion; while the hot Southern sun, which soon drives the white man away from his favorite "hole" to the umbrageous shelter of the nearest woods, never "fases the shell" of Cuffee, so to speak : to reverse the words of the poet, the black rascal seems to make a "shady place in the sunshine," and will lie down any day at noon, when the thermometer stands at 100° in the shade, and sleep as quietly as an infant, with the broiling eye of Phœbus glaring right down upon him, hot enough almost to singe his eye-lashes.

The negroes also set deadfalls for squirrels, snares for rabbits, traps for quail and ducks, and pens for wild turkeys; of all which they destroy large quantities, owing to their great abundance all through the South. We never cared any great deal for any of these pot-hunting schemes of the negroes, save the turkey-pens, which used to vex us amazingly. But, unlike the gentlemen sportsmen of Canada, who are said to wantonly destroy every turkey-pen they find, though built by English freemen; we never could feel that it was exactly honorable to do such a thing, even when the pens belonged to negro slaves. Certainly pot-hunting is a very sorry business, but a true sportsman will not forget, for all that, that he is, or ought to be at least, a *gentleman.*

Added to the wild game, of which, we presume, the negroes in the South eat more every year than one half of the whites of our large cities, the usual fare of the slaves is bacon and greens, with ash-cake and corn-pone in summer, and in winter bacon and turnips and the same bread, with an addition of wheat flour for the

Christmas holidays, except in the wheat-growing States, wherein it is customary to give the negroes about as much flour-bread as of that made from corn-meal. In the summer time, also, they are allowed to eat fruit *ad libitum*, since on most plantations there are large apple, pear, peach, and plum orchards, the productions whereof the planters rarely think of selling. The negroes are also very fond of roasted or boiled maize, and hominy, as well as of a bread made of corn-meal and persimmons mixed, which is quite palatable. In winter they have, besides, sweet potatoes more or less, and pumpkins all the time, of which latter they are fonder than the Down-Easters. Indeed, we will assert this in behalf of the Southern slaves, however much the assertion may be discredited; *they annually throw away food enough to feed during an entire winter the thousands of half-starved white laborers thrown out of employment in all the Free States during the months from December to March.* The proof of their well-fed condition is strikingly observable in their sleek skins, full cheeks, and general plumpness of physical development. You rarely see amongst them a haggard, thin-jawed starveling, but their very eyes on the contrary stand out with fatness. In consequence whereof they are nearly always jovial and smiling, indulging at all times in snatches of song, and giving vent to the most stunning peals of laughter, which to hear even produces a pleasurable sensation.

No matter where they may be or what they may be doing, indeed, whether alone or in crowds, at work or at play, ploughing through the steaming maize in the sultry heats of June, or bared to the waist and with deft hand mowing down the yellow grain, or trudging homeward in the dusky twilight after the day's work is done—always and every where they are singing and happy, happy in being free from all mental cares or troubles, and singing heartily and naturally as the birds sing, which toil not nor do spin. Their songs are usually wild and indescribable, seeming to be mere snatches of song rather than any long continuous effort, but with an often recurring chorus, in which all join with a depth and clearness of lungs truly wonderful. No man can listen to them, be his ear ever so cultivated, particularly to their corn-husking songs, when the night is still and the singers some distance off, without being very pleasantly entertained. But the wildest and most striking negro song we think we ever listened to, we heard while on board an Alabama river steamboat. We were steaming up from Mobile on a lovely day in the early winter, and came in sight of Montgomery just as the heavens were all a-glow with the last crimson splendors of the setting sun, and while the still shadows of evening seemed already to be stealing with noiseless tread along the hollows in the steep riverbanks, creeping slowly thence with invisible footsteps over the placid surface of the stream itself. A lovelier day or a more bewitching hour could not well be imagined. As we began to near the wharf, the negro boatmen collected in a squad on the bow of the boat, and one dusky fellow, twirling his wool hat above his head, took the lead in singing, improvising as he sang, all except the chorus, in which the whole crew joined with enthusiasm. And O Madame Jenny Goldschmidt, and Mademoiselle Piccolomini! we defy you both to

15*

produce, with the aid of many orchestras, a more soul-
stirring strain of melody than did those simple Africans
then and there! The scene is all before us now—the
purple-tinted clouds overhead—the dim shadows tread-
ing noiselessly in the distance—the gleaming dome of
the State Capitol and the church-spires of Montgomery
—the almost perfect stillness of the hour, broken only .
by the puff, puff of the engine and the wild music of the
dusky boatmen—and above all, the plump, well-defined
outlines of some sable Sally, who stood on the highest
red cliff near the landing-place, and, with joy in her
heart and a tear in her eye no doubt, (we hadn't any
opera-glass with us,) waved a flaming bandanna with
every demonstration of rejoicing at the return of her
dusky lover, whom we took to be our sooty *improvisa-
tore*, from the glow which mantled his honest countenance, and the fervor with which he twirled his old
wool hat in response to the fair one's signal. Ah! we
had then but recently left our adopted home in the
Free North, but, as we listened to the happy voices of
these children of oppression, we could not fail to contrast the same with the mournful wail at that very hour
going up from all the streets and parks of our greatest
metropolis—the wail of the unemployed clamoring for
Work or Bread!

Now, we feel persuaded the anti-slavery reader is
longing to ask why, if the slaves are so happy and contented, do they ever seek to run away and go North?
We might as well answer this question here as elsewhere. As a general thing no honest, industrious slave
ever desires to run away at all, even though solicited
to do so by the secret emissaries of the abolitionists;

and when such an one is seduced to leave the protecting care of his master, and all the• blessings and comforts of the "old plantation," for the freedom to enjoy
a precarious and hard-earned livelihood in the Free
States or Canada, he is almost sure to embrace the first
opportunity to return back again, a "sadder but a
wiser man." The vicious, however, the dissolute, the
lazy—these all are captivated by the glowing promises
of ease and plenty held temptingly out to them in the
"land of freedom;" nor will any student of human nature wonder that such vagabonds should prefer comforts earned without toil to those earned by the constant
sweat of the brow. But when these fugitives come to
realize the facts, and learn that white men hardly make
a subsistence in the Free States by the most ceaseless
labor, in proof of what we have said concerning their
characters, they invariably almost (a few praiseworthy
exceptions) take to petty stealing for a livelihood, pilfering from hen-roosts, or snatching coats and hats in
public halls. Will any Northern man deny this charge?
No: on the contrary they always plead in excuse of
such conduct on the part of their colored population,
that they are fugitives. Now, gentlemen agitators, allow
us to tell you, that every freeman who walks your
streets could be induced to sacrifice his present all, in
the hope of grasping some greater imaginary good—
such as a South Sea bubble or a Pike's Peak humbug.
Mankind, whether black or white, like the dog in the
fable, are ever ready to throw away a substantial good
to snatch at the shadowy forms delusive Hope or too
eager Desire is ever tempting them with, but which

dissolve themselves into thin air the moment they feel
the touch of Reality.

This all by way of parenthesis.

The religious and love-songs of the negroes are not
so peculiar and striking as those wild choruses and lul-
laloos, which their fathers must have brought with
them from Africa, but the words and meaning of which
are no longer remembered. Nevertheless, even their
tamest and most civilized efforts are surpassingly good;
and the loudest and most fervent camp-meeting singers
amongst the whites are constrained to surrender to the
darkeys in "The Old Ship of Zion" or "I want to go
to Glory." In singing these and other kindred songs,
the negroes usually keep time with the feet, or by clapping the hands or wagging the head, often shedding
tears freely in the fervency and rapture of their devo-
tions. And we may as well here remark, for the benefit of those philosophers and divines who pretend to
abhor slavery so greatly, that Christian slaves are rarely
found on the plantations of infidels, while it is equally
rare not to find them in the households of Christian
masters. This is a fact worth considering, particularly
when we add, that the slaves do not by any means always belong to the same denomination with their "masters according to the flesh." There is hardly a plantation of any size in the entire South, belonging to an
honest professor of Christianity, whereon you will not
find some two or three different sects of Christians
among the negroes; but these usually fraternize together much more harmoniously than do their white
brethren of the same rival creeds. On nearly all such

plantations, in fact, the negroes unite together without regard to differences of religious beliefs, and hold a common prayer-meeting two nights in every week, at which the master is sometimes present and expounds to them the Word of God. And it is notable what a change for the better Christianity produces in even the most degraded of them. They readily give up their banjos, their fiddles, their double-shuffles, and break-downs, and are eager to learn what is right and becoming. Of course we speak only of such as are sincere believers of the Gospel; for we have reason to know that they sometimes profess Christianity because *it pays*, and in particular is this true of just about one half the negro preachers. Believe us, amiable Mrs. Stowe, black people are no better than white people the world over.

It must not be denied, too, that few of the negroes entertain perfectly correct ideas concerning the Gospel of Jesus Christ; but, if we must speak plainly, we don't believe one white man in a hundred entertains ideas perfectly correct and rational in regard thereto. The whites can not get along without their creeds and their innovations, and their preachers with itching ears, (and pockets too;) and, as we think, the poor blacks are far less blameworthy, when they weave into the simple story of the Cross the tangled threads of their own crude fancies and imaginings. Hence we are much more inclined to pity than to censure, when we hear the poor creatures recount their dreams and visions about hell-hounds chasing them many a weary mile, with others equally apocryphal. But there is one thing which they always dwell on with peculiar de-

light, and in which there may be a grain of truth—
that after death they are to be changed into white folks.
Their idea of hell is, that the Devil is a black man,
with horns and a forked tail, a raw-head-and-bloody-
bones old fellow, who literally burns up the wicked
with fire and brimstone. Their idea of heaven is, that
in the New-Jerusalem they will walk along pavements
of gold with silver slippers on, and blessed with straight
hair and a fair complexion. And here we may remark,
this consciousness of the superiority of the white man
over the black seems to be pretty generally entertained
by all negro races whatever, and is not by any means
confined to our Southern slaves. The negroes in Africa told Dr. Livingstone that God made them first, but
hated them because they turned out so ugly and black,
and so left them to run about naked; but that He
loved the white man, he was so fair to look upon, and
in consequence gave him guns, houses, clothes, and
books. So too were the poor pagans of Ethiopia much
captivated with the Doctor's straight hair, just as our
Southern slaves are always carding their own woolly-
heads, twisting the wool out by means of cotton strings
six days in the week, all for the glory of having it
look straight like white folks' hair on Sunday! For
verily no Broadway dandy could be more attentive to
his own saponaceous curls than are some of the "Dandy
Jims of Caroline" to their kinky wool.

But, notwithstanding the negroes are ignorant, and
thousands of them use religion for a cloak simply, still
multitudes of them are devout and pious, as well as
intelligent Christians. In Savannah, Georgia, three
colored pastors, with salaries from eight hundred to a

thousand dollars, are supported by subscriptions and pew-rents among their own numbers. In 1853, fifteen thousand dollars were contributed by five thousand slaves in Charleston, to benevolent objects. These may serve as examples. A Northern writer was deeply interested in some prayer-meetings of slaves he attended; and furnishes us the following specimens of the prayers he heard: " Bless our dear masters and brothers who come here to read the Bible to us, and pay so much attention to us, though we ain't that sort of people as can interpret thy word in all its colors and forms." " O my heavenly Father!" said an old man, "I am thy dear child. I know I love thee. Thou art my God, my portion, and nothing else. O my Father, I have no home in this world; my home is very far off. I long to see it. Jesus is there; thou art there; angels, good men are there. I am coming home. I am one day nearer to it."

As a general rule, however, the old adage of " like master like man," applies with as much truthfulness to the negroes in the South, as to the hired servants of other places. The slaves of a gentleman of good family, (we mean those who are accustomed to come into daily contact with their master,) are not only more intelligent than the mass of blacks, but are both polite and well-bred, and in a measure refined and aristocratic. They scorn to associate with common darkeys, and are given to all the airs and stately mannerisms of a Yellowplush or a Jenkins. Their chief ambition is to become master's waiting-man, or *valet;* or, in case of a female, lady's maid; next they would prefer to act as housekeeper, chambermaid, steward, dining-room servant, or groom, or better still, carriage-driver. This last is considered a post of great honor, and the negroes are all capital fellows with the whip, being immoderately fond of horse-flesh, but much fonder of showy trappings—the silk tassels, the silver-plated buckles, the plumes, the costly harness, et cetera, et cetera, which usually constitute a gentleman's equipage. Even to be wagoner, to drive the plantation mules and oxen, often becomes a fruitful source of rivalries and ill-feeling. But the chief ambition of a field hand, or plantation slave, is to become a head-man. No king on his throne feels more his own importance, than does a big buck negro feel his, when he finds himself mounted on a sleek mule with close-cropped mane, and holding in his hand a stout New-England cow-skin, and having under his direct super-vision a "gang" of from twenty to thirty fellow-slaves.

The slaves of persons of the middle class do not carry their heads quite so high as those who belong to the "raal quality," but they are, as a general thing, from being brought into closer contact with their own-ers, more moral and tractable than the slaves of very wealthy gentlemen, when the latter live in "quarters" under the control of an overseer, and, in consequence, seldom enjoy the advantages of daily intercourse with educated white persons. The worst slaves, however, the most degraded, thieving, impudent, and utterly worthless, are those who belong to men in moderate circumstances. This may seem strange to many, but it is true in most cases nevertheless. Such slaves in the main, enjoy greater liberties than other negroes, are over-familiar with their masters, do not begin to work as hard as the latter, and the consequence is that they grow up to be sleek, and saucy, and rascally. They never feel the lash, even in infancy, are permitted to leave home at all times without a "pass," and to run about at night pilfering from hen-roosts, pig-pens, and dairies; and even when caught by the "paterollers," and basted as they deserve, ten chances to one but the ministers of the law are sued for damages by the indignant and too indulgent masters. In view of such facts, is it at all strange such spoiled and petted blacks should sometimes deflour a poor and friendless white girl, or even in a moment of uncurbed passion knock out their master's brains? For, singularly enough, nearly all the crimes of this nature are committed by negroes of the above class. And the worst of it is, just among such a class of slaves, in the mountainous districts of Tennessee, Kentucky, and Virginia, the emissaries of Northern fanaticism are casting broadcast their incendiary firebrands; deluding the poor simple-minded blacks into a belief that, by murdering their masters and mistresses, they shall be raised to the condition of ladies and gentlemen themselves, with plenty of lands and money, and nothing to do but to eat and to sleep. And this too, despite the sad spectacle of Hayti, which, since the rule of the blacks began, has changed its form of government *ten times*, and from exporting, as a French slave colony, 225,687,952 lbs. of produce, has now actually to *import* sugar for its home consumption! Yet Wendell Phillips, in Beecher's church, Brooklyn, while making a saint of John Brown, for his murders in Kansas and

Virginia, cited the bloody example of St. Domingo as the fairest page upon the scroll of time!! How eloquently did the pure Edward Everett reply to the frenzied madman in his great speech in Faneuil Hall; we quote his closing words:

"Sir, I have been admitted to the confidence of the domestic circle in all parts of the South, and I have seen there touching manifestations of the kindest feelings, by which that circle, in all its members, high and low, master and servant, can be bound together; and when I contemplate the horrors that would have ensued had the tragedy on which the curtain rose at Harper's Ferry been acted out, through all its scenes of fire and sword, of lust and murder, of rapine and desolation, to the final catastrophe, I am filled with emotions to which no words can do justice. There could, of course, be but one result, and that well deserving the thoughtful meditation of those, if any such there be, who think that the welfare of the colored race could by any possibility be promoted by the success of such a movement, and who are willing to purchase that result by so costly a sacrifice. The colored population of St. Domingo amounted to but little short of half a million while the whites amounted to only thirty thousand. The white population of the Southern States alone, in the aggregate, outnumbers the colored race in the ratio of two to one; in the Union at large, in the ratio of seven to one, and if (which Heaven avert) they should be brought into conflict, it could end only in the extermination of the latter after scenes of woe, for which language is too faint, and for which the liveliest fancy has no adequate images of horror."

In regard to the holidays usually granted the negroes, we find there prevails a pretty general misapprehension in all parts of the North. It is almost universally believed in the Free States, that the only holiday allowed the slaves is Christmas: but there could be no greater mistake. Some masters make it a rule to give their negroes every Saturday afternoon, while nearly all masters give them certain established holidays, such as Easter Monday, the Fourth of July, the Eighth of January, and others. Indeed, if this custom did not prevail, the slaves could never find time to put in their little crops, a practice almost universal with them. After the crops are once seeded, they can manage to work them of moonlight nights, if so disposed, and in case the regular holidays should prove too wet or otherwise unsuitable. Those who plant no crops (we are speaking of the industrious negroes) either work at basket-making, chair-making, or other similar trades, by which they make considerable money. Of a truth there is not an adult male slave in the entire South, provided he possess the necessary energy, who can not lay up more ready money in a twelvemonth than most day-laborers in the North or elsewhere, and at least double as much as the poor Coolies can at their four dollars per month, even granting they ever get their pay. In order to comprehend this assertion, you must consider that the slaves are not of necessity put to any expense whatever, either for themselves or their families. Their masters are compelled by law as well as by self-interest to house them well, clothe them warmly, feed them bountifully, and pay all their doctor's bills; hence, whatever they make for themselves is so much clear gain.

The charge of the abolitionists that every thing the negroes make, is the property of their masters, is the sheerest gammon. It may be true in theory, (for we have not taken the trouble to examine the law on the subject,) but the Southerner who should rob a slave of what he had earned for himself in the hours allotted him for his own use, would be pelted with rotten eggs out of the community in which he might reside, nor would he find a resting-place for the soles of his feet south of Mason's and Dixon's line. We have never heard yet of such a mean-spirited wretch, and we should dislike much to believe that he exists on the face of the globe. But we do know on the contrary, that the negroes sometimes make for themselves during a twelvemonth as much as one hundred dollars; while in any of the Cotton States, nothing is easier than for a negro man and his wife to make for themselves a bale of cotton, and at present prices a bale is worth sixty dollars at the gin. Besides, the negroes have always (nearly) a little garden close to their cabins, in which they raise whatever kind of vegetables they please; and are also great raisers of poultry, receiving at all times good prices for their eggs and chickens from their own masters and mistresses or from the neighbors.

Why, then, asks the inquisitive reader, do so few of them make enough money to buy their freedom? *It is because they do not know how to keep their money.* You must not forget that the negro race in Africa, has been from time immemorial the most degraded of all the human family, and that the semi-civilization which it has attained in this country is owing entirely to the sustaining and protecting care of the white race, without which the blacks would assuredly relapse again into barbarism. Even in our Free States, although the free negroes are made much of by the abolitionists, and although their numbers are constantly augmented by fugitives from the South; still the census returns prove that they are gradually passing away from before the presence of their white brothers, just as the poor Red-men have already passed away.

As a general thing, the great mass of slaves do not know or care any thing at all about freedom, and spend their money just as fast as they get it. A great many of them are even too indolent to strive to make any money for themselves, but spend their holidays sleeping, fishing, or playing like so many children; while the evenings are devoted almost wholly to dancing, banjo-playing, singing, chit-chatting, or to coon-hunting and night-fishing. Many a night have we lain awake until near twelve o'clock, listening to the distant " thrum, tumpe tum" of the merry banjo, may be accompanied by a flute or violin, or "patting," and always more or less by singing and uproarious shouts of laughter: until we have been led to wonder how the simple creatures ever manage to find time to sleep, for at the blowing of the headman's horn at cock-crowing they are obliged to be found every man at his post. Although usually accounted somewhat nappy-headed we are confident they sleep less than white persons, and that they do not require as much. Indeed, we have known a slave girl, while standing behind her mistress' chair during the dinner hour, go fast asleep and startle the assembled guests by a veritable snore, while the same girl would dance in the moon-light for hours together, and yet be up bright and early the next morning, and with her eyes wide open so long as her duties required that she should keep bustling about. The moment they cease from work, unless eating or in conversation, they begin to nod—to sleep, verily snoring with a forty-horse power. It is also remarkable that any kind of sedentary habit very soon undermines a negro's constitution. Seamstresses and weavers, in particular, seem to fade soonest, and masters are constrained oftentimes to send such out into the field, to labor with the field hands for the benefit of their health, which is always recruited greatly thereby.

But, as we stated just now, even those slaves who make money, spend it as soon as it is made. In case they are addicted to strong drink, whenever they can by any means elude the watchfulness of the overseer, they pretty soon pour all their hard earnings into the till of the groggery-keeper, and in exchange pour the vilest of "bald-face" and "rot-gut" down their own throats. And even when they spend their money for dry goods, groceries, shoes, hats, or other useful articles, instead of allowing their masters to invest their money for them, they invariably prefer to spend it themselves, except in a few rare cases, and just as invariably pay dearly for their foolish love of display, or independence, or whatever you may please to call it. They are wholly at the mercy of those unconscionable scamps, the clerks of country store-keepers, and are swindled accordingly, just as many a more enlightened white man has been ere this, we dare say. However, if it be any pleasure to the simple souls to be cheated, (and we maintain with Butler that it is a pleasure to all of us,) why, let them continue to enjoy the luxury, say we. But for conscience' sake don't let us suffer them to be cheated out of their present happy though humble condition, by those mistaken philanthropists, who are blindly laboring to help the negroes to become like their pagan ancestors—worshippers of snakes, monkeys, *thunder* and other *reptiles*, as our Liberian friends have recently expressed it in a government edict against such abominations.

A word in regard to the manner in which the negroes celebrate the Christmas holidays, and we shall soon bring our present labors to a close.

As is well known to most of our readers, Christmas, owing to the difference of opinion between the early Cavaliers and Puritans regarding the propriety of religious feasts, has always been a day of much greater renown in the South than in the North. Of late years, 'tis true, the Free States are changing in this regard very much, but still there is not in them that general *abandon*, that universal merry-making which always characterizes Christmas in the Slave States. More particularly, however, is Christmas acceptable to the slaves, for at each return of the memorable day, as was customary during the old Roman saturnalia, the negroes are permitted to enjoy a week of freedom; in some localities even the necessary household duties, such as cooking, washing and the like, have to be performed by the whites, or else must be paid for with a good round sum. The negroes generally begin to prepare for the great occasion about six weeks beforehand. As the time draws near, their mistresses make them presents of extra allowances of flour, sugar, coffee, etc.

etc.; while they themselves replenish their beer barrels, (they brew a sort of beer from persimmons, malt, and other things, which is quite palatable,) or smuggle fresh bottles of rum or whisky into their cabins; have all their "Sunday-go-to-meeting" clothes done up in the neatest manner, and have their houses, also, scrubbed, washed, and generally furnished inside and out. The night preceding Christmas they are all busy as bees, sweeping their little yards, running hither and thither in a fever of excitement, laughing and jumping about in a delirium of joy. Many of them hardly go to bed at all, but remain up during the entire night, snatching a nap by chance while sitting in a chair or lounging on a wooden bench before the fire.

Long before the morrow's dawn they are all astir, and robing in their Sunday's best toggery, every mother's son or daughter darts straight for the "Great House;" and in a trice the old mansion rings from cellar to garret with the merry sounds of "Chrismus Giff, Mas'r!" "Chrismus Giff, Mistis!" which term of salutation is used in the South instead of the customary "merry Christmas" of the Free States. And we do not care how drowsy you may be, how cross, or determined—even though you should swear worse than the troops did in Flanders—still the inevitable "Chrismus Giff" will continue to ring in your ears, and the grinning ivory will be thrust in your face, until you have conformed to the universal custom of making a donation on such occasions. Those of the darkeys who do not intrude upon your slumbers, lie in wait behind every door and corner, and the moment the end of your nose appears, they pounce upon you with a whoop, shouting

furiously, "Chrismus Giff, Mas'r! ah! I cotch you dis
time!" And as you begin leisurely to open your purse
and to clink the silver pieces inside, it does one's heart
good to hear their ringing laughter, and their inimitable and hearty "Thankee, Mas'r! Mas'r's a raal gen'l'-
man. God bless you, Sar, an' gib you many happy
Chrismuses!" And receiving your liberal donation,
(for if you are a *gentleman*, it will be liberal,) the poor
souls humbly bow themselves almost to the ground in
your august presence, pulling off their hats at the same
time, or in case their hats are not on, politely plucking
at a kinky lock of wool in the place where the hats
ought to be.

By ten o'clock every body is wild with delight, having entered body and soul into the spirit of the occasion, while not a few of both whites and blacks are
"unco fou' thegither." Procuring powder from their
young masters, the blacks proceed to bore holes in
large oak logs, filling the same with the powder, and,
having set a slow match, stand off at a little distance
until their big Christmas guns go off, when they shout
and hurrah in a perfect frenzy of delight. A few who
are accustomed to handling fire-arms either accompany
their young masters a-hunting, or borrowing the guns
belonging to the latter, go hunting themselves, followed
by a rabble of the more timid men and boys, to whom
a fowling-piece is about as great a mystery as it was to
those salvages Miles Standish frightened away from
Plymouth Rock, or is at this day to the natives of
Central Africa, who are accustomed to plant powder,
expecting to reap a crop of guns, bullets, etc. etc., in
due season.

16

Thus, for the seven days the carnival continues, by which time the negroes themselves have become weary of so much feasting and idleness; and hence return with eagerness to their shovels and hoes, feeling refreshed, strengthened, and fully prepared to undertake the labors of the New Year.

So much for the slaves in our Southern States. That they are not what every honest Christian would rejoice to see, we shall not gainsay; neither will we deny that every people, of whatever creed or color, on the face of the earth, are far other than what the true men of all ages would approve of or desire. However, after reviewing the whole subject in all its bearings, we are disposed to regard the institution of Negro Slavery in a light very different from most of our contemporaries. We are too apt, all of us, to confound the abuses of any system or institution with the system or institution so abused. Nothing could be more unwise or unphilosophic. Let us consider how the little busy bee manages to extract sweetest honey from even the most inodorous and hurtful of flowers, while man has learned to distill from the most useful of all seeds a deadly and damning poison. Now, God is wiser than bees, and he is infinitely greater and more just than man; but no one can point to a single passage in the only authentic revelation of his will to man, in which he has condemned as sinful the holding of a fellow-man in bondage. On the contrary, he has by statute especially approved of the same; and even while he undertook to lead his chosen people out of Egyptian bondage, (and about this exodus the Higher Law advocates make much ado,) read, O anti-slavery advocate, what the Almighty ordained to be a law among these fugitive bondmen, even while they still tarried in the land of their unfeeling taskmasters :

"And the Lord said unto Moses and Aaron, This is the ordinance of the passover : there shall no stranger eat thereof. BUT EVERY MAN'S SERVANT THAT IS BOUGHT FOR MONEY, when thou hast circumcised him, then shall he eat thereof. A foreigner and a hired servant shall not eat thereof."

In this connection we can not refrain from mentioning, that we once heard an honorable gentleman (by the bye, one of our cleverest Northern politicians, let his enemies denounce him as much as they please) deliver an harangue upon the Burdens of Society. Although several times during his performance, he won from us the applause of a smile at some of his inimitable mimicries and grimaces, still we felt persuaded once or twice, that he ventured beyond his proper avocation when he attempted to handle sacred subjects. For example, in speaking of slavery as one of the greatest burdens of society, he took occasion to remark that he had no objection to the system of slavery upheld by Moses, and that he would be perfectly willing to put all that concerns slavery to be found in the Old Testament, into the New. Now, we are charitable enough to suppose that the Honorable gentleman is much better read in the New-York *Tribune* than in either the Old or New Testament; for we find Moses has declared (Exod. 21 : 20, 21,) the following rather singular doctrine to be so emphatically indorsed by a leading champion of the anti-slavery men of the North. It is a doctrine, indeed, which would not be accepted by the most ultra Fire-eater in the South, and is besides opposed to the whole tenor and spirit of the New Testament. We furnish it for the benefit of the Honorable gentleman himself, who possibly has never read it—at least we hope he never has, for the contrary supposition would be even worse than what his bitterest enemy has ever uttered to his hurt; and yet he may not see it now, for we judge he is one of those men who read their own side only of every question, since he has neglected to read his Bible. But here is the passage:

"And if a man smite his servant, or his maid, with a rod, and he die under his hand, he shall be surely punished. Notwithstanding, *if he continue a day or two, he shall not be punished;* FOR HE IS HIS MONEY."

There, Sir! that is the kind of slavery you don't call a *burden.* That is the kind of slavery you declare to be humane as compared to Negro slavery. Alas! what intolerable *farceurs* are we all!

In conclusion, however, and merely for the sake of argument, let us suppose our African slavery to be an evil: but we have it still, and how are we to get rid of it? That's the question. Besides, notwithstanding this great evil, this great curse, we have as a people prospered more than any other people on the globe. Although the youngest of nations, we have already taken our place among the oldest as a first-class Power. From the very feeblest of beginnings, in little more than half a century we have grown to be of such gigantic stature, that we behold even now our lengthened shadow stretching entirely across the continent; while with the aid of our ubiquitous commerce, upheld by

invincible King Cotton, we have put a girdle of influence around the entire globe. All this we have achieved, divided as from the beginning into Free and Slave
States, and in the teeth of the opposition and ill-omened
vaticinations of the Old World dynasties, aided as
these always have been by home-traitors who do not
scruple to hold out blue-lights for the enemy in time
of war, and to continually predict in time of peace the
ultimate failure of our complex and artificial system of
government. Thus far the past history of the Republic has been one continuous succession of brilliant
achievements; and now, blessed as we are on every
hand, we see no cause why we can not reasonably look
forward to a boundless future of prosperity, provided
only we will consent as brethren to "dwell together in
amity." And why shall we not? We all have glass
houses enough, God knows, without daring to throw
stones at each other. Would it not be better, then, for
us all,

> " —— close-buttoned to the chin,
> Broadcloth without, and a warm heart within,"

to go about "doing good as we have opportunity"?
We will meet with opportunities every where, in the
North or the South, in town or country, on land or
sea. And when we slight those opportunities, to prat-
tle never so sweetly about sins which do not concern
us, and responsibilities which rest on other men's
shoulders, however much we may gain the applause of
men for our fine speeches, yet there is One who con-
demns us utterly for the miserable sham. Why, in a
great city, in which at the time there were hundreds of

poor white families in a state of semi-starvation for lack of employment, we once paid our two shillings, along with about two thousand other sleek and well-fed citizens, to hear a *quasi*-minister of the Gospel (whose yearly salary is about five thousand dollars) declaim in choicest billingsgate against a set of rascals some thousand miles off, although he had never seen them, (from *prudential* reasons, as he waggishly observed, which brought down the house;) but he denounced them nevertheless as the greatest oppressors in the world, to the inconceivable delight of his hearers, who every one went straightway home, blessing God that they were not born in that heathenish country a thousand miles away, and feeling particularly unctuous in the consciousness of their own good deeds! While the unctuous lecturer himself, pocketing the plethoric purse earned by his night's labor, went on his way rejoicing, not caring a bawbee for the hundreds of hollow-eyed, hungry beggars, who at every street-corner thrust their pleading eyes and cadaverous faces between his saintly Reverence and the biting winter air.

Ah! Hood! Thomas Hood! many a true word spakest thou in jest, but never a truer than is found in the following tale, "whereto is tied a moral:"

> " Once on a time a certain English lass
>   Was seized with symptoms of such deep decline,
>   Cough, hectic flushes, every evil sign,
>   That, as their wont is at such desperate pass,
>   The doctors gave her over to an ass.

> " Accordingly, the grisly Shade to bilk,
>   Each morn the patient quaffed a frothy bowl

Of assinine new milk,
Robbing a shaggy suckling of a foal,
Which got proportionably spare and skinny—
Meanwhile the neighbors cried: 'Poor Mary Ann!
She can't get over it! she never can!'
When lo! to prove each prophet was a ninny,
The one that died was the poor wet-nurse jenny.

" To aggravate the case,
There were but two grown donkeys in the place;
And most unluckily for Eve's fair daughter,
The other long-eared creature was a male,
Who never in his life had given a pail
Of milk, or even chalk and water.
No matter: at the usual hour of eight
Down trots a donkey to the wicket-gate,
With Mister Simon Gubbins on his back—
' Your sarvant, Miss—a werry springlike day—
Bad time for hasses tho'! good lack! good lack!
Jenny be dead, Miss—but I'ze brought ye Jack,
He doesn't give no milk—but he can bray.' "